Mergers and Acquisitions in Asia

T0316182

The investment climates of many Asian countries have changed substantially over the last ten years. Many changes such as deregulation, privatization, new free trade agreements, and new incentives for foreign direct investment have had a very positive impact on mergers and acquisitions (M&A) in Asia.

Mergers and Acquisitions in Asia provides the latest information on the investment climates and M&A activities in Japan, China, Hong Kong, Taiwan, and five Southeast Asian countries: Indonesia, Malaysia, the Philippines, Singapore, and Thailand. Roger Y. W. Tang and Ali M. Metwalli closely examine data from the Worldwide M&A Database maintained by Thomson Financial Service and draw comparisons among countries and regions. Special attention is paid to the United States as a major trading partner of the selected countries; US trade and investment relations with these countries are analyzed.

Roger Y. W. Tang is The Upjohn Chair Professor of Business Administration and **Ali M. Metwalli** is Professor of Finance at Western Michigan University, USA.

Routledge Studies in Global Competition
Edited by
John Cantwell
University of Reading, UK

David Mowery
University of California, Berkeley, USA

Mergers and Acquisitions in Asia

A global perspective

**Roger Y. W. Tang and
Ali M. Metwalli**

LONDON AND NEW YORK

First published 2006
by Routledge
2 Park Square, Milton Park, Abingdon, Oxon OX14 4RN

Simultaneously published in the USA and Canada
by Routledge
711 Third Avenue, New York, NY 10017

First issued in paperback 2013

*Routledge is an imprint of the Taylor & Francis Group,
an informa business*

© 2006 Roger Y. W. Tang and Ali M. Metwalli

Typeset in Times New Roman by
Newgen Imaging Systems (P) Ltd, Chennai, India

All rights reserved. No part of this book may be reprinted or
reproduced or utilised in any form or by any electronic,
mechanical, or other means, now known or hereafter
invented, including photocopying and recording, or in any
information storage or retrieval system, without permission in
writing from the publishers.

British Library Cataloguing in Publication Data
A catalogue record for this book is available
from the British Library

Library of Congress Cataloging in Publication Data
A catalog record for this book has been requested

ISBN13: 978–0–415–76996–9 (hbk)
ISBN13: 978-0-415-65009-0 (pbk)
ISBN13: 978–0–203–96635–8 (ebk)

Contents

Figures

Tables

Preface

In the past, mergers and acquisitions (M&A) in industrial countries have captured the attention of many corporate executives, investment bankers, business researchers, government regulators, and some international organizations such as the United Nations Conference on Trade and Development (UNCTAD). Many books, articles, and reports have been published to examine various aspects of M&A in the United States and Europe. The areas covered in existing literature include historical reviews of M&A activities, cross-border acquisitions, M&A theories and strategies, leveraged buyouts, acquisition methods, due diligence, integration, and other issues. In the last 10 years, some studies have also been carried out to review those same issues in Asia.

The main purpose of this book is to provide the latest information on the investment climates and M&A activities in Japan, China, Hong Kong, Taiwan, and five member countries of the ASEAN region: Indonesia, Malaysia, the Philippines, Singapore, and Thailand. M&A data available in the Worldwide M&A Database maintained by Thomson Financial Service will be reviewed and analyzed. Comparisons are made among countries and regions. Because the United States has strong economic ties with those selected countries, US trade and investment relations with those countries will also be examined. The new information provided by this book should be useful to potential investors, investment bankers, business faculties, and students studying mergers and acquisitions in Asia.

For this book, we are grateful to Western Michigan University (WMU) for granting us sabbatical leaves in the 2004–5 and 2005–6 school years. Roger Tang also wants to thank Lingnan University in Hong Kong for providing him a visiting scholarship in 2005 to visit Lingnan for five months and collect current information on M&A in Asia. The research on which this book is based was supported by research funds from the Upjohn Chair of Business Administration at WMU and a grant from the Project on South Asia and China Education Program funded by the US Department of Education. The views expressed in this book have nothing to do with our sponsors and we are solely responsible for any errors or omissions.

We want to thank Thomson Financial for allowing us to use its database. Our appreciation also extends to many individuals who provided suggestions and assistance for the book manuscript. Judy Beam offered professional editorial assistance, and skillful typing services were provided by Brianna Hollenkamp and Angela Phillips. Research assistance was provided by Brianna Hollenkamp, Joe Lake, and Matt Babbie.

We are thankful to the staff at Routledge and Taylor & Francis Books, especially Robert Langham and Terry Clague, for their assistance and encouragement. Last, but not least, this book is dedicated to the Tang family as well as to the Metwalli family. The book would not have been completed without their understanding and support.

Roger Y. W. Tang
Ali M. Metwalli

Acknowledgments

The authors and publishers would like to thank Thomson Financial for granting permission to reproduce financial data in this book:

Tables 1.2, 1.3, 1.4, 1.5, 1.6, 1.7, 1.8 and Figures 1.1, 1.2.
Tables 3.1, 3.2, 3.3, 3.4, 3.5, 3.6, 3.7, 3.8 and Figures 3.1, 3.2.
Tables 5.1, 5.2, 5.3, 5.4, 5.5, 5.8, 5.9, 5.10, 5.11, 5.12, 5.13, 5.14, 5.15, 5.16, 5.17, 5.18, 5.19, 5.20.
Tables 7.1, 7.2, 7.3, 7.4, 7.5, 7.6, 7.7, 7.8, 7.9, 7.10, 7.11, 7.12, 7.13, 7.14, 7.15, 7.16, 7.17, 7.18, 7.19, 7.20, 7.21, 7.22, 7.23, 7.24 and Figures 7.1, 7.2.
Tables 8.4, 8.5, 8.6, 8.7, 8.8.

The data for the above tables and figures were collected between May and June of 2005.

Every effort has been made to contact copyright holders for their permission to reprint material in this book. The publishers would be grateful to hear from any copyright holder who is not here acknowledged and will undertake to rectify any errors or omission in future editions of this book.

1 Mergers and acquisitions in a changing world

Mergers and Acquisitions (M&A) is a process or a range of activities for two companies to combine their operations to achieve specific business or strategic objectives. These objectives may include expanding into new products or markets, reducing production or administrative costs, and adding new research and development capabilities to the combined company. Cross-border M&A may allow the acquirer to expand into overseas markets and obtain new technology and brand names, or distribution networks.

M&A activities expanded rapidly in the United States and Europe during the 1990s. The M&A transaction value in the United States reached its peak of $2.3 trillion in 1999. In Britain, the M&A transaction value also reached a record of $802 billion in 1999. In Germany, its M&A record in 1999 was $518 billion. Unfortunately, the M&A boom in the 1990s was followed by a slow-down of the global economy and the stock market crash in the second half of the 1990s. The 9/11 tragedy in September 2001 and the recession in 2001 and 2002 also depressed worldwide M&A activities. M&A transaction values in the United States and Europe plummeted in 2002 and 2003.

In the last two decades, many writers have published hundreds of articles and dozens of books to explain the M&A activities in the United States and Europe. Some papers and books have also been published to explain cross-border M&A in Asia. For example, Zhan and Ozawa (2001) provide a comprehensive review of cross-border transactions in Indonesia, Malaysia, the Philippines, Thailand, and South Korea up to 1999. Mody and Negishi (2001), and Chen and Findlay (2003) reviewed the cross-border mergers and acquisitions in Asia up to the year 2000 and discussed their impact on the host economies in that region.

Chen and Findlay (2003) concluded that the rapid increase in cross-border M&A in the APEC economies in the 1990s was "driven by a combination of factors, including the liberalization of trade and investment regimes, the deregulation of the service sector, the privatization of state-owned enterprises (SOEs), and the relaxation of controls over cross-border M&As." These factors continue to impact M&A activities in the twenty-first century. Other factors including the economic expansion in China and the economic integration among the three regions of Greater China (Hong Kong, Taiwan, and Mainland China) also have significant impact on the M&A activities in East Asia. The main purpose of this book is to provide a comprehensive review of M&A activities in selected countries in Asia. These countries include Japan, Hong Kong, Taiwan, China, and selected countries in the ASEAN (Association of Southeast Asian Nations) region.

In the remainder of this chapter, we will discuss the following topics:

- global trends of M&A in industrial countries, Greater China, and the ASEAN region;
- cross-border M&A from a US perspective;
- the importance of East and Southeast Asia in global investment and trade;
- economic growth of developing countries in Asia;
- recent changes in the Asian-Pacific region that facilitate the expansion of M&A;
- the objectives and scope of this book.

An overview of the book is provided toward the end of this chapter.

Global trends of M&A

In the past, M&A activities in the United States and many other industrial countries included some periods of high merger activities (merger waves) followed by periods of relatively fewer activities. Many writers agree there have been five waves of M&A in the United States since 1890 (e.g. Weston and Weaver, 2001; Gaughan, 2003; Sudarsanam, 2003). However, they disagree slightly on the beginning and ending years of those five merger waves. Table 1.1 summarizes the views of three books: Weston and Weaver (2001), Sudarsanam (2003), and Gaughan (2003). Major characteristics of each of those five merger waves are also provided in Table 1.1. Detailed discussions can be found in Gaughan (2003), Sudarsanam (2003), Gilson and Black (1995), Salter and Weinhold (1979), and many other publications. Some major outcomes from these waves are summarized as follows:

- *The first wave (1890–1905)*: Many horizontal mergers took place during this wave. Industrial giants such as General Electric, Eastman Kodak, American Can, American Tobacco, and DuPont were established through consolidations.
- *The second wave (1920s)*: This wave was characterized by an increase in vertical mergers and a movement toward oligopolistic structure in some industries. According to Sudarsanam (2003), "the second wave accompanied economic growth and stock market boom. An estimated 12,000 firms disappeared during the period."
- *The third wave (1960s)*: During this period, there were many unrelated mergers to achieve growth through diversification into new product markets. This wave ended with the petroleum crisis in 1973 and the economic recession that followed.
- *The fourth wave (1980s)*: This wave witnessed many financial innovations including junk bonds and leveraged buyout (LBO) that made many firms vulnerable to hostile tender offers. This wave included acquisitions as well as divestitures that allowed companies to sell off some segments of their businesses.

Table 1.1 Five waves of M&A activities in the United States from 1893 to 2004

Wave	Time period			
	Weston and Weaver (2001)	Sudarsanam (2003)	Gaughan (2003)	Major characteristics
First wave	1893– 1904	1890– 1905	1897– 1904	M&A for monopoly: major horizontal mergers took place in the steel, oil, and basic manufacturing industries
Second wave	1920s	1920s	1916– 1929	M&A for oligopoly: large vertical mergers took place in the automobile, public utility, petroleum, and chemical industries
Third wave	1960s	1960s	1965– 1969	Conglomerate mergers: many M&A activities were undertaken to form conglomerates conducting business in different industries
Fourth wave	1980s	1980s	1981– 1989	Mega mergers: large mergers and acquisitions occurred in the telecommunications, banking, oil and gas, pharmaceutical, and airline industries
Fifth wave	1993– 2001	1990s	1992– 2001	Large strategic mega mergers in the banking, telecommunications and pharmaceutical industries with the intention to expand into new markets to obtain new technologies and business synergies

Sources: Weston and Weaver (2001); Sudarsanam (2003); Gaughan (2003), and other publications.

- *The fifth wave (1990s)*: This period witnessed the emergence and wide-spread use of many new technologies including the Internet, cable television, and satellite communication. Globalization of production, sales, and capital markets had also accelerated. Mature industries such as banking, automobiles, pharmaceuticals, and media were being downsized and restructured. M&A of the fifth wave reached its peak in 1999 with a world-wide M&A value of about $4.4 trillion, before declining to $3.9 trillion in 2000.

Historical reviews of M&A activities among member countries of the European Union (EU) and merger waves of the United Kingdom (UK) are provided in Sudarsanam (2003) who noted there were two merger waves among the EU. One small wave occurred from 1987 to 1992 and a much larger one existed from 1995 to 2001. These two merger waves almost parallel those of the fourth and fifth waves of the United States. Sudarsanam (2003) also found that the EU countries most active in M&A in the 1990s were the United Kingdom (31 percent of all EU deals), Germany (16 percent), France (14 percent), the Netherlands (7 percent), and Italy (6 percent).

In reviewing the merger waves in the United Kingdom, Sudarsanam (2003) discovered that "there is a striking parallel in the incidence and timing of the 1960s and 1980s waves in the US and the UK," and the UK merger wave in the 1990s "shares many of the characteristics of the 1990s wave in the EU."

Since the focus of this book is on M&A activities from 1990 to 2004, we will provide more discussion of the fifth wave and other global trends for that period. In the following sections, we will review recent worldwide M&A aggregate statistics, M&A in selected industrial countries and those in Greater China and the ASEAN region.

Worldwide M&A activities

Table 1.2 shows the announced worldwide M&A activity from 1990 to 2004. The table includes statistics on the number of deals, total M&A value, and average

Table 1.2 Announced worldwide M&A activity, 1990–2004

Year	Number of deals		Total value of M&A (millions US$)		
	Worldwide total	% change	Worldwide total	% change	Average value per deal (million US$)
1990	6,107	NA	644,006		105.5
1991	6,318	+3	483,253	−25	76.5
1992	6,538	+3	503,645	+4	77.0
1993	7,809	+19	665,228	+32	85.2
1994	9,299	+19	797,095	+20	85.7
1995	10,576	+14	1,203,673	+51	113.8
1996	12,047	+14	1,453,432	+21	120.7
1997	13,834	+15	2,072,449	+43	149.8
1998	15,589	+13	3,024,460	+46	194.0
1999	15,908	+2	4,447,684	+47	279.6
2000	16,758	+5	3,923,499	−12	234.1
2001	12,312	−27	2,132,196	−46	173.2
2002	11,486	−7	1,423,231	−33	123.9
2003	12,708	+11	1,635,369	+15	128.7
2004	13,260	+4	2,319,331	+42	174.9
1990–2004 total	170,549		26,728,550		156.7
Averages					
1990–4	7,214		618,645		86.0
1995–9	13,591		2,440,340		171.6
2000–4	13,305		2,286,725		167.0

Source: Thomson Financial.

Note
The value of M&A transactions listed in this table is limited to those with one million dollars or higher.

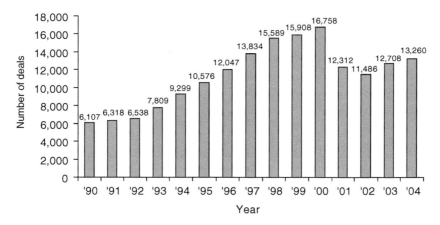

Figure 1.1 Worldwide M&A activity in number of deals, 1990–2004.

Source: Thomson Financial.

value per deal. The value of M&A transactions listed is limited to those with one million dollars or higher.

In 1990, there were 6,107 deals worldwide. The number of deals increased moderately in 1991 and 1992. Between 1993 and 1998, the number of deals recorded double-digit increases each year before slowing down in 1999. The number of deals reached its peak in 2000 and declined substantially in 2001 and 2002 before recovering in 2003. The changes in worldwide M&A transactions are also depicted in Figure 1.1. In 2004, there were 13,260 deals with values of US$ 1 million or higher.

As shown in Table 1.2, total M&A value declined by 25 percent from 1990 to 1991. It recorded a moderate increase of 4 percent in 1992. The fifth merger wave took place between 1992 and 2000. During this period, the annual worldwide total M&A value increased from $503 billion in 1992 to $4.4 trillion in 1999 before dropping to $3.9 trillion in 2000. Total M&A value declined substantially in 2001 and 2002. In 2002, the worldwide total of M&A value was about $1.4 trillion. The year 2003 witnessed a slow recovery of M&A activity, and total M&A value recorded an impressive gain of 42 percent in 2004. In 2004, worldwide total M&A value was about $2.1 trillion. Changes in worldwide M&A value from 1990 to 2004 are also shown in Figure 1.2.

The last column of Table 1.2 shows the average value per deal from 1990 to 2004. The average value fluctuated from $76.5 million in 1991 to $279.6 million in 1999. In 2004, the average value per deal was $174.9 million.

M&A activities in selected developed countries

Table 1.3 shows the announced M&A deals in eight selected industrial countries from 1990 to 2004. These countries are the United States, the United Kingdom, Japan, France, Germany, Italy, the Netherlands, and Sweden. During the period from

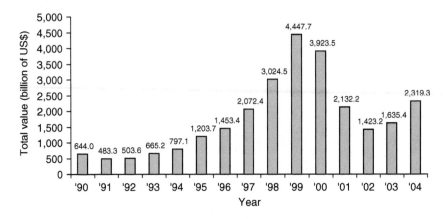

Figure 1.2 Worldwide M&A activity in transaction value, 1990–2004.

Source: Thomson Financial.

Table 1.3 Announced M&A deals in selected industrial countries[a], 1990–2004

Year	United States	United Kingdom	Japan	France	Germany	Italy	Nether-lands	Sweden
1990	3,416	1,587	286	262	158	108	120	98
1991	2,824	1,201	211	422	219	161	134	178
1992	3,314	1,136	116	379	180	272	123	118
1993	4,011	1,220	67	330	183	177	101	105
1994	5,087	1,550	91	300	169	176	113	132
1995	5,642	1,654	126	352	236	185	133	129
1996	6,660	1,741	166	344	230	188	156	144
1997	7,485	2,211	208	378	252	191	182	172
1998	8,305	2,436	277	473	360	205	243	186
1999	7,137	2,427	663	733	466	310	301	347
2000	6,601	2,617	955	664	552	423	369	410
2001	4,474	1,714	847	501	397	312	229	241
2002	3,912	1,412	1,117	380	377	254	176	141
2003	3,956	1,593	1,379	348	326	343	167	179
2004	4,120	1,664	1,225	420	361	311	155	211
1990–2004 total	76,944	26,163	7,734	6,286	4,466	3,616	2,702	2,791
Averages								
1990–4	7,046	2,094	154	456	309	216	203	196
1995–9	4,613	1,800	288	463	403	329	219	236
2000–4	4,116	1,596	1,105	412	365	305	182	193

Source: Thomson Financial.

Note
a Include only transactions of US$1 million or above.

1990 to 2004, the United States had a total of 76,944 announced deals and accounted for about 45 percent of the world's total as shown in Table 1.3. The British share of M&A for the same period was about 15 percent. Together, the United States and Britain accounted for 60 percent of worldwide M&A from 1990 to 2004.

Japan witnessed a remarkable growth in announced M&A deals from 1990 to 2004. In 1990, the announced M&A deals of $1 million or above were only 286. The number declined to 91 in 1994. Between 1995 and 2003, the number of deals increased from 126 to 1,379. In 2004, it decreased to 1,225. During the 1990–2004 period, Japan had a total of 6,213 deals, or about 4 percent of the world's total. Details of Japan's M&A activities will be provided in Chapter 3. France, Germany, Italy, the Netherlands, and Sweden are all member countries of the EU with significant M&A deals. Together, these five countries had about 12 percent of worldwide M&A deals.

Table 1.4 provides the statistics of M&A transaction values for the eight industrial countries from 1990 to 2004. In most of these countries, the fifth merger wave began in 1993 and ended in 2001. M&A transaction values of these countries reached their peaks in 1999. During 1999, the United States had a record transaction value of $2.3 trillion, while Britain also had a record of $802 billion in the same year. Between 2001 and 2003, M&A transaction values plummeted in many industrial countries. This trend coincided with the recession and stock market crash in the same period. The year 2004 witnessed a recovery of M&A transactions in most of these eight countries.

From 1990 to 2004, the United States had a total M&A transaction value of $14.8 trillion, or 55 percent of the world's total. Britain's total for the same period was $3.9 trillion, accounting for 15 percent of the world's total. Together, the United States and Britain had about 70 percent of the worldwide total M&A transaction value from 1990 to 2004. The other six industrial countries also had significant M&A transaction values during the same period.

Table 1.5 shows the twenty largest worldwide M&A during the 1990–2004 period. The largest transaction ($202.8 billion) was the takeover of Mannesmann AG (Germany) by Vodafone Airtouch PLC (UK). The merger between Time Warner and America Online was second with a transaction value of $164.7 billion. The third largest deal was the acquisition of Warner-Lambert by Pfizer in 1999 that had a transaction value of $89.2 billion.

All the acquirers and target companies of the twenty largest M&A were from industrial countries. Fourteen US companies were involved as acquirers and another 15 US firms as target companies. Three British companies were involved in three transactions as acquirers and another British firm (SmithKline Beecham) was involved as a target company. Other countries that had companies involved as acquirers or targets in the top 20 deals are France, Canada, and Germany.

Table 1.6 shows the 30 largest worldwide M&A in 2005. The largest transaction was the acquisition of Gillette by Proctor & Gamble in a $54.9 billion deal. The second largest transaction was the purchase of Mitsubishi Tokyo Financial by UFJ Holdings in Japan. The acquisition of MBNA by Bank of America was the third largest deal. The other 27 deals ranged in value from $7.6 billion to $35.4 billion.

Table 1.4 Announced M&A transaction values in selected industrial countries[a], 1990–2004 (value in millions of US dollars)

Year	United States	United Kingdom	Japan	France	Germany	Italy	Netherlands	Sweden
1990	307,176	140,807	43,089	47,674	27,050	31,541	21,773	17,951
1991	212,928	78,253	12,182	44,223	27,875	20,196	10,766	16,069
1992	229,061	75,040	7,868	39,424	36,811	27,953	22,788	17,362
1993	365,949	71,968	14,953	61,514	24,589	22,918	15,288	15,292
1994	496,818	86,309	15,149	51,427	18,154	29,437	9,304	12,186
1995	767,923	187,837	46,638	35,806	36,292	21,028	19,104	26,585
1996	918,798	182,638	19,973	72,394	42,824	29,597	28,895	25,709
1997	1,297,385	232,457	23,161	109,936	80,612	62,706	42,530	30,067
1998	2,045,345	372,429	27,718	153,982	181,248	71,123	101,297	64,987
1999	2,300,298	802,446	243,674	442,819	517,728	305,057	139,732	82,006
2000	2,138,962	653,309	151,275	269,505	268,093	141,937	134,118	61,298
2001	1,167,389	277,010	73,495	144,716	132,977	76,390	67,196	36,396
2002	631,794	212,890	77,945	114,105	101,857	63,634	33,582	17,987
2003	752,403	185,844	107,982	65,481	73,569	94,248	25,088	20,016
2004	1,183,179	321,572	138,521	150,497	88,248	75,793	115,660	30,573
1990–2004 total	14,815,408	3,880,809	1,003,623	1,803,503	1,657,927	1,073,558	787,121	474,484
Averages								
1990–4	322,386	90,475	18,648	48,852	26,986	26,409	15,984	15,772
1995–9	1,465,950	355,561	72,233	162,987	171,741	97,902	66,312	45,871
2000–4	1,174,745	330,125	109,844	148,861	132,949	90,400	75,129	33,254

Source: Thomson Financial.

Note
a Include only transactions of US$1 million or above.

Table 1.5 Twenty largest worldwide M&A deals, 1990–2004

Date announced	Date effective	Target name and nationality	Acquirer and nationality	Transaction value (US$ billion)
11/14/1999	6/19/2000	Mannesmann AG (Germany)	Vodafone Airtouch PLC (UK)	202.8
1/10/2000	1/12/2001	Time Warner (US)	America Online Inc (US)	164.7
11/4/1999	6/19/2000	Warner-Lambert Co (US)	Pfizer Inc (US)	89.2
12/1/1998	11/30/1999	Mobil Corp (US)	Exxon Corp (US)	78.9
1/17/2000	12/27/2000	SmithKline Beecham PLC (UK)	Glaxo Wellcome PLC (UK)	76.0
4/6/1998	10/8/1998	Citicorp (US)	Travelers Group Inc (US)	72.6
7/8/2001	11/18/2002	AT&T Broadband & Internet Svcs (US)	Comcast Corp (US)	72.0
5/11/1998	10/8/1999	Ameritech Corp (US)	SBC Communications Inc (US)	62.6
4/13/1998	9/30/1998	BankAmerica Corp (US)	NationsBank Corp, Charlotte, NC (US)	61.6
1/18/1999	6/30/1999	AirTouch Communications Inc (US)	Vodafone Group PLC (UK)	60.3
1/26/2004	8/20/2004	Aventis SA (France)	Sanofi/Synthelabo SA (France)	60.2
1/26/2000	5/1/2000	Nortel Networks Corp (Canada)	Shareholder Investor Groups (Canada)	60.0
7/15/2002	4/15/2003	Pharmacia Corp (US)	Pfizer Inc (US)	59.5
1/14/2004	7/1/2004	Bank One Corp, Chicago, IL (US)	JP Morgan Chase & Co (US)	58.8
6/14/1999	6/30/2000	US WEST Inc (US)	Qwest Commun Intl Inc (US)	56.3
6/24/1998	3/9/1999	Tele-Communications Inc (US)	AT&T Corp (US)	53.6
7/28/1998	6/30/2000	GTE Corp (US)	Bell Atlantic Corp (US)	53.4
7/5/1999	3/27/2000	Elf Aquitaine (France)	Total Fina SA (France)	50.1
4/22/1999	6/15/2000	MediaOne Group Inc (US)	AT&T Corp (US)	49.3
10/27/2003	4/1/2004	FleetBoston Financial Corp, MA (US)	Bank of America Corp (US)	49.3

Source: Thomson Financial.

Table 1.6 Thirty largest worldwide M&A in 2005

Target company (country)	Acquiring firm (country)	Date announced	Transaction value (in US$ billion)
Gillette (US)	Proctor & Gamble (US)	Jan. 28	54.9
UFJ Holdings (Japan)	Mitsubishi Tokyo Fal (Japan)	Feb. 18	41.4
MBNA (US)	Bank of America (US)	June 30	35.8
Burlington Resources (US)[a]	ConocoPhillips (US)	Dec. 12	35.4
O2 (UK)[a]	Telefonica (Spain)	Oct. 31	31.7
Endesa (Spain)[a]	Gas Natural SDG (Spain)	Sept. 5	28.3
Guidant (US)	Boston Scientific (US)	Dec. 5	24.9
HypoVereinsbank (Germany)	Unicredito Italiano (Italy)	May 30	18.3
Adelphia Commun (US)[a]	Investor Group (US)	April 21	17.6
Unocal (US)	ChevronTexaco (US)	April 4	17.1
AT&T (US)	SBC Communications (US)	Jan. 31	14.7
Allied Domecq (UK)	Goal Acquisitions (France)	April 5	14.4
Electrabel (Belgium)	Suez (France)	Aug. 9	14.3
OAO Sibneft (Russia)	OAD Gazprom (Russia)	Sept. 28	13.1
Georgia-Pacific (US)	Koch Forest Products (US)	Nov. 13	12.6
Seven-Eleven Japan (Japan)	Ito-Yokado (Japan)	April 20	12.5
TDC (Denmark)[a]	Nordic Telephone (US)	Nov. 30	12.0
Travelers (US)	MetLife (US)	Jan. 31	11.7
Constellation Energy (US)[a]	FPL Group (US)	Dec. 19	11.3
Falconbridge (Canada)[a]	Inco (Canada)	Oct. 11	11.0
SunGard Data Systems (US)	Investor Group (US)	March 28	11.0
May Department Stores (US)	Federated Dept Stores (US)	Feb. 28	10.5
Placer Dome (Canada)[a]	Barrick Gold (Canada)	Oct. 31	10.2
Innovene (US)	INEOS Group (UK)	Oct. 7	9.0
Cincrgy (US)[a]	Duke Energy (US)	May 9	8.8
MCI (US)	Verizon Communications (US)	Feb. 14	8.5
Texas Genco Holdings (US)[a]	NRG Energy (US)	Oct. 2	8.3
Auna (Spain)	Orange (France)	July 27	7.7
Jefferson-Pilot (US)[a]	Lincoln National (US)	Oct. 10	7.7
Daiichi Pharmaceutical (Japan)	Sankyo (Japan)	Feb. 25	7.6

Source: Thomson Financial.

Note
a Pending transactions.

Of the 30 largest deals, 11 were still pending as of March 1, 2006. Preliminary statistics from Thomson Financial also show that total worldwide M&A transaction value for 2005 was more than $2.7 trillion, and the number of deals worldwide increased by 38 percent compared with 2004.

M&A activities in Greater China

In this book, Greater China is defined to include Hong Kong, Taiwan, and Mainland China. In the past, many authors have used this definition to discuss the economic growth, economic integration, and cultural aspects of Mainland China, Hong Kong, and Taiwan (e.g. Ash and Kueh, 1993; Ho and Tsui, 2004; and Sung, 2005). Details on investment and trade relations among the three regions of Greater China will be presented in Chapter 4. In Chapter 1, we will provide the aggregate statistics of M&A in Greater China. Details of M&A by region (or country) of Greater China will be discussed in Chapter 5.

Table 1.7 shows the announced M&A deals and transaction values of Greater China from 1990 to 2004. The number of deals increased rapidly from a low of 131 deals in 1990 to 2,195 deals in 2004. In recent years (2000–4), the average number of deals per year (1,417 deals) surpassed those in the first half and second half of the 1990s.

The M&A transaction values in Greater China had fluctuated from a low of $10.3 billion in 1990 to $167.1 billion in 2000. The transaction value dropped by 59 percent in 2001 before recovering a bit in 2002. In 2004, the annual transaction value was $56.4 billion.

The total M&A transaction value of Greater China from 1990 to 2004 was $675.2 billion, accounting for about 3 percent of the worldwide total. The

Table 1.7 Announced M&A deals and transaction values in Greater China, 1990–2004

Number of deals			*M&A transaction values*[a]		
Year	*Total*	*% change*	*Total (US$ million)*	*% change*	*Average value per (US$ million)*
1990	131	NA	10,377	NA	79.2
1991	248	+89	14,527	+40	58.6
1992	219	−12	12,024	−17	54.9
1993	370	+69	22,291	+85	60.3
1994	396	+7	13,597	−39	34.3
1995	318	−20	11,408	−16	35.9
1996	424	+33	24,974	+119	58.9
1997	605	+43	43,706	+75	72.2
1998	592	−2	34,627	−21	58.5
1999	698	+18	55,674	+61	79.8
2000	1,103	+58	167,107	+200	151.5
2001	857	−22	68,947	−59	80.5
2002	1,249	+46	80,020	+16	64.1
2003	1,683	+35	59,564	−26	35.4
2004	2,195	+30	56,399	−5	25.7
1990–2004 total	11,088		675,242		60.9
Averages					
1990–2004	273		14,563		53.3
1995–9	527		34,078		64.7
2000–4	1,417		86,407		61.0

Source: Thomson Financial.

Note

a Include only transactions of US$1 million or above.

average value per deal for the 1990–2004 period was about $60.9 million. Annual average value per deal varies significantly from year to year.

M&A activities in the ASEAN region

For the purpose of this book, the ASEAN region is defined to include the ten member countries of the Association: Brunei, Myanmar (Burma), Cambodia, Laos, Malaysia, Singapore, Thailand, Indonesia, the Philippines, and Vietnam. In Chapter 1, we will review only the aggregate statistics for the ASEAN region. Details for the five major ASEAN countries (Malaysia, Singapore, Thailand, Indonesia, and the Philippines) with significant M&A activities are discussed in Chapters 6 and 7.

Table 1.8 shows the announced M&A deals and transaction values in the ASEAN region from 1990 to 2004. The number of deals for the region fluctuated significantly from year to year and reached its peak of 1,020 deals in 2004. Total number of deals for the 1990–2004 period was 9,821 deals or about 6 percent of the worldwide total.

Table 1.8 Announced M&A deals and transaction values in ASEAN region, 1990–2004

Number of deals			*M&A transaction values*[a]		
Year	*Total*	*% change*	*Total (US$ million)*	*% change*	*Average value per (US$ million)*
1990	152	NA	15,299	NA	100.7
1991	301	+98	11,641	−24	38.7
1992	193	−36	8,977	−23	46.5
1993	418	+117	26,955	+200	64.5
1994	567	+36	24,607	−9	43.4
1995	780	+38	32,489	+32	41.7
1996	870	+12	41,121	+27	47.3
1997	787	−9	46,517	+13	59.1
1998	639	−19	32,244	−31	50.5
1999	818	+28	59,363	+84	72.6
2000	897	+10	48,904	−18	54.5
2001	775	−14	68,692	+40	88.6
2002	780	+1	26,383	−62	33.8
2003	824	+6	36,032	+37	43.7
2004	1,020	+24	41,692	+16	40.9
1990–2004 total	9,821		520,916		53.0
Averages					
1990–2004	326		17,495		53.6
1995–9	778		42,346		54.4
2000–4	859		44,340		51.7

Source: Thomson Financial.

Note
a Include only transactions of US$1 million or above.

The M&A transaction values vary from a low of $9.0 billion in 1992 to a record of $68.7 billion in 2001. The transaction values dropped to $26.4 billion in 2002 before recovering to $36.0 billion in 2003. The amount for 2004 was $41.7 billion. The average value per deal for the entire 1990–2004 period was about $53.0 million. The total M&A transaction values of ASEAN for the 1990–2004 period was about $521 billion, accounting for only 2 percent of the world's total.

Cross-border M&A from a US perspective

Cross-border M&A is a popular route for global growth and overseas expansion. Cross-border M&A is also playing an important role in global M&A. This is especially true for developed countries such as the United States and those in the EU. As explained by Eiteman *et al.* (2006):

> The 1992 completion of the European Union's Internal Market stimulated many of these investments, as European, Japanese, and US firms jockeyed for stronger market positions within the EU. However, the long-run US growth prospects and political safety in the United States motivated more takeovers of US firms by foreign firms, particularly from the United Kingdom and Japan, than vice versa.

Other major factors that motivate multinational companies to engage in crossborder M&A in Asia include the following:

- Globalization of production and distribution of products and services.
- Economic integration of the three regions of Greater China.
- Expansion of trade and investment relationships among the ASEAN member countries and their major trading partners: China, Japan, and the United States.
- Many countries are reforming their economic and legal systems, and providing generous investment and tax incentives to attract foreign investment.
- Privatization of state-owned enterprises and consolidation of the banking industry in China and other Asian countries.

To illustrate the importance of cross-border M&A, we are providing some statistics of the United States in Tables 1.9 and 1.10. Table 1.9 shows the statistics on US acquisitions of foreign businesses from 1990 to 2004. Data on foreign acquisitions of US companies are shown in Table 1.10.

Table 1.9 shows that from 1990 to 2004 there were 13,353 US acquisitions of foreign businesses with a total value of about $1 trillion. Table 1.10 indicates that from 1990 to 2004, there were 9,306 foreign acquisitions of US companies with a total value of $1.4 trillion. In terms of number of deals, cross-border M&A accounted for about 30 percent of US M&A during the period from 1990 to 2004.

Table 1.9 US acquisitions of foreign business enterprises[a], 1990–2004

Year	Total no. of deals	Dollar value offered (US$ million)
1990	266	18
1991	244	6
1992	403	14
1993	400	13
1994	399	18
1995	483	50
1996	837	52
1997	1,107	79
1998	1,194	93
1999	1,398	173
2000	1,400	137
2001	1,265	65
2002	1,023	92
2003	1,236	106
2004	1,698	111
1990–2004 total	13,353	1,027

Source: Compiled by the authors from various sources.

Note
a Include only transactions of US$1 million or above.

Table 1.10 Foreign acquisitions of US companies[a], 1990–2004

Year	Total no. of deals	Value (US$ million)
1990	266	33.1
1991	188	12.3
1992	167	9.3
1993	190	12.4
1994	219	35.8
1995	218	39.5
1996	333	73.5
1997	526	51.8
1998	572	194.7
1999	959	272.1
2000	1,248	299.2
2001	1,143	119.7
2002	995	86.6
2003	1,031	69.7
2004	1,251	105.0
1990–2004 total	9,306	1,414.7

Source: Compiled by the authors from various sources.

Note
a Include only transaction of US$1 million or above.

During the same period, the value of cross-border M&A accounted for about 17 percent of the US total.

The importance of East and Southeast Asia in global trade and investment

In 2004, Japan, Greater China and the ASEAN region together accounted for 15.9 percent of the world's M&A deals and 7.7 percent of the world's M&A transaction values. These percentages were calculated based on the data reported in Tables 1.2, 1.3, 1.4, 1.7, and 1.8. The percentages may seem small when compared with those of the United States, Britain, and other industrial countries. However, things will change in the foreseeable future because the economies of East Asia and Southeast Asia are growing faster than other regions of the world. In addition, they are playing more important roles in international trade and global investment. Because of these reasons, there will be more cross-border M&A involving the companies in East and Southeast Asia in the future.

Table 1.11 shows the leading exporters and importers in world merchandise trade for 2004. Intra-EU trade between the 25 EU countries was excluded. Among the 30 leading exporters, ten were from East and Southeast Asia. Together, the exports from these ten countries accounted for 35.9 percent of the world's total excluding intra-EU trade. Among the top 30 importers, 11 were from East and Southeast Asia. The combined imports of these 11 countries accounted for 31.1 percent of the world's total excluding intra-EU trade.

Inward and outward direct investment of major East Asia and Southeast Asian countries are shown in Table 1.12. For the purpose of comparison, we also show the US statistics and the world's totals for inward and outward direct investment. We can observe that the world's total inward and outward investments peaked in 2001, and declined in 2002 and 2003. The year 2004 witnessed moderate recoveries in the World's total inward and outward direct investments. In 2004, the World's total inward direct investment was $648 billion, and total outward investment was $730 billion.

For East and Southeast Asia, it was a different story. In 2004, total inward direct investment in East and Southeast Asia was a record $136.9 billion, while outward direct investment from this region was also a record of $98.1 billion. Among the countries in East and Southeast Asia, China received an inward investment of $60.6 billion (or 44 percent), and Hong Kong received $34.0 billion (or 25 percent). Surprisingly, in 2004, Hong Kong's outward direct investment ($39.8 billion) was the largest among all East and Southeast Asian countries. Other countries including Japan, Singapore, and Taiwan also had substantial outward direct investment in 2004.

As their trade and investments grow rapidly, countries in East and Southeast Asia may produce more opportunities for global M&A activities, especially cross-border M&A. For example, by May 30, 2005, M&A transaction value involving an Asia-Pacific target amounted to $179 billion, 69 percent more than the same period in 2004 (Jönsson, 2005). According to Todd Marin, head of

Table 1.11 Leading exporters and importers in world merchandise trade (excluding intra-EU (25) trade), 2004 (billions of US$ and percentages)

Rank	Exporters	Value	Share	Annual % change	Rank	Importers	Value	Share	Annual % change
1	Extra-EU (25) exports	1202.8	18.2	20	1	United States	1526.4	22.0	17
2	United States	819.0	12.4	13	2	Extra-EU (25) imports	1279.5	18.4	20
3	China[b]	593.4	9.0	35	3	China[b]	561.4	8.1	36
4	Japan[b]	565.5	8.5	20	4	Japan[b]	454.5	6.5	19
5	Canada	322.0	4.9	18	5	Canada	275.8	4.0	13
6	Hong Kong[b]	265.7	4.0	16	6	Hong Kong[b]	273.0	3.9	17
	Domestic exports	22.6	0.3	15		Retained imports[a]	29.9	0.4	24
	Re-exports	243.1	3.7	16					
7	South Korea[b]	253.9	3.8	31	7	South Korea[b]	224.4	3.2	26
8	Mexico	188.6	2.8	14	8	Mexico	206.4	3.0	16
9	Russian Federation	183.2	2.8	35	9	Taiwan[b]	167.9	2.4	32
10	Taiwan[b]	181.4	2.7	21	10	Singapore[b]	163.8	2.4	28
11	Singapore[b]	179.5	2.7	25		Retained imports[a]	82.8	1.2	30
	Domestic exports	98.5	1.5	23	11	Switzerland	111.5	1.6	16
	Re-exports	81.0	1.2	26					

12	Malaysia[b]	126.5	1.9	21
13	Saudi Arabia	119.6	1.8	28
14	Switzerland	118.4	1.8	18
15	Thailand[b]	97.7	1.5	22
16	Brazil	96.5	1.5	32
17	Australia	86.6	1.3	21
18	Norway	82.0	1.2	22
19	United Arab Em.	79.5	1.2	21
20	India	72.5	1.1	27
21	Indonesia[b]	69.7	1.1	14
22	Turkey	62.8	0.9	33
23	South Africa	45.9	0.7	26
24	Iran	42.5	0.6	26
25	Philippines[b]	39.6	0.6	7
26	Israel	36.9	0.6	17
27	Argentina	34.3	0.5	16
28	Ukraine	32.7	0.5	42
29	Chile	32.0	0.5	52
30	Algeria	31.7	0.5	29
	Ten East and S.E. Asian countries	2,372.9	35.9	—
	World	6,618.7	100.0	22

12	Australia	107.8	1.5	21
13	Malaysia[b]	105.2	1.5	26
14	Turkey	97.2	1.4	40
15	Thailand[b]	95.4	1.4	26
16	India	95.2	1.4	34
17	Russian Federation	94.8	1.4	28
18	Brazil	65.9	0.9	30
19	South Africa	55.2	0.8	34
20	Norway	48.2	0.7	22
21	United Arab Em.	47.4	0.7	20
22	Indonesia[b]	46.2	0.7	42
23	Israel	43.4	0.6	20
24	Saudi Arabia	43.0	0.6	16
25	Philippines[b]	42.6	0.6	8
26	Iran	32.7	0.5	25
27	Romania	32.7	0.5	36
28	Vietnam[b]	31.0	0.4	23
29	Ukraine	29.0	0.4	26
30	Chile	24.8	0.4	28
	Eleven East and S.E. Asian countries	2,165.4	31.1	—
	World	6,953.5	100.0	22

Source: WTO.

Notes
a Retained imports are defined as imports less re-exports.
b Countries from East and Southeast Asia.

Table 1.12 Inward and outward direct investment of selected countries, 2001–4 (millions of US dollars)

Country		1985–95 annual average	2001	2002	2003	2004
Japan	Inward	642	6,241	9,239	6,324	7,816
	Outward	24,214	38,333	32,281	28,800	30,951
China	Inward	11,715	46,878	52,743	53,505	60,630
	Outward	1,687	6,885	2,518	(152)	1,805
Taiwan	Inward	1,009	4,109	1,445	453	1,898
	Outward	2,671	5,480	4,886	5,682	7,145
Hong Kong	Inward	4,093	23,777	9,682	13,624	34,035
	Outward	7,884	11,345	17,463	5,492	39,753
Indonesia	Inward	1,364	(2,978)	145	(597)	1,023
	Outward	532	125	182	15	107
Malaysia	Inward	2,924	554	3,203	2,473	4,624
	Outward	676	267	1,905	1,369	2,061
Philippines	Inward	727	899	1,792	347	469
	Outward	86	(160)	59	197	412
Singapore	Inward	4,529	14,122	5,822	9,331	16,060
	Outward	1,505	22,711	4,095	3,705	10,667
Thailand	Inward	1,428	3,886	947	1,952	1,064
	Outward	213	346	106	486	362
Vietnam	Inward	633	1,300	1,200	1,450	1,610
	Outward	—	—	—	—	—
South Korea	Inward	697	3,692	2,975	3,785	7,687
	Outward	1,278	2,420	2,617	3,426	4,792
East and	Inward	29,761	102,480	89,193	92,647	136,916
Southeast Asia	Outward	40,746	87,752	66,112	49,020	98,055
United States	Inward	44,109	159,461	71,331	56,834	95,859
	Outward	43,102	124,873	134,946	119,406	229,294
World	Inward	182,438	825,925	716,128	632,599	648,146
	Outward	203,256	743,465	652,181	616,923	730,257

Source: UNCTAD.

M&A at JP Morgan Asia, several factors are driving the Asia M&A for the moment. These factors include "the continued interest in the region, particularly China, shown by Western firms" (Jönsson, 2005). At the same time, many Asian firms also look for opportunities to grow and consolidate their positions in home markets.

Economic growth of developing countries in Asia

Many developing countries in Asia experienced rapid growth in their GDP from 1990 to 2005 with the exception of 1997 and 1998 when some of these countries were confronted with financial and currency crises. Details of the 1997 economic crises will be provided in Chapter 6 when we discuss the economic environment of the ASEAN countries.

Table 1.13 shows the GDP growth rates of selected developing countries in Asia from 1990 to 2005. The data were obtained from several sources including the International Monetary Fund (IMF), the Ministry of Commerce of China, United Nations Conference on Trade and Development (UNCTAD), and the World Bank. While the growth rates shown in the table for 1990–2004 are actual numbers, most of the rates for 2005 are estimates.

We can observe that China had the fastest GDP growth rate among all the countries (or regions) reported in Table 1.13. China's GDP growth rate from 1990 to 2000 averaged about 10.4 percent per year. In recent years (from 2003 to 2005), China's GDP growth rates have been at a rate close to the 9 percent level. The 9.9 percent growth rate in 2005 took into account revisions made by China's Census Bureau. The new census data indicate that China's expanding service sector plays a bigger role in the economy than previously thought. The GDP in Taiwan and Hong Kong was growing during the same period but at a much slower pace.

The growth rates for six Southeast Asian countries are also reported in Table 1.13. These countries are Indonesia, Malaysia, Philippines, Singapore, Thailand, and Vietnam. The average annual growth rates of these six countries from 1990 to 2000 ranged from 3.3 percent in the Philippines to 7.9 percent per year in Vietnam. All these countries (with the exception of Vietnam) suffered severely from the financial crisis in 1997 and 1998. That was the reason why these five Southeast Asian countries had negative growth rates in 1998.

Table 1.13 GDP growth rates in selected developing countries in Asia, 1990–2005 (percentage change over previous year)

Country	1990–2000	1998	1999	2000	2001	2002	2003	2004	2005[a]
China	10.4	7.8	7.0	8.0	7.5	8.3	10.0	10.1	9.9
Taiwan	6.3	4.6	5.3	5.8	(2.2)	3.9	3.3	5.7	3.4
Hong Kong	4.0	(5.0)	3.4	10.2	0.5	1.9	3.2	8.1	6.3
Indonesia	4.2	(13.1)	0.8	4.9	3.8	4.4	4.9	5.1	5.8
Malaysia	7.0	(7.4)	6.1	8.9	0.3	4.4	5.4	7.1	5.5
Philippines	3.3	(0.6)	3.4	4.4	1.8	4.4	4.5	6.0	4.7
Singapore	7.7	(0.9)	6.4	9.6	(1.9)	3.2	1.4	8.4	5.7
Thailand	4.2	(10.5)	4.4	4.8	2.2	5.3	6.9	6.1	5.5
Vietnam	7.9	5.8	4.8	6.8	6.9	7.0	6.0	7.7	7.0
South Korea	5.8	(6.7)	10.9	9.3	3.1	6.4	3.1	4.6	3.5
India	6.0	6.0	7.1	4.0	5.5	4.3	7.8	6.7	6.5
Pakistan	3.5	2.5	4.3	2.6	2.9	5.8	5.3	6.3	7.5
East and South Asia (excluding Japan)	6.7	0.3	6.5	7.0	3.8	5.6	6.0	6.9	NA

Source: The IMF, Ministry of Commerce of China, UNCTAD, the World Bank, and the Wall Street Journal.

Notes
a Estimates.
NA = Not available.

Hong Kong and South Korea also had negative growth rates in 1998. In recent years, these Southeast Asian countries have enjoyed robust growth rates with the exception of Singapore and Thailand.

The growth rates for South Korea, India, and Pakistan are also reported in Table 1.13. Their statistics are for reference purpose only. The M&A activities of these three countries are not covered by this book.

Changes in the Asian-Pacific region that facilitate M&A expansion

Besides enjoying high growth rates in their GDPs, many countries in Asia have also changed their investment climates over the last ten years. Details of these changes in Japan, Greater China, and the ASEAN region will be reported in Chapters 2, 4, and 6. In this section, we provide some important examples of changes that will facilitate M&A expansion in the Asian-Pacific region.

In Japan, changes in corporate law have reduced legal barriers to M&A and venture capital and private equity investments. Japan has also relaxed many foreign investment restrictions and other related regulations including antitrust restrictions on M&A activity by enacting the Industrial Revitalization Law in 2003. In addition, Japan has made significant changes to the *Commercial Code* to introduce stock swaps between Japanese corporations and new rules to reduce restrictions on corporate spin-offs, treasury stock, and so forth.

In China, the State Council approved and implemented the Interim Regulation on Foreign Investment and Industrial Guidelines for Foreign Investments in 1995. As a result of this and other measures, foreign investments grew considerably in all regions in China. In 2003, China became the largest host country of foreign investment. In 2004, foreign direct investment (FDI) in China accounted for about 10 percent of the world's total FDI outflow. One important policy of China is to restructure and privatize all but the largest and most strategic state-owned enterprises (SOEs). The State Council established the State Assets Supervision and Administration Commission (SASAC) in March 2003 and turned over the equities in 1,895 national and thousands of provincial and municipal SOEs to the new Commission (Woodard and Wang, 2004). This Commission is seeking foreign acquisitions of selected SOEs to make them more competitive and financially more transparent.

At the end of 2001, both China and Taiwan joined the WTO (World Trade Organization) and are committed to open key sectors including finance, trade, and distribution to greater foreign participation. As a result, there should be more cross-border M&A in China, Taiwan, and Hong Kong.

Between 1997 and 1999, many member countries of ASEAN were negatively impacted by the financial crisis in East Asia. At that time, those countries encouraged cross-border M&A to "speed up corporate and financial restructuring and facilitate faster economic recovery" (Chen and Findlay, 2003). In recent years, many countries in the same region have provided very attractive investment incentives that may allow 100 percent ownership, tax exemptions, and generous capital allowances to new industries. These measures should attract more FDI into the ASEAN region. Details of these measures are explained in Chapter 6.

Objective and scope of the study

The primary goal of this book is to provide the latest information on the investment climates and M&A activities in selected countries (or regions) of Asia: Japan, Greater China, and the ASEAN. There are three specific objectives for publishing this book. First, we would like to provide the latest information on M&A in Asia by analyzing the M&A trends in Japan, Greater China, and Southeast Asia from 1990 to 2004. Countries selected for extensive analysis are shown in Figure 1.3. M&A data are available in the Worldwide Mergers and Acquisitions Database maintained by SDC Platinum of Thomson Financial Service. Comparisons will be made among regions and between countries of a particular region.

Second, we will provide a brief economic profile of selected countries shown in Figure 1.3 and discuss the investment climates of these countries. Many issues will be examined from the perspectives of US-based investors because they play a significant role in M&A activities in all regions of the world. Major trade and investment issues between these regions (countries) and the United States, will be reviewed. Important economic issues and recently released laws and regulations on investment and M&A will also be examined.

The third objective is to review taxation issues and provide practical guidelines on how to deal with some due diligence and integration issues. The taxation issues include tax incentives and specific tax considerations for equity acquisition, asset acquisition, or merger. The integration issues may include reconciling

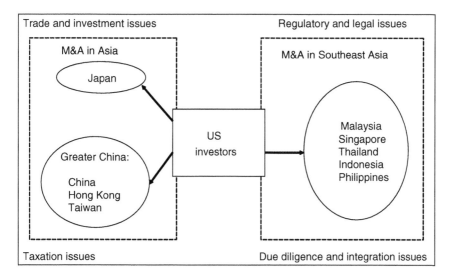

Figure 1.3 M&A in Asia: a global perspective.

cultural differences of M&A partners, and integrating human and physical resources. All of these issues are critical to the success of a merger or acquisition. When appropriate, the M&A practices in Asia will be compared with those observed in the United States. Implications for US-based investors will be explained.

An overview of the book

This book contains eight chapters. The first chapter reviews the global trends of M&A activities in selected industrial countries, Greater China, and the ASEAN region. The importance of East and Southeast Asia in global investment and trade will be discussed. Objectives and scope of the book will be explained.

Chapter 2 covers the economic environment of Japan. US trade and investment relations with Japan will be discussed. Japan's trade and investment relations with East Asian countries will also be reviewed. New M&A regulations and taxation issues will be presented.

Chapter 3 examines the M&A activities in Japan from 1990 to 2004. Transactions by target firms and acquiring firms will be discussed. Acquisition methods and the twenty largest M&A will be presented. Some unique features of Japanese M&A will also be discussed.

Chapters 4 and 5 cover materials related to Greater China (Hong Kong, China, and Taiwan). Chapter 4 provides an economic profile of the three regions of Greater China. Trade and investment relations between Greater China and the United States, will be reviewed. Investment climates of the three regions of Greater China and new investment and M&A regulations will be reviewed. Chapter 5 examines the M&A activities and practices in Hong Kong, Taiwan, and China.

Chapters 6 and 7 focus on Southeast Asia. Economic profiles and recent developments of the ASEAN countries will be explained in Chapter 6. Investment climates in the original five ASEAN countries (Malaysia, Singapore, Thailand, Indonesia, and the Philippines) will be discussed. Chapter 7 will analyze recent M&A trends and practices in Southeast Asia and a five-country comparison will be provided.

Chapter 8 compares major economic indicators and M&A activities and practices in Japan, Greater China, and Southeast Asia. The areas covered include growth in GDP, investment and trade, industrial distribution of the target firms, acquisition methods and the largest M&A in each country. Implications for US-based investors will be discussed. The chapter will also discuss future prospects for M&A activities in Asia, due diligence, and integration issues. General conclusions will also be provided.

2 Economic environment of Japan

Today, Japan is considered the second largest economy in the world. With a population exceeding 127 million and a GDP of well over $4 trillion, the country will remain a formidable economic power both in Asia and globally in the foreseeable future. It is important to view the Japanese economy and its performance in the context of a broader society.

Most Japanese live on four main islands (Hokkaido, Honshu, Shikoku, and Kyushu) and a number of smaller islands. About 50 percent of the population is concentrated in or around the three major cities of Tokyo, Osaka, and Nagoya. In Japan, the proportion of senior citizens aged 65 and older will reach 20 percent in 2006, compared with 10 percent just 20 years ago. This number is anticipated to reach its highest level of 35 percent in the year 2050. At the same time, a decreasing fertility rate means a shrinking work force that may undermine future economic growth.

Japanese society has a rich cultural heritage and a distinct social pattern. The family is of prime importance within the hierarchical society. The Japanese are relationship and group orientated people that place strong emphasis on interpersonal responsibility, orderliness, harmony, and respect for others, especially elders.

A deep sense of vertical and reciprocal personal obligations permeates both its society and the economy. Japanese workers place a high value on the work ethic. Relationships and behavior within the company tend to be hierarchical and stress a personal respect for authority. There is also a strong bond between workers and a high degree of identification of individual workers with their companies. A firm's obligation to the tradition of "lifetime employment" causes the employees to identify with their firms and make them unwilling to leave when they are offered a higher paying job to work for a foreign firm. However, today's economic problems are causing Japanese firms to downsize and impose pressure on the existing tradition of "lifetime employment." In spite of this, loyalty still plays an important part in worker-company relationships. Lifetime employment, seniority wages, and company unions are referred to as the three "treasures" of Japanese business relations that have assisted the country to achieve its remarkable economic growth. Yet in the global environment today, these three "treasures" entail limitations that may hinder the long-term development of the economy.

In the following sections, we will discuss topics relevant to the economic environment of Japan:

- an economic profile of the country;
- the business and investment environment in Japan;
- Japan's trade and investment relations with the United States and important Asian countries;
- M&A and reforms of M&A regulations;
- taxation issues.

Summary and conclusions will be provided toward the end of the chapter.

An economic profile of Japan

Strong government–industry cooperation, mastery of high technology, a strong work ethic, and a relatively small defense budget (1 percent of GDP) have helped Japan achieve considerable growth over the past 50 years. This rapid growth was achieved at the expense of an increase in government borrowing. Now the government is working to reduce the national debt and plans a slow but steady growth with an improved standard of living.

One of the important characteristics of the Japanese economy is the working relationship among manufacturers, suppliers, and distributors in closely-knit groups called *Keiretsu* (business group). *Keiretsus* are huge, vertically integrated corporations. They are held together by a variety of devices including the use of a single group bank, dependence on a trading company for sales, cross-holding of shares, close working relationships of CEOs in a presidential council, and the foundation of joint ventures. There are essentially three types of *Keiretsus*: manufacturing firms, industrial firms, and banks or financial companies, which are grouped around and led by a major trading company that creates a center for the group.

Table 2.1 shows the world's 25 largest companies ranked by revenue in 2004. Three of them are Japanese: Toyota Motor, Nippon Telephone & Telegraph, and Hitachi. In addition, Japan also has other powerful trading firms such as Mitsubishi, Mitsui, Itochu, Sumitomo, Marubeni, and Nissho, which generate billions of dollars in exports and imports. Their large trading volume accounts for almost a quarter of Japan's GDP.

After 1945, Japan experienced a rapid growth and economic expansion for over 40 years. However, in recent years Japan has faced an economic slowdown. The average growth of GDP dropped from 4.3 percent in the 1970s to 4.0 percent in the 1980s. GDP growth continued to decline in the 1990s and turned negative by 1998. The annual increase or decrease in the three economic indicators (including domestic corporate price index and consumer price index) for the years from 1995 to 2005 are shown in Table 2.2. In 2004, growth continued to improve and the fear of deflation in prices and economic activities lessened. In 2005, Japan's GDP grew at a rate of 2.8 percent. Government statistics published in February 2006 also show that the Japanese economy grew at a stunning 5.5 percent annual rate in the fourth quarter of 2005 (Kageyama, 2006). Robust economic growth in

Table 2.1 The world's 25 largest companies ranked by revenue in 2004

Rank	Company	Industry	Country	Revenues (US$ billion)	Market value (US$ billion)
1	Wal-Mart Stores	Retailing	United States	285.22	218.56
2	BP	Oil & gas operations	United Kingdom	285.06	231.88
3	Royal Dutch/ Shell Group	Oil & gas operations	Netherlands/ United Kingdom	265.19	221.49
4	ExxonMobil	Oil & gas operations	United States	263.99	405.25
5	General Motors	Consumer durables	United States	193.45	20.15
6	DaimlerChrysler	Consumer durables	Germany	192.75	47.04
7	Ford Motor	Consumer durables	United States	170.84	23.15
8	Toyota Motor	Consumer durables	Japan	165.68	140.89
9	General Electric	Conglomerate	United States	152.36	372.14
10	Chevron Texaco	Oil & gas operations	United States	142.90	131.52
11	Total	Oil & gas operations	France	131.64	151.13
12	Volkswagen Group	Consumer durables	Germany	120.71	19.03
13	ConocoPhillips	Oil & gas operations	United States	118.72	76.54
14	Allianz Worldwide	Insurance	Germany	112.35	46.55
15	Citigroup	Banking	United States	108.28	247.66
16	Nippon Tel & Tel	Telecommunications service	Japan	106.30	68.38
17	AXA Group	Insurance	France	97.92	51.45
18	IBM	Technology hardware & equipment	United States	96.29	152.76
19	American Intl Group	Insurance	United States	95.04	173.99
20	Siemens Group	Conglomerate	Germany	93.49	69.94
21	ING Group	Diversified financials	Netherlands	92.01	68.04
22	Carrefour Group	Food markets	France	88.66	37.02
23	Hitachi	Conglomerate	Japan	82.70	20.97
24	Hewlett-Packard	Technology hardware & equipment	United States	81.85	60.48
25	ENI	Oil & gas operations	Italy	79.31	104.71

Source: The websites of Fortune and Forbes Magazines and other sources.

China and solid growth in the United States has created a strong demand for Japanese exports. Demand for Japanese cars and flat panel televisions is very strong in the United States. Corporate profits have improved after many Japanese companies reduced their costs and major banks wrote off significant amounts of bad debts. However, deflation (declining prices) worsened during the last quarter of 2005 compared to one year ago.

Table 2.2 Japan's real GDP growth rates and price indexes, 1995–2005

Year	Real GDP growth rate over previous year	Domestic corporate goods price index[a]	Consumer price index[b]
1995	2.0	104.1	98.5
1996	3.4	102.4	98.6
1997	1.8	103.0	100.4
1998	(1.0)	101.5	101.0
1999	(0.1)	100.0	100.7
2000	2.4	100.0	100.0
2001	0.2	97.7	99.3
2002	(0.3)	95.7	98.4
2003	1.4	94.9	98.1
2004	2.6	96.1	98.1
2005	2.8	NA	97.8

Sources: Bank of Japan, Japanese External Trade Organization (JETRO), and Japan Statistical Bureau.

Notes
a The Bank of Japan has revised the 1995 base Wholesale Price Index into the 2000 base Corporate Goods Price Index.
b Base year for Consumer Price Index in 2000.
NA = Not available.

Today, Japan is still the second largest world economy with a GDP per capita of $36,190 in 2004. Table 2.3 shows that the service industry is the dominant sector of the economy and is also important for future growth and development. The service industry employed 70 percent of the total labor force of 66.9 million and contributed 74 percent of the total GDP in 2004. The industrial sector employed a quarter of the work force and contributed about 25 percent of the total gross domestic product.

Japan has enjoyed a balance of payment surplus for the past four decades. As discussed earlier, the role of the large trading firms within the *Keiretsu* are unique and significant in identifying market demand as they search the globe for sales opportunities, input, and new materials. They also help companies with their business group in forming joint ventures with other firms in an attempt to produce new products for exporting purposes. In short, they research the global markets, provide opportunities to increase trade and play an important role in the economic growth and development in Japan. Table 2.4 provides a profile of the merchandise and commercial service trades for Japan in 2004.

Merchandise exports increased by 5 percent from 2003 to 2004 to reach a total of $565.8 billion, or 6.2 percent of the world's total exports. In 2004, about 93 percent of the total exports from Japan were manufactured commodities such as transportation equipment, motor vehicles, electrical machinery, chemicals, and semiconductors. Key trading partners included the United States (22.7 percent), the European Union (25) (15.8 percent), China (13.1 percent), South Korea (7.8 percent), and Taiwan (7.4 percent).

Table 2.3 Japan's economic profile in 2004

Basic economic indicators	
Land area	374,744 sq. km.
Population (thousands 2004)	127,764
GDP (million current US$ 2004)	4,623,398
GDP (PPP current US$ 2004)	3,774,086
GDP per capita (US$ 2004)	36,190
GDP by sector (2004)	
Agriculture	1.3%
Industry	24.7%
Service	74.0%
Labor force (2004)	66.97 million
Labor force by occupation	
Agriculture	5.0%
Industry	25.0%
Service	70.0%
Unemployment rate (2004)	4.7%
Inflation rate (2004)	(0.1%)
Public debt (2004)	164.3% of GDP
Current account balance (million US$ 2004)	127,058

Sources: The CIA World Factbook, the IMF, and the World Bank.

Japan has limited farmland, forest, natural mineral, and energy resources. It depends heavily on imports of agricultural products, raw materials, timber, minerals, and most of its energy needs. Merchandise imports increased by 19 percent from 2003 to 2004 to reach a total of $454.5 billion, or 4.8 percent of the world's total imports.

The table shows that in 2004, 56 percent of all imports is from various manufacturing commodities while over 27 percent is related to energy and mining products. Imports of agricultural products accounted for over 14 percent of total imports. China, the United States, and the EU (25) are the top three partners in providing Japan with most of its merchandising trade imports. Commercial services trade experienced a huge annual percentage increase from 2003 to 2004. Exports increased by 25 percent while imports increased by 22 percent in 2004. In 2004, Japan's commercial services trade imports exceeded exports by $39.1 billion or 29 percent. In summary, Japan enjoyed a huge surplus ($111 billion) in merchandise trade in 2004, and incurred a large deficit in service trade during the same year.

Business and investment environment in Japan

Japan's business environment is based on an established free enterprise and free trade system firmly supported by the government and the people. The economy is relatively stable and oriented toward the service industry with a greater focus on rapid growth in the high tech industries. Public utilities, manufacturing, and

Table 2.4 Japan's merchandise and commercial service trade profile in 2004

Merchandise trade (US$ billion)	2004	Annual percentage change		
		1995–2004	2003	2004
Merchandise exports, f.o.b.	565.8	3	13	20
Merchandise imports, c.i.f.	454.5	3	14	19
Share in world's total merchandise exports (2004)	6.18%			
Share in world's total merchandise imports (2004)				4.79%

Breakdown of economy's total exports
(a) by main commodity group
- agriculture products — 1.0%
- fuels and mining products — 2.0%
- manufacturing products — 92.7%

(b) by main destination
- United States — 22.7%
- European Union (25) — 15.8%
- China — 13.1%
- Korea, Republic of — 7.8%
- Taiwan — 7.4%

Breakdown of economy's total imports
(a) by main commodity group
- agriculture products — 14.4%
- fuels and mining products — 27.6%
- manufacturing products — 56.3%

(b) by main destination
- China — 20.7%
- United States — 14.0%
- European Union (25) — 12.7%
- Korea, Republic of — 4.8%
- Australia — 4.3%

Commercial services trade (US$ billion)	2004	Annual percentage change		
		1995–2004	2003	2004
Commercial services exports	94.9	4	8	25
Commercial services imports	134.0	1	3	22
Share in world's total service exports (2004)	4.46%			
Share in world's total service imports (2004)				6.40%

Breakdown of economy's total exports by principal services item
- transportation — 33.9%
- travel — 11.9%
- other commercial services — 54.3%

Breakdown of economy's total imports by principal service item
- transportation — 31.9%
- travel — 28.5%
- other commercial services — 39.6%

Sources: WTO, UNCTAD, and the IMF.

financial services sectors are dominated by large corporations. The government is supportive of the business community and is totally committed to reforms and future economic development.

In response to the current economic slow down, the government outlined structural reform plans that focus on IT revolution, activation of local government, and deregulation with an emphasis on the financial sector. The financial system was highly regulated by very restrictive rules established to control the banks and restrict foreign competition. In June 1997, the government introduced a comprehensive package known as the "big bang" to reform the financial market. According to Kennett (2004), "Measures phased in over a five-year period ending in 2002 were expected to transform the Japanese financial landscape. However, in reality the reforms were more cosmetic than substantive, and a weak and over-regulated financial sector still lies at the heart of the troubled economy."

The Japanese labor force is considered skilled, disciplined, highly motivated, well-trained, and generally available. Managers and supervisors are educated, committed to work hard, and motivated. Japan will continue to be a high-labor cost country because of pensions, fringe benefits, and the elevated cost of social security.

Labor unions organized for each company are called "Company Unions." These unions can affiliate with major national federal organizations. Over 22 percent of the total labor force belongs to one of the over 31,000 unions in the country.

In 1964, after joining the Organization for Economic Cooperation and Development (OECD), the Japanese government intensified its commitment to free trade and free movement of capital. The Foreign Trade and Exchange Law was first amended in December 1980 and was further revised in April 1998 to "free in principle" foreign trade and investment between Japan and other foreign countries. Also, in April 1996 the government extended the effective period of the Import Promotion/Foreign Direct Investment Law for ten years ending December 2006. The law grants foreign investment a special tax incentive and guarantees a seven-year loss carryover period for qualified firms. Japan's basic tax system is considered neutral toward inward foreign investment or foreign enterprises.

It is clear that in recent years, the Japanese government has made numerous structural reforms to encourage inward foreign direct investment (FDI) in an attempt to achieve its economic growth and development. The following incentives for inward FDI are available under the Import Promotion and Inward Investment Promotion law:

- tax concessions for carrying over tax losses;
- availability of loan guarantees through the industrial structure improvement fund (ISIF) for up to 95 percent of the loan up to ¥1 billion;
- Credit guarantees are provided by the Credit Guarantee Association for small and medium size enterprises (SMEs).

Table 2.5 shows that foreign direct investment inflows into Japan have increased in the latter half of the 1990s. From 1990 to 1992, direct investment in

Table 2.5 Japan's direct investment inflows and outflows, 1990–2004 (amounts in US$ billion)

Year	Direct investment inflows	Direct investment outflows	Inflow/outflow ratio
1990	1.8	48.1	0.04
1991	1.3	31.6	0.04
1992	2.8	17.3	0.16
1993	0.2	13.9	0.02
1994	0.9	18.1	0.05
1995	0.2	22.6	0.00
1996	0.2	23.4	0.01
1997	3.2	26.0	0.12
1998	3.2	24.2	0.13
1999	12.7	22.7	0.56
2000	8.3	31.6	0.26
2001	6.2	38.3	0.16
2002	9.2	32.3	0.29
2003	6.3	28.8	0.22
2004	7.8	31.0	0.25
Total	64.3	409.9	0.16

Source: UNCTAD.

Japan remained at an average of $1.9 billion annually. This figure reached over $3 billion in 1997 and peaked at $12.7 billion in 1999. This inflow has since decreased, but is still at a level that ranges from $6 billion to $9 billion per year through 2004.

Table 2.5 also compares the inward FDI with the outward FDI. Based on the figures for 2004, Japan's ratio of inward FDI to outward FDI was 0.25. This compares to ratios for the United States and Britain of 0.42 and 1.2, respectively. Japan's inward FDI is extremely small compared to its outward FDI.

Many developing countries recognize the positive impact of growing inflows of FDI on the nation's capital investments and the future economic growth. In Japan, although FDI inflow has increased in the last few years, it is still considered insignificant because it is a very small fraction of a percent of the country's GDP as shown in Table 2.6.

Japan's central and local governments are making an attempt to increase the FDI inflow (inward) on a continuous basis. The central government utilizes the Japan External Trade Organization (JETRO) and the Development Bank of Japan (DBJ) to provide support services such as financial, matchmaking, and information to companies interested in investing in Japan and the local municipalities. The Japan Investment Council was established in 1994 to improve the investment environment and outline programs to promote foreign direct investment into Japan to revitalize the economy.

It will be a challenge to achieve the government's target of doubling inward FDI in five-years' time based on the recent trends in FDI inflow. To achieve

Table 2.6 Japan's foreign direct investment inflows, stock, and GDP, 1990–2004

Year	FDI		GDP (US$ billion)
	Inflows (US$ billion)	Inward investment stock (US$ billion)	
1990	1.75	9.85	3,210
1991	1.28	12.30	3,554
1992	2.76	15.52	3,883
1993	0.22	16.88	4,458
1994	0.89	19.21	4,946
1995	0.04	33.53	5,216
1996	0.23	29.94	4,575
1997	3.22	27.08	4,246
1998	3.19	26.06	4,031
1999	12.74	46.12	4,572
2000	8.32	50.32	4,652
2001	6.24	50.32	4,011
2002	9.24	78.14	4,080
2003	6.32	89.73	4,447
2004	7.82	96.98	4,110
Total	64.62		63,991

Source: UNCTAD and the IMF.

this target, both private and public sectors will have to remove many obstacles, including eliminating regulations that hinder mergers and acquisitions and changing the negative public opinion regarding investments to speed up the inward FDI into the country.

US trade and investment relations with Japan

In recent years, Japan has accumulated a significant surplus on its trade with the United Sates. Table 2.7 shows that in 2004, Japan's exports recorded an annual increase of 20 percent to $565.5 billion, marking the third consecutive year of increase. Imports grew by 19 percent to $454.5 billion, an increase recorded for the second consecutive year. As a result, Japan's trade surplus increased by 25 percent to $111 billion in 2004.

Table 2.7 reflects a continuous increase in the ratio of export to the GDP. In 2004, Japan's ratio recorded an annual increase of 14 percent, making it the second consecutive year of increase.

Figure 2.1 shows the composition of Japan's foreign trade by commodity in 2004. Electrical machinery accounted for 23.5 percent of Japan's total export value, followed by transportation equipment with 23.1 percent and general machinery with 20.6 percent. During the same year, mineral fuels such as liquefied gas and petroleum accounted for 21.7 percent of the total import value, followed by electrical machinery with 13.9 percent, and foodstuffs with 10.8 percent.

Table 2.7 Japan's foreign trade and GDP, 1990–2004

Year	Exports (US$ billion)	% change	Imports (US$ billion)	% change	Balance Ex−Im	GDP (US$ billion)	Ratio of exports to GDP %
1990	287.6	9	235.4		52.2	3,210	9
1991	314.8	9	236.9	1	77.9	3,554	9
1992	339.9	2	233.2	(2)	106.7	3,883	9
1993	362.3	7	241.6	4	120.7	4,458	8
1994	397.1	10	275.2	14	121.9	4,946	8
1995	443.1	12	335.9	22	107.2	5,216	8
1996	410.9	(7)	349.2	4	61.7	4,575	9
1997	420.9	2	338.8	(3)	82.1	4,246	10
1998	387.9	(8)	280.5	(17)	107.4	4,031	10
1999	419.4	8	311.3	11	108.1	4,572	9
2000	479.2	14	379.5	22	99.7	4,652	10
2001	403.5	(16)	349.1	(8)	54.4	4,011	10
2002	416.7	3	337.2	(3)	79.5	4,080	10
2003	471.8	13	382.9	14	88.9	4,447	11
2004	565.5	20	454.4	19	111.0	4,110	14

Sources: WTO and UNCTAD.

Japan's foreign trade with many countries has recorded a trade surplus in recent years. Table 2.8 shows that in 2004, US imports from Japan increased by 10 percent to $129.6 billion after three consecutive years of decline in imports. Imports had peaked in 2000 to a record high of $146.6 billion. In 2005, US imports from Japan increased to $138.1 billion. General and electrical machinery mainly accounted for the considerable growth in imports. In 2004, US exports to Japan increased only by 4 percent to $54.4 billion after three years of continuous decline. Beverages, tobacco, and meat exports to Japan have experienced a decline in the last few years. In 2005, US exports to Japan increased slightly to $55.4 billion.

Figure 2.2 shows the US trade deficit with Japan, which ranges from a low of $41.8 billion in 1990 to a high of $82.7 billion in 2005. This yearly deficit creates friction in the economic relationship between the two countries. The United States is exerting pressure on Japan to open up its market or it will be faced with new trade sanctions. Many economists believe that the only way for the United States to reduce the trade deficit with Japan lies not in creating trade barriers, but rather in the US companies' ability to work harder to satisfy the needs of consumers with quality products at reasonable prices. Today, the Japanese government is working hard to open up its market and deregulate its industries. This would allow foreign businesses to find growth opportunities in Japan and reduce the relevance of the foreign trade deficit issue, not only with the United States, but also with the rest of the world.

Table 2.9 shows the bilateral direct investment between Japan and the United States. The statistics shown are direct investment positions calculated on a historical cost basis. These statistics were published by the US Bureau of Economic

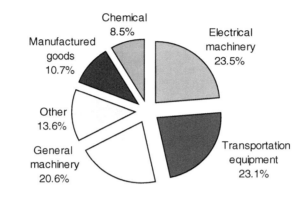

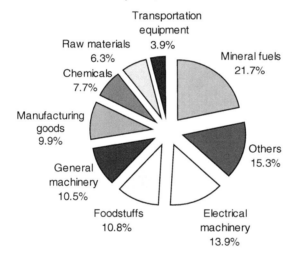

Figure 2.1 Composition of Japan's foreign trade by commodity in 2004.

Source: Ministry of Finance, Japan.

Analysis. We can observe that in the year 2000, the US direct investment in Japan was about $57 billion, while Japan's direct investment in the United States was $59.7 billion. US direct investment in Japan declined in 2001, but increased gradually from 2002 to 2004. Japan's direct investment in the United States increased by 151 percent in 2001. Since then, Japanese direct investment has also increased gradually and reached $176.9 billion in 2004. At the end of 2004, the US direct investment in Japan ($80.2 billion) was equivalent to about 45 percent of Japan's direct investment in the United States.

Table 2.8 Japan's trade with the United States, 1990–2005 (amounts in US$ billions)

Year	Imports from Japan	% change	Export to Japan	% change	US trade deficit
1990	90.4		48.6		41.8
1991	92.3	2	48.1	(1)	44.2
1992	97.2	5	47.8	(1)	49.4
1993	107.3	10	47.9	—	59.4
1994	119.1	11	53.5	12	65.6
1995	123.6	3	64.3	20	59.3
1996	115.2	(7)	67.5	5	47.7
1997	121.4	5	65.7	(3)	55.7
1998	122.0	1	57.9	(12)	64.1
1999	131.4	8	57.5	(1)	73.9
2000	146.6	12	65.3	14	81.3
2001	126.6	(14)	57.6	(12)	69.0
2002	121.5	(4)	51.4	(11)	70.1
2003	118.0	(3)	52.1	(1)	65.9
2004	129.6	10	54.4	4	75.2
2005	138.1	7	55.4	2	82.7

Source: US Department of Commerce, trade statistics.

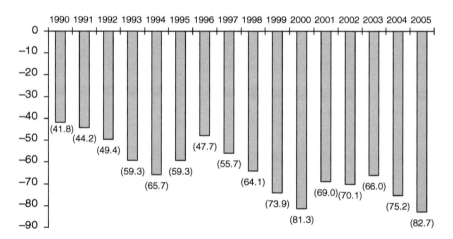

Figure 2.2 The US trade balances with Japan, 1990–2005 (US$ billions).

Source: The IMF and others.

Japan's investment and trade relations with East Asia

As an Asian country, Japan has strong investment and trade relations with other countries in East and Southeast Asia. Table 2.10 shows Japan's FDI in Asia and other regions at year end from 1996 to 2004. Japan's FDI in China was $8.1 billion in 1996, increased to $21.2 billion in 1997, but declined to $7.3 billion in 1999. Since 2000, the number has been going up and reached $20.2 billion in 2004.

Table 2.9 Bilateral direct investment between Japan and the United States[a]

Year	US DI in Japan	Japanese DI in the United States	US DI as a % of Japanese DI in the United States
2000	57,091	59,690	96
2001	55,651	149,859	37
2002	66,468	151,333	44
2003	68,097	160,452	42
2004	80,246	176,906	45

Source: US Bureau of Economic Analysis.

Note
a On a historical-cost basis.

Table 2.10 Japan's FDI position in Asia and other regions at year end, 1996–2004 (amounts in US$ billion)

Region and country	1996	1997	1998	1999	2000	2001	2002	2003	2004
China	8.1	21.2	17.9	7.3	8.6	10.0	12.4	15.3	20.2
Hong Kong	9.4	8.3	9.2	6.2	6.5	5.5	5.5	5.7	6.3
ASEAN Big Five	52.9	31.4	33.5	23.0	24.5	27.7	29.2	31.3	35.0
Singapore	11.4	11.0	9.5	8.4	8.9	10.2	10.4	9.8	11.2
Thailand	15.7	5.7	5.7	4.6	4.8	6.1	6.3	7.7	9.9
Indonesia	17.2	7.9	11.5	4.4	4.8	5.0	5.6	6.7	6.5
Malaysia	5.8	4.7	4.4	3.6	4.0	4.3	3.9	4.0	4.1
Philippines	2.8	2.1	2.4	2.0	2.0	2.1	3.0	3.2	3.3
ASEAN Small Five	0.3	0.9	0.6	0.5	0.5	0.7	0.7	0.7	0.8
United States	94.3	102.3	111.1	118.4	132.2	140.7	136.2	139.2	142.3
Europe	47.5	55.6	51.9	49.7	56.4	70.6	72.4	87.6	101.9
Latin America	12.0	14.5	17.4	17.9	21.0	20.7	18.2	22.0	26.5
Others	34.2	37.8	28.5	26.1	28.7	25.0	30.9	34.1	38.8
Total	258.7	272.0	270.1	249.1	278.4	300.9	305.6	335.9	371.8

Source: JETRO and Bank of Japan.

Notes
1 Percentages may not add up to 100 percent due to rounding.
2 ASEAN Small Five comprises Brunei, Vietnam, Laos, Myanmar, and Cambodia.

Japan's total FDI position in the ASEAN Big five countries (Singapore, Thailand, Indonesia, Malaysia, and the Philippines) was $52.9 billion in 1996. It dropped by about 41 percent to $31.4 billion in 1997 mainly due to the financial crisis in Southeast Asia. At the end of 2004, Japan's total FDI position in the ASEAN Big Five was $35.0 billion. Japan's investment in the ASEAN Small Five (Vietnam, Laos, Cambodia, Myanmar, and Brunei) was minimal. For example, at the end of 2004, Japan's FDI position in the ASEAN Small Five was only about $800 million.

At the end of 2004, Japan's FDI position in the United States was $142.3 billion, less than the $176.9 billion reported by the US Bureau of Economic Analysis as shown in Table 2.9. Japan's FDI position in Europe was about $101.9 billion at the end of 2004. About two-thirds of Japan's FDI position at the end of 2004 was in Europe and the United States.

Japan has traded heavily with many East Asian countries in recent years. Table 2.11 shows Japan's trade with China, South Korea, Taiwan, Hong Kong, Singapore, and the ASEAN 4 from 2000 to 2004. The ASEAN 4 is comprised of Indonesia, Thailand, the Philippines, and Malaysia. In other words, the ASEAN 4 plus Singapore are equal to the ASEAN Big Five countries.

Japan exported $191.0 billion of goods to the nine East Asian countries in the year 2000, and imported $150.8 billion in the same year. Japan's trade with these countries declined substantially in 2001 due to a global recession. The situation began to improve in 2003, and by the year 2004, Japan's total trade with the nine East Asian countries amounted to $460.7 billion. Japan also enjoyed a surplus of $68.9 billion on its trade with those nine countries. The expansion in East Asian trade was a key factor for Japan's economic growth in 2004.

On January 13, 2002, Japan signed a Free Trade Agreement (FTA) with Singapore that became effective on November 30, 2002. On December 13, 2005, Japan and Malaysia also signed a comprehensive Economic Partnership

Table 2.11 Japan's trade with China and selected Asian countries, 2000–4 (amounts in US$ billion)

	2000	*2001*	*2002*	*2003*	*2004*
Japan's exports					
China	30.4	31.1	39.9	57.2	73.8
South Korea	30.8	25.4	28.5	34.7	44.2
Taiwan	36.1	24.3	26.2	31.2	42.0
Hong Kong	27.3	23.4	25.4	29.8	35.3
Singapore	20.9	14.8	14.2	14.8	18.0
ASEAN 4	45.5	37.7	38.8	43.3	51.5
East Asia total	191.0	156.7	173.0	211.0	264.8
Japan's imports					
China	55.3	58.1	61.7	75.2	94.2
South Korea	20.5	17.3	15.5	17.8	22.0
Taiwan	18.0	14.3	13.5	14.2	16.7
Hong Kong	1.7	1.5	1.4	1.3	1.6
Singapore	6.5	5.4	5.0	5.4	6.3
ASEAN 4	48.8	44.8	42.3	47.8	55.1
East Asia total	150.8	141.4	139.4	161.7	195.9
Japan's trade balance with East Asia	40.1	15.3	33.6	49.1	68.9

Source: Japan JETRO.

Notes
1 Percentages may not add up to 100 percent due to rounding.
2 The ASEAN 4 comprises Indonesia, Thailand, the Philippines, and Malaysia.
3 East Asia includes China, S. Korea, Taiwan, Hong Kong, Singapore, and the ASEAN 4.

Agreement (EPA) to liberalize and facilitate trade in goods and services, and to mutually protect and expand investment. As of February 2006, Japan was also negotiating FTAs with Indonesia and Thailand.

Japan's trade with China has been growing rapidly since the year 2000. In 2000, the bilateral trade total between Japan and China was only $85.7 billion. By 2004, the bilateral trade total had increased to $168.0 billion. In the first 11 months of 2005, Japan exported $90.6 billion of goods to China, and imported $76.4 billion of merchandise from China. In 2005, Japan was the second largest trading partner of China after the United States.

Japan exported about $66.4 billion of goods to Singapore and the ASEAN 4 in 2000, and imported $55.3 billion of goods from the ASEAN Big Five countries in the same year. Japan's trade with the ASEAN Big Five declined in 2001 and 2002. However, their bilateral trade recovered in 2003 and by 2004, and the two-way trade total was about $130.9 billion.

Mergers, acquisitions, and reforms of M&A regulations

In the past, most M&A in Japan were in reality a domestic M&A and as a result the level of activities has been comparatively low. In recent years, starting from the 1990s, there has been a surge in the level of M&A activity but this surge is less common than in other developed countries. In fact, the total value of M&A by foreign companies between 1990 and 2004 came to $139.7 billion in Japan, much lower than the $1,676.7 billion in the United States during the same period. Details of M&A activity will be presented in Chapter 3.

Until the 1990s, foreign Japanese M&A (out-in M&A) were rare events. Only after the deregulation of various industries and the subsequent decade long recession did the number of out-in M&A deals increase. Japanese firms in financial distress accept the foreign companies' mergers and acquisitions as the only option for them to survive.

For a long time, the image of M&A has been negative in the Japanese culture. The word acquisition has been associated with the Japanese word *nottori*, which means "hijacking" in English. Public opinion feels that the financially weak firms are going to be acquired by a "hijacking" firm. More recently, however, after the IT sector crisis that led to market concentration through many mergers and acquisitions, M&A has become less of a bad idea among Japanese firms. In contrast to the young entrepreneurs of the IT sector, the traditional manufacturing and service industries are still laden with traditional values.

Japan's economic recession is the main contributing factor in the increase in M&A activities between Japanese firms (in-in M&A). The traditional rationale for domestic M&A deals is financial rescue for distressed companies. As explained in the next chapter, there have been overwhelmingly more in-in M&A (72 percent) compared with out-in M&A (14 percent) during the period 1990–2004.

The future macroeconomic performance in Japan will determine the level of M&A market development and the continued participation of foreign firms. As a result, the future development and success of in-in M&A activity is greatly dependent on the future development of out-in M&A.

In recent years, Japan's corporate law reform has been accelerated. The Commercial Codes have significantly changed. Some of these changes are:

1   allowing Japanese firms to use stock swaps;
2   easing the procedural rules on corporate spin-offs;
3   easing the rules for issuing new shares;
4   loosening the restrictions on treasury stock;
5   introduction of new stock subscription options and class shares.

These changes will facilitate corporate restructuring by minimizing legal barriers to mergers and acquisitions as well as private equity investments and venture capital. In 2003, the Industrial Revitalization Act was introduced to reduce restrictions on M&A activity that involve firms with heavy indebtedness. Also, the Japanese government has relaxed many foreign investment regulations and antitrust restrictions on M&A activities.

Codes and statutes are the main source for Japanese law. The Commercial Code, the Securities and Exchange Law, and the Anti-Monopoly Law are the essential codes and statutes applicable to mergers and acquisitions in Japan. The Foreign Exchange and Trade Law regulates certain reporting and approval of inward foreign investments in a limited situation depending on the investor's country of origin, the industry of the target firm, and the nature of the asset in the case of asset acquisition.

The Commercial Code does not provide for mergers between foreign corporations and Japanese firms. However, a foreign investor can participate in a merger as the acquiring party through a wholly owned or controlled Japanese subsidiary. If a foreign investor attempts to start a new firm with the objective of acquiring the asset of a Japanese firm through a merger, the acquisition of shares in the new company will be subject to the reporting requirements and restrictions that apply under the Foreign Exchange and Fair Trade Law (FEFTL) for share acquisitions.

The Anti-Monopoly Law prohibits mergers and acquisitions if competition in any area or trade may be greatly reduced, or if such a merger or acquisition brings unfair trade practices. To ensure the effectiveness of the prohibition, the law demands specific reporting and approval requirements on certain mergers and acquisitions. The notification and approval requirements have been reduced as a result of recent amendments to the Anti-Monopoly Law. It is important to note that in certain industries the responsible regulatory authority may have to be notified, and in some situations its consent or approval is required for an acquisition or merger.

Taxation issues

In 2001, special rules for tax free corporate reorganization were introduced by an amendment to the Japanese Corporate Tax Law. The new reorganization tax rules apply to qualified group reorganizations such as mergers. Taxation of mergers in the Japanese tax law is considered a very complex area because of the involvement of the following three taxable entities:

- the target company;
- the surviving company;
- the target's shareholders.

A merger can be considered a qualified corporate reorganization as long as it does not involve cash transactions. Assets and liabilities can be transferred on a book value/tax basis (carry-over basis). Under the new rules, no step-up in the cost basis is allowed in a tax-free merger. As a result, the capital gain or loss that would be realized on the transfer will be deferred. It is also possible, under certain conditions, to preserve tax loss carry-forward. Mergers will be a subject to stamp duty at a flat rate of ¥40,000 per document. In addition, a reduced rate may be applicable for merger registration and license tax for real estate and/or intangibles.

According to JETRO (2004), other reforms planned for FY 2004 include the following:

- extending eligibility of loss carry-forwards from 5 to 7 years;
- abolishing the consolidated surtax;
- reducing the tax rate on capital gains of unlisted shares from 26 to 20 percent,
- expanding the scope of aggregation of profits and loss through financial taxation integration;
- extending incentives to promote small and medium enterprise investment through a 7 percent tax deduction and a 30 percent special depreciation;
- expanding new tax incentives governing "angel" investments to include regional taxes;
- enhancing and extending incentives to promote investments in new energies and conservation.

Summary and conclusions

In this chapter, we have reviewed the economic environment and investment climate of Japan. Our general overview of the Japanese society focused on the components and the priorities of the country's rich culture and discussed the three treasures (life-time employment, seniority wages, and company unions) that govern a worker's relationship and loyalty to the work place.

The Japanese government plays a crucial role in the fundamental restructuring and deregulation reforms in its attempt to stimulate economic growth and development. In addition, the distinct and powerful position of the *Keiretsu* system is vertically integrated and oriented around the production, distribution, and financing of a single product. Within the economy, the service sector is a dominant force, employing 70 percent of the total labor force in Japan. The United States received 22.7 percent of Japan's total exports in 2004 and has experienced a large trade deficit for the last 16 years. Today, the Japanese government is committed to support free trade and open its markets to foreign businesses to reduce tension on the issues of foreign trade deficit, not only with the United States, but also with the rest of the world.

In an attempt to encourage more inflow of foreign direct investment, the Japanese government has introduced a number of incentives to free capital movement and create a stronger investment environment. It is clear that inward FDI is still very small compared to the country's outward FDI, which impacts its future economic growth and development. The Japanese government's future plans are to double the FDI inflow in the next five years. To achieve this target both the private and public sectors need to work on removing most of the obstacles standing in the way.

We also reviewed Japan's investment and trade relations with the United States and other East Asian countries. Japan has accumulated a significant surplus on its merchandise trade with the United States since the early 1980s. In 2005, the US trade deficit with Japan was $82.7 billion.

Japan also has strong investment and trade relations with other East Asian countries. For example, Japan's FDI position in China at the end of 2004 was $20.2 billion. Japan's FDI position in the ASEAN Big Five was about $35 billion at the end of 2004. In 2004, Japan's exports to nine East Asian countries were $264.8 billion and imports from those countries were $195.9 billion.

We also discussed the current pattern of mergers and acquisitions in Japan. We noted that M&A activities are less common in Japan as compared to other developed countries. Japan's economic recession is the main driving force in increasing its domestic M&A activities (in-in M&A). These M&A activities mainly focus on the financial rescue of distressed and weak firms. Overall, foreign and Japanese M&A (out-in M&A) are considered rare and much fewer than domestic M&As (in-in M&A). In discussing M&A, we found that cultural factors are critically important in Japan.

We noted that the basic tax system in Japan is considered neutral toward inward foreign firms and investments. Reforms of corporate law and changes in tax law implemented in recent years are quite extensive. These reforms and changes should facilitate the expansion of domestic and cross-border M&A activity in the future.

3 Merger and acquisition activity in Japan

With a GDP of about $4.95 trillion (at official exchange rate) in 2005, Japan has the second largest economy in the world. However, M&A activity in Japan has historically been less active than in other industrialized countries. For example in 2001, Japanese M&A value as a percentage of its stock-market capitalization was 5.9 percent, compared to 7.7 percent in Europe and 8.4 percent in the United States. Major contributing factors include foreign ownership restrictions, corporate relationships involving cross shareholdings, and economic recession. In recent years, we have also witnessed significant changes in the legal and financial systems that facilitate more corporate restructuring and M&A activity in Japan. The changes began with financial system reform (or the Japanese version of the Big Bang) that started on June 13, 1997. One major goal was to revitalize the Japanese economy and to find more efficient ways of investing private assets which reach up to ¥1,200 trillion (MOF, 2005). This financial reform included a progression of deregulation such as liberalization of deposit interest rates, amendment of the foreign exchange and foreign trade control law, and changing the consolidated accounting requirements. Over the last three years, the Japanese government has also introduced the following measures:

- the new Commercial Code of Japan now allows stock swaps between Japanese companies. The rules for issuing new shares have also been streamlined;
- the Industrial Revitalization Law enacted in 2003 has relaxed restrictions on M&A activity under some circumstances;
- antitrust restrictions on M&A activity have also been eased.

As a result, M&A activity in Japan is expected to accelerate in the future. The main purpose of this chapter is to provide an overview of the M&A activity in Japan from 1990 to 2004. Another objective is to explain some unique characteristics of M&A activity in the country. We will analyze all known M&A transactions announced from January 1, 1990, to December 31, 2004, in which the target firm or acquirer was located in Japan.

An overview of M&A in Japan

Table 3.1 shows the number of M&A deals and transaction values announced in Japan from 1990 to 2004. The trends of M&A numbers and transaction values are also depicted in Figures 3.1 and 3.2. We can observe that there were 286 M&A

Table 3.1 Number of M&A deals and transaction values announced in Japan[a], 1990–2004

Year	Number of deals		M&A transaction values	
	Total for the year	*% change*	*Total for the year (US$ million)*	*% change*
1990	286	NA	43,089	NA
1991	211	−26	12,182	−72
1992	116	−45	7,868	−35
1993	67	−42	14,953	90
1994	91	36	15,149	1
1995	126	38	46,638	208
1996	166	32	19,973	−57
1997	208	25	23,161	16
1998	277	33	27,718	−20
1999	663	139	243,674	779
2000	955	44	151,275	−38
2001	847	11	73,495	−51
2002	1,117	32	77,945	6
2003	1,379	23	107,982	39
2004	1,225	−11	138,521	28
Total	7,734		1,003,623	

Source: Thomson Financial.

Note
a Only transactions of one million US$ or higher are included.

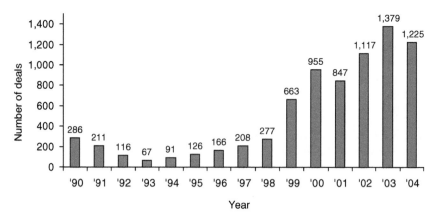

Figure 3.1 Number of M&A announced in Japan, 1990–2004.
Source: Thomson Financial.

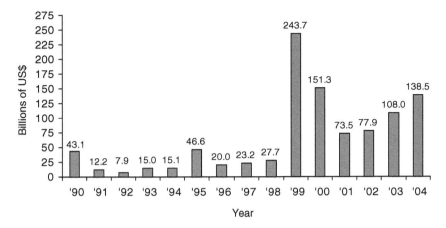

Figure 3.2 Changes in M&A values in Japan, 1990–2004.

Source: Thomson Financial.

deals in 1990. After 1990, the number decreased continuously until it reached 67 in 1993. The main reason for the low M&A activity in the first half of the 1990s was the general economic recession in Japan. M&A activity recovered gradually in the second half of the 1990s. The number reached its peak of 1,379 M&A deals in 2003. There were 1,225 deals that exceeded $1 million each in 2004.

From 1990 to 1998, the value of M&A deals fluctuated between a low of $7.9 billion and a high of $46.6 billion. The expansion in M&A value from $27.7 billion in 1998 to $243.7 billion in 1999 looks very dramatic in Figure 3.2 because there were many mega-mergers during 1999. The list of those mega-mergers will be presented later in this chapter.

The M&A value boom in 1999 was followed by a dramatic slowdown in 2000 and 2001 in line with the global economic recession. M&A activity started to recover in 2003, and the M&A value in 2004 in Japan was $138.5 billion.

M&A transactions by the nationality of the target firms

Table 3.2 shows the M&A transaction value in Japan by the nationality of the target firms from 1990 to 2004. During that 15 year period, there were 7,734 M&A transactions in Japan, with a total value of about $1,004 billion. The M&A value for target firms from Japan amounted to $865.9 billion (or 86 percent) while the subtotal for target firms from other countries was $137.7 billion (or 14 percent). The average value per deal for target firms from Japan was about $137.8 million, substantially higher than the average value of $94.9 million for target firms from all other countries combined.

As shown in Table 3.2, many target firms from the United States, the Netherlands, the United Kingdom, South Korea, Indonesia, Hong Kong, Australia, China, Brazil, and France were involved in the M&A activity related to

Table 3.2 M&A transaction value in Japan by the nationality of the target firms, 1990–2004

Nationality/ region	Transaction value (US$ million)	% of total	Number of deals	% of total	Average value per deal
Japan	865,888	86	6,282	81	137.8
United States	63,672	6	557	7	114.3
Netherlands	13,716	1	24	0	571.5
United Kingdom	10,372	1	95	1	109.2
South Korea	7,728	1	54	1	143.1
Indonesia	4,605	0	30	0	153.5
Hong Kong	4,458	0	88	1	50.7
Australia	3,679	0	67	1	54.9
China	3,089	0	71	1	43.5
Brazil	2,542	0	14	0	181.6
France	2,640	0	28	0	94.3
Other countries	21,234	2	424	5	50.1
Total	1,003,623	100	7,734	100	129.8

Source: Thomson Financial.

Note
Percentages may not add up to 100 percent due to rounding.

Japan. There were 557 deals involving US target firms with M&A transaction value of $63.7 billion. British target firms were involved in 95 deals with M&A value of $10.4 billion.

Home countries of the acquiring firms

Table 3.3 shows that acquiring firms from Japan accounted for 93 percent of the deals and 86 percent of the M&A transaction value during the 1990–2004 period. Acquiring firms from other countries accounted for 7 percent of the deals but 14 percent of the transaction value. Acquiring firms from the United States ranked first with 3 percent of the M&A deals and 4 percent of the transaction value. Acquiring firms from the United Kingdom were involved in 53 deals valued at $16.7 billion. A comparison between Tables 3.2 and 3.3 shows that more Japanese firms were involved in M&A transactions as acquiring firms than as target firms.

Acquisition methods

Table 3.4 shows the M&A transactions by acquisition methods in Japan for the 1990–2004 period. It is apparent that 33 percent of the M&A transactions (in value) were done by asset acquisition, with an average value per deal of $80 million. In Japan, asset acquisitions are divided into two types: one that involves a business transfer of all or substantially all of a company's business, and one that does not. Asset acquisitions involving the disposition of "important" property or substantial portion of the selling company's assets require the approvals of (1) the board of

Table 3.3 M&A transaction value in Japan by the nationality of the acquiring firms, 1990–2004

Nationality/ region	Transaction value (US$ million)	% of total	Number of deals	% of total	Average value per deal
Japan	863,916	86	7,195	93	120.1
United States	43,225	4	206	3	209.8
United Kingdom	16,743	2	53	1	315.9
France	10,075	1	18	0	559.7
Germany	4,467	0	26	0	171.8
Canada	1,238	0	6	0	206.3
Hong Kong	1,189	0	45	1	26.4
Unknown	51,518	5	35	0	1,471.9
Other countries	11,252	1	150	2	75.0
Total	1,003,623	100	7,734	100	129.8

Source: Thomson Financial.

Note
Percentages may not add up to 100 percent due to rounding.

Table 3.4 M&A transaction methods used by the acquiring firms in Japan, 1990–2004

Transaction method	Transaction value (US$ million)	% of total	Number of deals	% of total	Average value per deal (US$ million)
Asset acquisition	329,371	33	4,099	53	80
Merger	328,949	33	426	6	772
Acquisition of majority interest	116,399	11	880	11	132
Acquisition of partial interest	168,415	17	1,539	20	109
Acquisition of remaining interest	60,489	6	790	10	77
Total	1,003,623	100	7,734	100	130

Source: Thomson Financial.

directors of the target company, (2) the shareholders of the target company, and (3) the board of directors of the acquiring firm.

Mergers also accounted for 33 percent of the M&A transaction value but only 6 percent of the number of deals. The average value per deal for mergers was $772 million, significantly higher than that for any other acquisition method. According to the Japanese Commercial Code, there are two types of mergers: (1) merger by absorption when the acquiring firm takes over all the assets and liabilities of the target company which is then dissolved after the deal is closed; (2) merger by incorporation when the assets and liabilities of the target company and acquiring firm are transferred to a newly incorporated company. A majority of the mergers in Japan are mergers by absorption.

As shown in Table 3.4, the other three methods are acquisitions of majority interest, partial interest, or the remaining interest. These three methods accounted for 34 percent of all M&A transaction values. Acquisitions of majority interest or partial interest can be done through share acquisitions or joint ventures.

According to the Baker and McKenzie and Aoyama Aoki (2005) Guide to Mergers and Acquisition in Japan, share acquisitions of a listed company may involve one or more of the following transactions:

- purchase of existing shares on or off-market;
- purchase of stock subscription rights on or off-market;
- purchase of shares from a major stockholder or stockholders;
- issue of new shares;
- a stock swap or stock transfer.

The Baker and McKenzie and Aoyama Aoki (2005) Guide suggests that "a joint venture is often preferred where access to local distribution networks and marketing know-how is sought, where the market is highly regulated, or where the market is dominated by a small number of powerful players."

The 20 largest M&A in Japan

The 20 largest mergers and acquisitions in Japan during the 1990–2004 period are shown in Table 3.5. The value of these largest M&A deals varied from $5.5 billion (the acquisition of Japan Telecom, J-Phone by the Vodafone Group PLC UK) to $45.5 billion (the acquisition of Sakura Bank by Sumitomo Bank). The acquirers in the six largest deals were Japanese firms. Two of the other 14 largest M&A transactions involved acquirers from unknown investors' groups. It is interesting that one US firm was involved as acquirer (General Electric Capital) and three as target companies: AT&T Wireless, MCA, and Verio.

Table 3.5 also shows that 8 of the 20 largest deals involved consolidation of the banking industry in Japan. This coincided with the large bank mergers in the United States. For example, in 1998, Citicorp was acquired by Nations Bank, and First Chicago NBD was purchased by Bank One. In September 2000, J. P. Morgan was acquired by Chase Manhattan.

M&A activity by the industries of the target firms and the acquirers

Table 3.6 shows the industries of target firms in Japan, from 1990 to 2004. In terms of transaction value, 91 percent of the target firms were from three industries: financial (34 percent), manufacturing (28 percent), and services (29 percent). However, in terms of number of deals, 43 percent of the target firms were in manufacturing industries while 27 percent of the target companies were in service industries. Target companies in financial industries accounted for only 7 percent of the deals.

Table 3.5 Twenty largest mergers and acquisitions in Japan, 1990–2004

Announced year	Effective year	Target and nationality	Acquirer and nationality	Amount (US$ million)
10/13/1999	4/1/2001	Sakura Bank Ltd (Japan)	Sumitomo Bank Ltd (Japan)	45,494
8/20/1999	9/29/2000	Dai-Ichi Kangyo Bank Ltd (Japan)	Fuji Bank Ltd. (Japan)	40,097
3/27/1995	4/1/1996	Bank of Tokyo Ltd (Japan)	Mitsubishi Bank Ltd (Japan)	33,788
8/20/1999	9/29/2000	Industrial Bank of Japan (Japan)	Fuji Bank Ltd (Japan)	30,760
6/10/2003	7/1/2003	Resona Bank Ltd (Japan)	Deposits Corp. of Japan (Japan)	16,650
12/16/1999	10/1/2000	KDD Corp. (Japan)	DDI Corp. (Japan)	15,822
7/13/1999	11/12/1999	Nippon Telegraph & Telecorp (Japan)	Group of Investors (unknown)	15,080
3/14/2000	4/1/2001	Tokai Bank Ltd (Japan)	Sanwa Bank Ltd (Japan)	14,984
12/16/1999	10/1/2000	IDO Corp. (Japan)	DDI Corp. (Japan)	10,659
4/18/2000	4/1/2001	Mitsubishi Trust & Banking (Japan)	Bank of Tokyo-Mitsubishi Ltd (Japan)	10,373
11/30/2000	1/22/2001	AT&T Wireless Group (US)	NTT DoCoMo Inc. (Japan)	9,805
11/13/1990	4/1/1991	Saitama Bank Ltd. (Asahi Bank) (Japan)	Kyowa Bank Ltd (Japan)	8,093
2/24/2004	4/1/2005	Fujisawa Pharmaceutical Co. Ltd (Japan)	Yamanouchi Pharmaceutical Co. (Japan)	7,940
3/8/1999	5/12/1999	RJ Reynolds International (Netherlands)	Japan Tobacco, Inc. (Japan)	7,832
9/24/1990	1/3/1991	MCA, Inc. (US)	Matsushita Electric Industrial (Japan)	7,406
4/1/2000	5/9/2000	J-Phone Kansai, Tokai, Tokyo (Japan)	J-Phone Communications (Japan)	6,635
1/26/1999	3/5/1999	Japan Leasing Corp. (Japan)	General Electric Capital Corp. (US)	6,566
5/5/2000	9/13/2000	Verio Inc. (US)	NTT Communications Corp. (Japan)	5,694
7/2/1999	8/2/1999	East Japan Railway Co. (Japan)	Investors Group (unknown)	5,594
5/1/2001	6/1/2001	Japan Telecom, J-Phone (Japan)	Vodafone Group, PLC (UK)	5,486

Source: Thomson Financial.

Table 3.6 M&A transactions by the industry of the target firms, 1990–2004

Industry type	Transaction value (US$ million)	% of total	Number of deals	% of total	Average value per deal (US$ million)
Financial	336,602	34	558	7	603.2
Manufacturing	276,211	28	3,308	43	83.5
Services	296,017	29	2,092	27	141.5
Retail	36,249	4	669	9	54.2
Wholesale trade	26,016	3	685	9	38.0
Natural resources	21,211	2	169	2	125.5
Others	11,317	1	253	3	44.7
Total	1,003,623	100	7,734	100	129.8

Source: Thomson Financial.

Note
Percentages may not add up to 100 percent due to rounding.

Table 3.7 M&A transactions by the industry of the acquiring firms, 1990–2004

Industry type	Transaction value (US$ million)	% of total	Number of deals	% of total	Average value per deal (US$ million)
Financial	452,334	45	1,561	20	289.8
Manufacturing	257,722	25	3,045	39	84.6
Services	216,858	22	1,651	21	131.3
Wholesale trade	26,965	3	691	9	39.0
Natural resources	22,471	2	135	2	166.5
Retail	19,785	2	461	6	42.9
Others	7,487	1	190	2	39.4
Total	1,003,623	100	7,734	100	129.8

Source: Thomson Financial.

Note
Percentages may not add up to 100 percent due to rounding.

Table 3.7 lists the industries of acquiring firms from 1990 to 2004. We can observe that acquirers from financial industries participated in 20 percent of the deals and 45 percent of the transaction value. On the other hand, acquirers from manufacturing industries participated in 39 percent of the deals and 25 percent of the transaction value. Acquiring firms from service industries accounted for 21 percent of the deals and 22 percent of the transaction values.

Comparing Tables 3.6 and 3.7, we can observe a similarity in industry ranking of target and acquiring firms. In terms of transaction value, the financial industry was first followed by manufacturing and service industries. Over 90 percent of all M&A activity in Japan occurred in those three groups of industries. Table 3.5 also shows that most of the largest 20 Japanese M&A deals have acquirers or target firms from financial, manufacturing, and service industries.

Table 3.8 compares the extent of domestic versus cross-border M&A activity in four countries or regions. We can observe that most M&A activity in Japan during the 1990–2004 period were Japanese firms buying other Japanese companies. This type of transaction accounted for 72 percent of all transaction value. The rest are cross-border transactions. Japanese firms acquiring non-Japanese companies accounted for 14 percent of the value. Non-Japanese firms acquiring Japanese companies also accounted for 14 percent of all transaction value.

In Table 3.8, data on domestic versus cross-border M&A mergers are also provided for Hong Kong, China, and Malaysia. We can observe that domestic mergers (Hong Kong firms acquiring other Hong Kong firms) only accounted for 49 percent of all M&A activity in Hong Kong from 1990 to 2004. About 64 percent of all M&A activity in Mainland China were cross-border transactions during the same period. On the other hand, only 26 percent of the M&A in Malaysia were cross-border mergers.

Some unique features of Japanese M&A

In Table 3.8, we noted that about 72 percent of Japanese M&A activity from 1990 to 2004 were domestic M&A deals (Japanese firms acquiring other Japanese target companies). According to Nakamura (2002), one key reason of this phenomenon is that large corporate groups (or *keiretsu*) have been engaging in numerous M&A deals for many years. The main purpose of these M&A deals has been to consolidate the business of a *keiretsu* or to rescue a sister company within the corporate group. However, the trend may be changing. Foreign investors have shown increased interests in Japanese companies after the Japanese Government started the deregulation process in various industries in the late 1990s. An example is the successful acquisition of the Japanese life insurance company Dai Jyaku Seimei Hokew by Manulife from Canada in 1998. General Electric Capital Corporation was able to acquire Japan Leasing Corporation in 1999. In 2001, Vodafone also acquired a majority stake in J-Phone of Japan Telecom.

In studying Japanese M&A activity, Nakamura (2002) suggested that we distinguish between large firms and small- and medium-sized firms (SMFs) because the circumstances surrounding their M&A deals are different. Many large companies are multinational firms so they can identify a suitable M&A partner. In fact, many large company M&A deals are really *de facto* rescuing of ailing companies. A good example is the acquisition of Nissan's stocks by Renault that began in the late 1990s. The cross-ownership with Renault has provided Nissan significant cost advantage over other Japanese auto makers. On the other hand, SMFs exist typically in the agricultural, manufacturing, and service industries. Many SMFs are managed by their founders or their extended families. The main problem of SMFs are finding competent successors or searching for venture capitalists in times of financial difficulties. These SMF owners are reluctant to sell their businesses. Many SMF owners consider "selling one's firm is like selling your own son" and a seller might be seen as a failure by fellow

Table 3.8 Domestic versus cross-border M&A: comparison among Japan, China, Hong Kong, and Malaysia, 1990–2004 (M&A value in US$ Millions)

Japan	M&A value (US$ million)	%	Mainland China	M&A value (US$ million)	%	Hong Kong	M&A value (US$ million)	%	Malaysia	M&A value (US$ million)	%
Japanese firms acquiring other Japanese firms	726,181	72	Mainland Chinese firms acquiring other Mainland Chinese firms	73,054	36	Hong Kong firms acquiring other Hong Kong firms	187,721	49	Malaysian firms acquiring other Malaysian firms	146,359	74
Japanese firms acquiring non-Japanese firms	137,735	14	Mainland Chinese firms acquiring non-Mainland Chinese companies	17,040	8	Hong Kong firms acquiring non-Hong Kong companies	133,068	34	Malaysian firms acquiring non-Malaysian firms	37,635	19
Non-Japanese firms acquiring Japanese companies	139,707	14	Non-Mainland Chinese firms acquiring Chinese firms	113,290	56	Non-Hong Kong firms acquiring Hong Kong companies	65,958	17	Non-Malaysian firms acquiring Malaysian firms	13,936	7
Total	1,003,623	100		203,384	100		386,747	100		197,930	100

Source: Thomson Financial.

entrepreneurs in the local community (Nakamura, 2002, p. 8). SMFs usually keep their M&A discussions very discreet and they may contact an M&A consultant only during the final stages of negotiation. In recent years, many SMF M&A deals have been reported and they have occurred in the pharmaceutical, wholesale, and retail industries.

Summary and conclusions

This chapter has provided an overview of Japanese M&A activity from 1990 to 2004. We noted that M&A activity in Japan was substantially higher during the 1999–2004 period than in the 1990–8 period. Most M&A activity in Japan occurred in three industries: financial, manufacturing, and services. About 72 percent of Japanese M&A deals are domestic transactions. Recent changes in Japanese commercial code and other regulations have created a more favorable environment for corporate restructuring and M&A activity.

In the future, we think M&A activity in Japan will continue to grow for the following reasons:

1   China's economy has been growing at a rate of about 10 percent for the last three years. As China continues to expand its economy, Japanese exports to China, Hong Kong, and Taiwan will increase rapidly in the future. This should improve Japan's economy and create more M&A opportunities for Japan.
2   Japan's economy is also strengthened by the economic recovery in the United States and the expansion of the EU because many large Japanese firms are major players in the global markets.
3   Japan has an FTA with Singapore, and a comprehensive Economic Partnership Agreement with Malaysia. Japan is also negotiating an FTA with Indonesia and Thailand. These FTAs, if implemented, should expand Japan's trade and investment relations with Southeast Asian countries.
4   In recent years, Japan has implemented tax reform measures to reduce corporate tax rates on income, capital gains, and estate taxes on inheritances. Tax incentives were provided for small and medium business investment and investments in new energies and conservation.
5   Many US and European companies want to expand their business activities in Japan and the Japanese Government will continue to streamline its regulations that restrict takeovers by foreign firms. The new Industrial Revitalization Law also supports programs for corporate restructuring and consolidation.

According to a report published by the JETRO (2005), Japanese M&A activity in the first half of 2005 totaled $108.9 billion, more than twice the $49.8 billion recorded in the same period of 2004. In the future, we think Japan has great potential to create many new M&A opportunities for investors from both inside and outside of Japan.

4 Greater China and its investment and trade relations with the United States

A key to understanding M&A practices in Greater China is to have some knowledge about the economic and business environments of the three regions of Greater China: Hong Kong, Taiwan, and Mainland China. It is also important to understand China's investment and trade relations with its major trading partners: Japan, the United States, Hong Kong, and Taiwan.

China started its economic reform and opened its door to foreign investors in 1978. Since then, China's economy has been growing at an average rate of about 9.6 percent per year. In 2005, its GDP growth rate was 9.9 percent. In 1978, it accounted for less than 1 percent of the world's economy and China's foreign trade was only $21 billion. Today, China accounts for more than 4 percent of the world's economy. Its foreign trade in 2005 was $1.4 trillion, the third largest in the world, behind the United States and Germany.

Hong Kong Island was ceded to the United Kingdom in 1842 after China lost the First Opium War and signed the Nanking Treaty. Later, Britain also managed to add the Kowloon Peninsula, the New Territories, and many surrounding islands to its holdings. Hong Kong was a British colony until it reverted to China on July 1, 1997. On that day, Hong Kong became the Hong Kong Special Administrative Region (SAR) of China. Under the principle of "one country, two systems," Hong Kong enjoys a very high degree of autonomy and will be able to preserve its economic and social systems for 50 years beginning July 1, 1997. Hong Kong has a free market economy. It is highly dependent on international trade and tourism. As a gateway to China, Hong Kong's re-export business to and from China is a major driver for economic growth and prosperity.

Taiwan is an island that has had an independent government since President Chiang Kai-Shek of the Nationalist Government fled to Taiwan in 1949. Using the 1946 constitution drawn up for all China, the Nationalist Kuomingtang (KMT) Government established a government with Taipei as its capital. Over the next five decades, Taiwan has successfully transformed itself from an agricultural economy to a dynamic capitalist economy. In 1996, Taiwan completed its first direct presidential election. The 2000 presidential election ended more than five decades of KMT rule and the power was transferred to the Democratic Progressive Party. In recent years, some large Taiwanese government-owned banks and industrial firms have been privatized, creating an important impetus for

M&A activity. Currently, Taiwan has formal diplomatic relations with about 25 countries even though China considers Taiwan as a renegade province. Taiwan may not have a seat at the United Nations, but it is a member of the WTO and of the Asia-Pacific Economic Council (APEC). The United States maintains unofficial commercial and cultural relations with Taiwan through the American Institute in Taiwan (AIT) that has offices in both Taiwan and the United States. Many other countries including Japan, France, Britain, and Australia also have similar unofficial relations with Taiwan.

Despite their political differences, the three regions of Greater China have enjoyed close economic ties since China opened its door to foreign investors in 1978. Hong Kong remains the primary source of foreign investment in China. Taiwanese investors have also invested more than $40 billion in China over the last 25 years. There are substantial trade relationships among the three regions of Greater China. According to Sung (2005), "the fusion of know-how and capital from Hong Kong and Taiwan with the abundant labor resources of the Chinese Mainland has led to the emergence of a dynamic economy of Greater China rivaling the USA, the European Union, and Japan." On the synergies of Greater China, Shenkar (2005) also noted that "those economies possess complementary and synergetic attributes of capital, skill, knowledge, human resources, and market savvy that can deliver development on a magnitude and at a pace never before seen in a developing economy."

As a group, the three regions of Greater China have also traded heavily with Japan, the United States, and some Southeast Asian countries. The United Kingdom and the British Virgin Islands also have substantial investment relationships with Hong Kong. For the remainder of Chapter 4, we will cover the following topics related to the three regions of Greater China and their major trading partners:

- economic profile of China, Hong Kong, and Taiwan;
- investment relations among the three regions of Greater China;
- merchandise trade between Hong Kong, Taiwan, and Mainland China;
- US investment relations with Greater China;
- US trade with China;
- new regulations and institutional changes that facilitate M&A activities in Hong Kong;
- major economic indicators and new regulations that impact M&A activities in Taiwan;
- tax incentives and new regulations in Mainland China.

Most of the above have significant impact upon both the M&A and cross-border merger activities in China, Hong Kong, and Taiwan.

An economic profile of China, Hong Kong, and Taiwan

Table 4.1 provides an economic profile of Mainland China, Hong Kong, and Taiwan. It is obvious that the three regions of Greater China are very different in

Table 4.1 Economic profiles of Mainland China, Hong Kong, and Taiwan

Economic profile	Mainland China	Hong Kong	Taiwan
Land area	9,596,960 sq. km	1,092 sq. km	35,980 sq. km
Population (2004)	1.3 billion	6.9 million	22.6 million
GDP in US$ (2004 est.)	1,980 billion	164 billion	282 billion
GDP per capita (2004 est.)	$1,523	$23,880	$12,585
Export (2004)	$593 billion	$226 billion	$144.2 billion
Import (2004)	$561 billion	$230 billion	$127.2 billion
Key trading partners	United States, Hong Kong, Japan, Taiwan	China, Japan, United States	China, Hong Kong, United States, Japan
Principal exports	Computers, clothing, textiles, footwear, machinery and equipment, iron and steel, toys	Clothing, textiles, footwear, electrical appliances, watches and clocks, toys	Machinery and electrical equipment, computers, metals, textiles, plastics, chemicals
Foreign exchange reserve (November 2005)	$794 billion	$123 billion	$253 billion
Mobile phones	394 million (2005)	7.2 million (2004)	22 million (2004)
Internet users	103 million (2004)	3.2 million (2003)	13.8 million (2005)

Sources: From the websites of the respective governments, The CIA World Factbook and *China Statistical Yearbook*, China Statistics Press, Beijing, various years, and other sources.

land areas, population sizes, and per capita income. For example, Mainland China's land area (9.6 million sq. km.) is about 265 times the size of Taiwan. Hong Kong is even smaller with a land area of about 1,092 sq. km. China's population is also substantially larger than either that of Taiwan or Hong Kong. On the other hand, Hong Kong had the highest GDP per capita of $23,880 in 2004, compared to $12,585 in Taiwan and $1,523 in Mainland China during the same year.

In 2005, Hong Kong, Taiwan, Japan, and the United States were the major trading partners of China. As a gateway to China, Hong Kong traded heavily with Taiwan and other Asian countries. Taiwan's economy also relies heavily on foreign trade. In 2005, Taiwan's major trading partners included China, Hong Kong, Japan, South Korea, and the United States. Principal exports from the three regions of Greater China vary somewhat as shown in Table 4.1. At the end of November 2005, China had a large foreign exchange reserve of $794 billion, second largest in the world behind Japan that had $824 billion. Both Taiwan and Hong Kong also had sizable foreign exchange reserves at the end of November 2005. A large portion of China's foreign exchange reserve is invested in US Treasuries. For example, at the end of October 2005, China held $247.6 billion of US Treasury securities, second only to Japan, that held $681.6 billion (Oster, 2006).

There are many mobile phone users in the three regions of Greater China and the cell phone markets are still expanding, especially in China. China's cell phone market is the largest in the world. In Hong Kong and Taiwan, more than half of the population now has access to the internet. At the end of 2004, there were about 103 million internet users in China.

Investment relations among the three regions of Greater China

Hong Kong and Taiwan have been the two largest sources of FDI in China since China opened its door in 1978. Before we look at the details of Hong Kong and Taiwan's investment in China, we will review the changes in total contracted and utilized FDI in China since 1979. As shown in Table 4.2, contracted FDI in China was only about $2.8 billion in 1986. It increased steadily until 1993 and then suffered a significant decline during the 1994–9 period. Beginning in 2000,

Table 4.2 Foreign direct investment in China, 1979–2005

Year	Contracted FDI		Utilized FDI	
	Amount (US$ million)	% change	Amount (US$ million)	% change
1979–85	16,325		4,721	
1986	2,834		1,875	
1987	3,709	31	2,314	23
1988	5,297	43	3,194	38
1989	5,600	6	3,392	6
1990	6,596	18	3,487	3
1991	11,977	82	4,366	25
1992	58,124	385	11,008	152
1993	111,436	92	27,515	150
1994	82,680	−26	33,767	23
1995	91,282	10	37,521	11
1996	73,277	−20	41,725	11
1997	51,004	−30	45,257	8
1998	52,102	2	45,463	0
1999	41,223	−21	40,319	11
2000	62,380	51	40,715	1
2001	69,195	11	46,878	15
2002	82,768	20	52,743	13
2003	115,070	39	53,505	1
2004	153,500	33	60,600	13
1979–2004	1,096,379		560,365	
2005	NA		60,330	(0.5)

Source: *China Statistical Yearbook*, China Statistics Press, Beijing, various years.

Note
NA = Not available.

contracted FDI started to soar and reached $153.5 billion in 2004. From 1979 to 2004, the total contracted FDI in China was about $1.1 trillion.

Utilized FDI in China has increased steadily from about $1.9 billion in 1986 to $60.6 billion in 2004. Beginning in 2003, China has been the largest recipient country of FDI outflows from all countries. From 1979 to 2004, the total utilized FDI in China was $560 billion. Preliminary statistics show that China received $60.3 billion of utilized investment in 2005. Investment funds continued to come to China despite the 2.1 percent appreciation of the Chinese Yuan in July 2005. According to the Ministry of Commerce statistics, Hong Kong remained the top source of China's FDI in 2005, accounting for $17.9 billion (or 29.8 percent) of the total. FDI from 15 EU member countries jumped 22.5 percent, while FDI from the United States dropped by 22.3 percent in 2005.

The substantial increase in FDI in recent years has stimulated rapid growth in China's economy and its foreign trade. From 1979 to 2004, China's economy grew at an average annual rate of 9.6 percent. In 2005, China's economy grew by another 9.9 percent, taking into account revisions from China's census data which showed that China's service sector played a much larger role than had been previously thought (*Wall Street Journal*, 2006). According to the National Statistic Bureau of China, service sectors (real estate, banking, restaurants, and others) accounted for about 40 percent of the GDP in 2005.

Table 4.3 presents the top 10 countries (or regions) with most FDI in China by the end of 2004. Hong Kong provided a total of $241.6 billion or 43.1 percent of the utilized FDI in China by the end of 2004. More than half of Hong Kong's direct investment is invested in the neighboring Guangdong Province. According to one estimate (Sung, 2005), Hong Kong companies employed directly or indirectly an estimated 10 million workers in Guangdong at the end of 2001.

Table 4.3 The top 10 countries/regions with most foreign direct investment in China by the end of 2004 (amounts in US$ million)

Countries/ regions	Projects		Contractual foreign investment		Actual utilized foreign investment	
	Number	*% total*	*Amount*	*% total*	*Amount*	*% total*
Total	506,358	100.0	1,096,379	100.0	560,365	100.0
Hong Kong	239,228	47.2	464,652	42.4	241,573	43.1
United States	45,265	8.9	98,608	9.0	48,028	8.6
Japan	31,855	6.3	66,649	6.1	46,846	8.4
Taiwan	64,188	12.7	79,334	7.2	40,428	7.2
Virgin Islands	11,518	2.3	81,408	7.4	36,894	6.6
Singapore	13,150	2.6	47,991	4.4	25,539	4.6
South Korea	32,753	6.5	50,564	4.6	25,935	4.6
United Kingdom	4,344	0.9	22,126	2.0	12,239	2.2
Germany	4,112	0.8	17,995	1.6	9,908	1.8
France	2,591	0.5	8,037	0.7	6,804	1.2

Source: The Ministry of Commerce of China.

During the same period, Taiwan provided about $40.4 billion or 7.2 percent of utilized FDI in China. The United States provided $48.0 billion or 8.6 percent of utilized FDI in China by the end of 2004. Other countries providing substantial FDI in China includes Japan, Singapore, and South Korea. But, according to Sung (2005), there are several potential biases in FDI statistics in China:

1   China's total inward FDI are exaggerated by the round tripping of China's own capital through offshore financial centers, Hong Kong, and elsewhere. One incentive for this form of round tripping is to capture the benefits (tax and nontax incentives) offered by China to foreign investors.
2   Taiwan's investment in China is grossly understated because some Taiwanese capital was channeled to Mainland China from Hong Kong, the United States, and other offshore financial centers, primarily because the Government of Taiwan restricted large-scale investment in China from 1996 to 2001.
3   As a result of 1 and 2 above, FDI in China from Hong Kong, other offshore financial centers and other countries are correspondingly overstated.
4   China's FDI from Hong Kong may be understated because some Hong Kong capital is channeled through other offshore financial centers. These offshore centers include the British Virgin Islands, the Cayman Islands, Bermuda, and other tax haven jurisdictions.

Because of the above four biases, it is difficult to determine the exact amount of direct investment in China from Hong Kong and Taiwan. Table 4.4 offers a slightly different view of outward DI of Hong Kong by major recipient country or territory at market value. We can observe that by the end of 2004, Hong Kong's DI in China had a market value of $155.3 billion according to Hong Kong's Census Statistics Department. On the other hand, at the end of 2004, the market value of Hong Kong's investment in the British Virgin Islands was $179.8 billion. Together, Hong Kong's outward direct investment in the British Virgin Islands and China accounted for 83 percent of all of Hong Kong's outward direct investment by the end of 2004.

Table 4.4 also shows that Hong Kong's outward DI in Britain had a market value of $7.1 billion at the end of 2004. At that time, Hong Kong's DI in the United States was worth $2.9 billion. According to the Taiwan Government's statistics, Hong Kong's cumulative investment in Taiwan was about $4.0 billion by the end of 2004. Table 4.4 also shows that Hong Kong's total outward DI increased substantially to $45.7 billion, compared to $5.5 billion recorded in 2003.

Table 4.5 shows the inward DI of Hong Kong by major investor country or territory at market value from 2001 to 2004. It appears that the British Virgin Islands is the largest investor territory and had $132.0 billion of DI in Hong Kong at the end of 2004. Mainland China is second with a total of $130.8 billion. Other offshore financial centers such as the Netherlands, Bermuda, and the Cayman Islands also have substantial investments in Hong Kong. US investment position in Hong Kong at the end of 2004 was $31.2 billion, and British investment

Table 4.4 Outward DI of Hong Kong by major recipient country/territory at market value, 2001–4 (amounts in US$ billion)

Major recipient country/territory	Position of outward DI at end of year (market value)				DI outflow during the year			
	2001	*2002*	*2003*	*2004*	*2001*	*2002*	*2003*	*2004*
British Virgin Islands	183.9	147.0	162.6	179.8	3.3	1.3	3.2	17.5
Mainland China	108.0	107.9	119.2	155.3	8.5	15.9	7.7	18.6
Bermuda	11.8	9.8	11.3	16.6	−2.5	−0.6	−0.4	3.4
United Kingdom	2.6	2.6	6.1	7.1	0.1	0.5	0.6	0.6
Singapore	3.1	3.3	3.8	4.4	0.5	0.6	0.3	0.6
Malaysia	3.7	3.6	3.1	2.9	0.8	0.6	−0.4	0.2
Panama	4.1	5.0	3.1	3.7	1.2	0.3	−1.2	−0.4
Thailand	2.6	2.7	2.8	3.2	0.3	0.3	−0.1	0.4
United States	3.2	4.1	2.6	2.9	−0.3	0.9	−1.2	0.4
Japan	1.5	1.5	1.9	5.4	−0.2	−2.2	0.1	3.6
Others	27.3	21.3	21.0	20.4	−0.4	−0.1	−3.2	0.8
Total	351.9	308.9	337.5	401.7	11.3	17.4	5.5	45.7

Source: Census and Statistics Department, Hong Kong.

Notes
1 Individual figures may not add up exactly to the total due to rounding.
2 Country/territory here refers to the immediate destination economy. It does not necessarily reflect the country/territory in which the funds are ultimately used.
3 Negative outflow does not necessarily relate to equity withdrawal. It may be the result of repayment of loans by nonresident affiliates.

position at that time was $7.9 billion. Table 4.5 also provides the DI inflow by year. In 2004, the total DI inflow was $34.0 billion, with investors from the British Virgin Islands, Mainland China, and the United States investing a total of $22.1 billion.

The Government of Taiwan publishes statistics regularly on Taiwan's approved investment in Mainland China. Table 4.6 shows such statistics for the combined years of 1991–2003, the year 2004, and cumulative totals as of the end of 2004 by province or region. In the table, numbers in brackets represent percentages to the total. We can observe that by the end of 2004, Taiwanese companies have invested $41.2 billion in Mainland China with the approval of the Government in Taiwan. This amount included the $6.9 billion invested in 2004. Of the $41.2 billion invested by the end of 2004, $17.9 billion (or 43.3 percent) was invested in Shanghai and the connected Jiangsu Province. About 28.9 percent (or $11.9 billion) was invested in the Guangdong Province, and $3.5 billion (or 8.5 percent) was invested in the Fujian Province. A substantial portion of Taiwan's investments (87.3 percent) in China is in the coastal provinces.

Table 4.7 shows Taiwan's approved 33,155 investment cases by industry. We can observe that about 34.1 percent (or $14 billion) of Taiwan's investment in China was invested in the electronics and electric equipment industry, 9 percent (or $3.7 billion) was in basic metals and metal products, and 6 percent was in the

Table 4.5 Inward DI of Hong Kong by major investor country/territory at market value, 2001–4 (amounts in US$ billion)

Major investor country/territory	Position of inward DI at end of year (market value)				DI inflow during the year			
	2001	2002	2003	2004	2001	2002	2003	2004
British Virgin Islands	120.8	99.8	120.2	132.0	9.6	7.6	2.5	8.0
Mainland China	122.6	76.1	99.0	130.8	4.9	4.1	4.9	7.9
Netherlands	25.6	26.2	32.9	39.4	−0.3	1.3	3.2	1.1
Bermuda	40.4	35.0	32.8	34.9	1.3	0.3	−1.7	1.1
United States	24.8	23.9	24.1	31.2	0.2	−1.4	2.8	6.2
Japan	14.9	18.1	18.3	19.0	1.1	2.0	1.8	1.4
Singapore	11.4	9.4	7.5	11.2	1.5	1.5	−1.3	0.4
Cayman Islands	15.3	5.7	6.8	9.0	1.4	−8.8	0.4	0.8
United Kingdom	5.8	7.1	6.2	7.9	0.9	1.1	0.6	2.3
Others	36.9	34.30	32.8	36.1	1.9	3.0	0.5	4.8
Total	418.5	335.7	380.5	451.5	23.7	9.7	13.6	34.0

Source: Census and Statistics Department, Hong Kong.

Notes
1 Individual figures may not add up exactly to the total due to rounding.
2 Country/territory here refers to the immediate source economy. It does not necessarily reflect the country/territory in which the funds are initially mobilized.
3 Negative inflow does not necessarily relate to equity withdrawal. It may be the result of repayment of loans by nonresident affiliates.

Table 4.6 Taiwan's approved investments in Mainland China by province (or region) (amounts in US$ million) (numbers in brackets represent percentages to the total)

	1991–2003	2004	1991–2004 cumulative total
Guangdong	10,512 (30.6)	1,403 (20.2)	11,915 (28.9)
Jiangsu-Shanghai	14,189 (41.4)	3,662 (52.8)	17,851 (43.3)
Fujian	3,032 (8.8)	453 (6.5)	3,485 (8.5)
Zhejiang	2,055 (6.0)	686 (9.9)	2,741 (6.6)
Subtotal	29,788 (86.8)	6,204 (89.4)	35,992 (87.3)
Other regions	4,521 (13.2)	736 (10.6)	5,257 (12.7)
Total	34,309 (100.0)	6,940 (100.0)	41,249 (100.0)

Source: Ministry of Economic Affairs, Investment Commission, Taiwan.

Table 4.7 Taiwan's approved investments in Mainland China by industry, 1991–2004

Industry	Approved cases	Approved investment (US million)	% of total investment
Electronics and electric equipment	6,009	14, 044	34.1
Basic metals and metal products	2,841	3,704	9.0
Chemicals	2,023	2,801	6.8
Plastic products	2,697	2,585	6.3
Precision instrument	2,998	2,202	5.3
Nonmetallic minerals	1,435	2,144	5.2
Food and beverage processing	2,467	1,934	4.7
Transport equipment	1,058	1,580	3.8
Textile	1,187	1,446	3.5
Services	1,869	1,428	3.5
Machinery equipment	1,319	1,321	3.2
Paper products and printing	831	917	2.2
Rubber products	599	915	2.2
Lumber and bamboo products	599	915	2.2
Wholesale retail	777	734	1.8
Garment and footwear	1,055	570	1.4
Banking and insurance	96	407	1.0
Others	2,739	1,686	4.0
Total	33,155	41,249	100.0

Source: Ministry of Economic Affairs, Investment Commission, Taiwan.

plastic product industry. Taiwanese firms also invested in many other industries in China. Some researchers maintain that the actual amount invested by Taiwanese firms in Mainland China is much higher than the official number published by the Government of Taiwan because Taiwanese firms may invest in China through their overseas subsidiaries in Hong Kong, in tax haven jurisdictions, or in the United States and Japan (Sung, 2005).

Merchandise trade among the three regions of Greater China

China's foreign trade has expanded rapidly over the last 25 years. As shown in Table 4.8, in 1980, China's export was only $18.1 billion, and imports about $19.9 billion. Trade continued to expand throughout much of the 1980s and 1990s. By 2000, China's exports were $249.2 billion, and imports $225.1 billion. Since then, it has taken only four years for China to more than double its exports to $593.4 billion in 2004, and more than double its imports to $561.4 billion. By the end of 2004, China had surpassed Japan to become the third largest trading nation, after the United States and Germany.

China's foreign trade continued to grow at a rapid rate in 2005. Statistics published on the websites of the Ministry of Commerce show that in 2005, China's exports increased by 28 percent to $762 billion and imports grew by

Table 4.8 China's foreign trade, 1978–2005

Year	Exports		Imports		Ratio of exports to GDP (%)
	Amount (US$ million)	% change	Amount (US$ million)	% change	
1978	9,955		11,131		4.6
1979	13,614	37	15,621	40	5.2
1980	18,099	33	19,941	28	6.0
1981	22,007	22	22,015	10	7.5
1982	22,321	1	19,285	−12	7.5
1983	22,226	0	21,390	11	7.2
1984	26,139	18	27,410	28	8.1
1985	27,350	5	42,252	54	9.2
1986	30,942	13	42,904	2	10.7
1987	39,437	27	43,216	1	12.5
1988	47,516	20	55,268	5	12.0
1989	52,538	11	59,140	7	11.9
1990	62,091	18	53,345	−10	16.3
1991	71,910	16	63,791	20	18.0
1992	84,940	18	80,585	26	18.1
1993	91,744	8	103,959	29	15.3
1994	121,006	32	115,614	11	22.3
1995	148,780	23	132,084	14	21.3
1996	151,048	2	138,833	5	18.4
1997	182,792	21	142,370	3	20.2
1998	183,712	1	140,237	−1	19.3
1999	194,931	6	165,699	18	19.5
2000	249,203	28	225,094	36	23.2
2001	266,098	7	243,553	8	25.2
2002	325,591	22	295,171	21	26.3
2003	438,371	35	412,836	40	35.4
2004	593,400	35	561,400	36	42.4
2005	761,999	28	660,118	18	42.4

Source: IMF, International Financial Statistics, Washington, DC and the WTO.

18 percent to $660 billion compared to the same period in 2004. In 2005, China's trade surplus surged to $101.9 billion. Government statistics for 2005 show that 58.3 percent of the exports were initiated by foreign-invested enterprises, 23 percent by state-owned companies, and 19 percent by other enterprises. In other words, more than half of China's exports are conducted by foreign multinational companies that set up shop in China to supply their home and global markets. As explained by Shenkar (2005), "Foreign invested enterprises account for a big chunk of China's export growth because they have the know-how, quality level, reputation, distribution channels, and markets necessary for foreign market entry." Because Hong Kong and Taiwan are the two largest investors in Mainland China, we will review their trade relations with China next in the following sections.

Hong Kong's merchandise trade with China

Hong Kong's aggregate trade statistics for the recent years of 1996–2005 are shown in Table 4.9. We can observe that Hong Kong's merchandise trade has been expanding in recent years. In 2005, Hong Kong's total imports were $298.6 billion, and its total exports were $288.4 billion, making Hong Kong the eleventh largest trading entity of the world. Of the $288.4 billion export total for 2005, $271.0 billion (or 91 percent) were re-exports. Re-exports are goods purchased by Hong Kong companies outside Hong Kong for resale elsewhere after the goods are processed, packaged, or inspected.

Hong Kong's merchandise trade by country or territory for 1999, 2003, and 2004 is shown in Table 4.10. In 2004, Mainland China was the largest trading partner, accounting for 43 percent (or 117.7 billion) of the imports, and 42.9 percent (or $114 billion) of total exports. Japan, the United States, European Union, and Taiwan were the next three largest trading partners of Hong Kong in 2004.

Bilateral trade statistics between Hong Kong and Mainland China for 2000–5 are shown in Table 4.11. We can observe that the two-way trade between Hong Kong and China amounted to $264.3 billion in 2005. More than 90 percent of goods imported from China were re-exported. In 2005, only 4 percent of Hong Kong's exports to China were domestic exports, the rest were re-exports. To strengthen trade and investment cooperation between Mainland China and Hong Kong, the two sides have signed and implemented several Closer Economic Partnership Arrangement (CEPA) agreements. The first CEPA was signed on June 29, 2003 and became effective on January 1, 2004. CEPA grants zero tariff on 90 percent of Hong Kong's domestic exports to Mainland China. Initially, it covered 273 types of products made in Hong Kong. The first agreement also provided easier market access for 18 service sectors: management consulting, convention and exhibition, advertising, accounting, construction and real estate, medical and dental, distribution, logistics, freight forwarding, storage and warehousing, transport, tourism, audio-visual, legal, banking, securities, insurance, and value-adding telecommunications services.

Table 4.9 Hong Kong's aggregate merchandise trade statistics, 1999 and 2002–5 (amounts in US$ billion)

Type of trade	1999	2002	2003	2004	2005
Imports (c.i.f.)	178.6	207.6	231.5	272.9	298.6
Domestic exports (f.o.b.)	21.9	18.3	15.6	20.0	17.4
Re-exports (f.o.b.)	151.1	181.8	207.8	245.6	271.0
Total exports (f.o.b.)	173.0	200.1	223.4	265.5	288.4
Total trade	351.6	407.7	454.9	538.4	587.1
Merchandise trade balance	(5.6)	(7.5)	(8.1)	(7.4)	(10.1)

Source: Hong Kong Census and Statistics Department, and the WTO.

Table 4.10 Hong Kong's merchandise trade by country/territory, 1999 and 2003–5 (amounts in US$ billion)

Type of trade/main country or territory	1999	2003	2004	2005
Imports	178.6	231.5	272.9	298.6
Mainland China	74.7	97.1	117.7	134.5
Japan	20.9	27.4	32.8	32.9
Taiwan	12.9	16.1	19.7	21.6
United States	12.6	12.7	14.4	15.3
Singapore	7.7	11.6	14.2	17.3
European Union	16.5	19.8	21.8	NA
Domestic exports	21.9	15.6	20.0	17.4
United States	6.6	5.0	4.9	4.8
Mainland China	6.5	4.7	4.8	5.7
United Kingdom	1.3	1.0	1.1	0.9
Germany	1.1	0.6	0.6	0.6
Taiwan	0.6	0.5	0.6	0.7
European Union	4.2	2.7	2.8	NA
Re-exports	151.1	207.8	245.6	271.0
Mainland China	51.2	90.5	109.1	124.1
United States	34.5	36.6	38.8	41.4
Japan	8.7	11.7	13.4	14.6
Germany	5.7	6.6	7.4	8.8
United Kingdom	5.8	6.4	7.4	7.9
European Union	24.2	28.0	33.4	NA
Total exports	173.0	223.4	265.5	288.4

Source: Hong Kong, Census and Statistics Department.

Note
NA = Not available.

Table 4.11 Hong Kong and Mainland China's merchandise trade, 2000–5 (amounts in US$ million)

Year	Hong Kong's imports from China			Hong Kong's exports to China		
	Total	Retained in Hong Kong	Re-exported elsewhere	Total	Hong Kong goods	Hong Kong re-exports
2000	87,741	9,779	77,962	69,613	6,943	62,670
2001	83,616	7,961	75,655	70,016	6,352	63,663
2002	88,251	5,731	82,520	78,621	5,304	73,317
2003	97,115	2,603	94,512	95,357	4,720	90,637
2004	117,728	NA	NA	113,916	4,859	109,057
2005	134,530	NA	NA	129,816	5,723	124,093

Source: Hong Kong Census and Statistics Department and Hong Kong Trade Development Council.

Note
NA = Not available.

Under CEPA II, signed on August 27, 2004, the two sides agreed to open up eight more areas for preferential access to Hong Kong's service suppliers: airport services, cultural entertainment, information technology, job referral agencies, job intermediaries, patent agencies, trademark agencies, and professional qualification examinations. When CEPA II became effective on January 1, 2005, 1,087 types of products made in Hong Kong could be exported to Mainland China free of tariff.

On October 18, 2005, Hong Kong and Mainland China reached an agreement on the third phase of further trade liberalization measures (CEPA III) which became effective on January 1, 2006. Under CEPA III, Mainland China agreed to give all products of Hong Kong origin tariff-free treatment except for prohibited articles such as used or waste electrical machinery and medical/surgical products, chemical residue, and municipal waste.

The three phases of the CEPA agreement will provide new business opportunities in Mainland China for Hong Kong firms and service providers. CEPA will also make Hong Kong more attractive to overseas investors because they can set up businesses in Hong Kong and enjoy easy access to the Mainland market as well as export goods to China free of tariff. In summary, CEPA will provide substantial direct and indirect benefits to Hong Kong for years to come.

Taiwan's trade with China and Hong Kong

Taiwan is a small island nation with few natural resources. It has to rely on trade and multinational investment for its survival and prosperity. Figure 4.1 shows that in 2004, Taiwan's total merchandise imports were $167.9 billion while merchandise exports amounted to $174 billion. The total trade volume ($341.9 billion) is equivalent to about 1.2 times Taiwan's GDP in 2004. Figure 4.1 also shows the major sources of Taiwan's imports: Japan, the United States, China, South Korea, and Germany. Together, these five countries supplied about 60 percent of Taiwan's imports in 2004. The five largest markets of Taiwan's exports in 2004 included China (19.5 percent), Hong Kong (17.1 percent), the United States (16.2 percent), Japan (7.6 percent), and Singapore (3.6 percent).

Table 4.12 summarizes Taiwan's merchandise trade with Mainland China and Hong Kong from 2001 to 2005. We can observe that Taiwan's exports to and imports from both China and Hong Kong have experienced double digit increases over the last four years. In 2005, merchandise trade between Taiwan and China plus Hong Kong reached an all time record of $93.4 billion according to the Taiwan Government's trade statistics. From 2001 to 2005, Taiwan enjoyed a substantial trade surplus for trading with China and Hong Kong. Taiwan's trade surplus for 2005 was close to $50 billion. This trade surplus with China and Hong Kong is vital to the survival of Taiwan because its foreign trade with the other countries in 2005 had a $42 billion deficit. Preliminary statistics show that

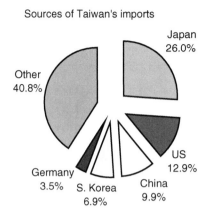

Sources of Taiwan's imports

Japan 26.0%

Other 40.8%

US 12.9%

Germany 3.5%

S. Korea 6.9%

China 9.9%

Total imports in 2004
$167.9 billion

Major import commodities (2004)
Machinery and electrical equipment
Electronic products
Minerals
Chemicals

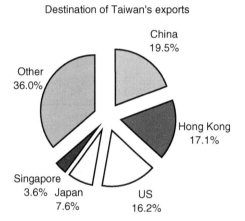

Destination of Taiwan's exports

China 19.5%

Other 36.0%

Hong Kong 17.1%

Singapore 3.6%

Japan 7.6%

US 16.2%

Total exports in 2004
$174 billion

Major export commodities (2004)
Computer products
Electrical equipment
Machinery
Metals
Textiles
Plastics and rubber products
Chemicals

Figure 4.1 Taiwn's major trading partners in 2004.

Source: Bureau of Foreign Trade, Taiwan.

Taiwan's total imports in 2004 were $167.9 billion and exports $174 billion. Table 4.12 also shows that Taiwan's economy is closely integrated with those of Hong Kong and Mainland China. More than 25 percent of Taiwan's foreign trade in 2005 was trade with China and Hong Kong.

US investment relations with Greater China

Table 4.13 shows the US direct investment abroad in selected countries from 2000 to 2004. The amounts shown are cumulative and on an historical-cost basis. At the end of 2004, US direct investment abroad totaled $2,064 billion. Most of US foreign direct investment was in Europe, Canada, Asia and Pacific, and Latin

Table 4.12 Taiwan's merchandise trade with Mainland China and Hong Kong, 2001–5 (amounts in US$ billion)

Merchandise trade	2001	2002	2003	2004	2005
Taiwan exports to					
Mainland China	4.7	9.9	21.4	34.0	40.9
Hong Kong	27.0	30.8	28.4	29.8	30.7
Subtotal	31.7	40.7	49.8	63.8	71.6
% increase over previous year		28	22	28	12
Taiwan imports from					
Mainland China	5.9	7.9	11.0	16.7	19.9
Hong Kong	1.8	1.7	1.7	2.1	1.9
Subtotal	7.7	9.6	12.7	18.8	21.8
% increase over previous year		25	32	48	16
Trade balance	24.0	31.1	37.1	45.0	49.8

Source: Bureau of Foreign Trade and Ministry of Finance, Taiwan.

Table 4.13 US DI position abroad[a], 2000–4 (amounts in US$ billion)

	2000	2001	2002	2003	2004
All countries	1,316	1,460	1,617	1,792	2,064
Canada	132	153	166	190	217
Europe	687	772	859	983	1,090
United Kingdom	231	228	248	279	303
Netherlands	115	148	158	186	202
Others	341	396	453	518	585
Latin America and other Western Hemisphere	267	280	289	301	326
Asia and Pacific	207	227	270	282	390
China	11.1	12.1	10.6	11.5	15.4
Hong Kong	27.4	32.5	40.3	37.6	43.7
Taiwan	7.8	9.3	10.1	12.1	D
Japan	57.1	55.7	66.5	68.1	80.2
Australia	34.8	27.8	39.1	48.9	D
Singapore	24.1	40.8	51.0	50.3	56.9

Source: US Department of Commerce and Bureau of Economic Analysis.

Notes
a Calculated on a historical-cost basis.
D = Data suppressed to avoid disclosure of data of individual companies.

America. Only $15.4 billion was invested in China, $43.7 billion was invested in Hong Kong, and about $12.1 billion (2003 figure) was invested in Taiwan. The US direct investment position in Hong Kong ($43.7 billion), reported by the US Bureau of Economic Analysis for 2004, is larger than that reported by Hong Kong Government in Table 4.5 ($31.2 billion). It is possible that some US investments channeled through tax haven jurisdictions were reported by the Hong Kong Census and Statistics Department as coming from those tax havens.

Using the US Government's data reported in Table 4.13 we can observe that US direct investment in Greater China at the end of 2004 was about $60.7 billion or only 3 percent of the total. This is less than the $80.2 billion total invested in Japan in 2004. Table 4.14 provides statistics on foreign direct investment in the United States from 2000 to 2004. The amounts are also cumulative and calculated on a historical-cost basis. Table 4.14 shows that all foreign direct investment in the United States totaled US $1,526 billion at the end of 2004. A large percentage of foreign direct investment in the United States came from Europe, Canada, and Japan. Only about 5.4 billion, or 0.4 percent, were invested by investors from China, Hong Kong, and Taiwan. On the other hand, China is investing its huge trade surplus in US Treasury securities. As reported earlier, China held $247.6 billion of US Treasury securities at the end of October 2005.

According to a US Government Accountability Office (GAO), 2005 report, US investment in China was concentrated in manufacturing. About $8.2 billion of the $15.4 billion cumulative stock of US investment in China in 2004 was in

Table 4.14 Foreign direct investment position in the United States[a], 2000–4 (amounts in US$ billion)

	2000	*2001*	*2002*	*2003*	*2004*
All countries	1,257	1,344	1,345	1,411	1,526
Canada	114	92	95	101	134
Europe	887	999	980	1,021	1,078
United Kingdom	278	198	216	220	252
Netherlands	139	146	150	153	167
Others	470	655	614	648	659
Latin America and other Western Hemisphere	54	65	75	82	86
Asia and Pacific	93	179	185	196	219
China	0.3	0.5	0.4	0.3	0.5
Hong Kong	1.5	1.3	1.9	1.8	1.7
Taiwan	3.2	2.5	2.7	3.0	3.2
Japan	59.7	149.9	151.3	160.5	176.9
Australia	18.8	19.5	23.8	24.9	28.1
Singapore	5.1	1.2	0.8	1.5	1.8

Source: US Department of Commerce and Bureau of Economic Analysis.

Note
a Calculated on a historical-cost basis.

Table 4.15 US banking investments in China, 2003–5

Chinese bank	Foreign investor(s)	% shares held	Closing date	Investment (US$ billion)
Shanghai Pudong Development Bank	Citigroup	4.6	Dec. 2003	0.067
Bank of China	Merrill Lynch, others	10.0	Aug. 2005	3.1
China Construction Bank	Bank of America	9	Sept. 2005	3.0
Shanghai Pudong Development Bank	Citigroup	15.3	Dec. 2005	0.8
Industrial and Commercial Bank of China	Goldman Sachs, Allianz, Amex, and others	10	Sept. 2005	3.0
Guangdong Development Bank	Citigroup and others	85	TBA	3.0
Shenzhen Development Bank	GE Consumer Finance	7	TBA	0.1

Source: Moody's, CFO Asia, and other sources.

Note
TBA = To be announced.

manufacturing. The GAO (2005) study also discovered that "U.S. companies have established local affiliate companies that increasingly sold their goods and services to the Chinese market." For example, in 2003, US majority-owned affiliates in China sold about 75 percent of their goods and services ($38 billion) in China to the Chinese market. The remaining 25 percent were sold to other countries including 7 percent back to the US market. This $38 billion exceeded the total of US goods exported to China (US $35 billion) in 2003.

In recent years, many US banks have also increased their investments in Chinese banks. Some examples are provided in Table 4.15. The US banking institutions that have invested in China include Citigroup, Bank of America, Goldman Sachs, and GE Consumer Finance. Citigroup is also a major player in syndicated lending and other services to 1,700 Chinese companies. It also wants to expand its investment banking operations (Bremner, 2006). According to the US-China Bilateral WTO Agreement reached on February 2, 2000, China is committed to full market access for US banks and other foreign banks would be able to conduct local currency business with Chinese enterprises. Foreign banks will also have the same rights as Chinese banks within designated geographic areas. Therefore, more US banking investment may come to China within the next few years.

US trade with China

In an earlier section, we provided some trade statistics between Taiwan, Hong Kong, and the United States. We have also discussed some recent developments on merchandise trade among the United States, Taiwan, and Hong Kong. Therefore, in this section, we will focus on US trade relations with Mainland China. Table 4.16 shows the bilateral trade between the two countries in recent years. As shown in the table, US–China merchandise trade has more than doubled from $123.9 billion in 2000 to $285.3 billion in 2005. On the other hand, US trade deficit with China has increased from $91.3 billion in 2000 to $201.6 billion in 2005. US exports to China are primarily aircrafts, steelmaking materials, nonferrous metals, plastic materials, and semiconductors. US imports from China include computer equipment, miscellaneous manufactured commodities (e.g. toys and games), audio and video equipment, footwear, and apparel.

The US trade statistics reported by the US Department of Commerce are different from those reported by China's National Bureau of Statistics which are shown in Table 4.17. One main reason for the differences between the US–China trade statistics is that a large portion of China's foreign trade is conducted through Hong Kong. In trade statistics, according to Sung (2005), "exports are usually classified by region of consignment, while imports are classified by region of

Table 4.16 China's merchandise trade with the United States, 1995 and 2000–5 (amounts in US$ billion)

	1995	2000	2001	2002	2003	2004	2005
US exports	11.8	16.3	19.2	22.1	28.4	34.7	41.8
% change	26.9	24.4	18.3	14.6	28.5	22.2	20.5
US imports	48.5	107.6	109.4	133.5	163.3	210.5	243.5
% change	17.1	22.6	1.6	22.0	22.3	29.0	15.7
Trade total	60.3	123.9	128.6	155.6	191.7	245.2	285.3
% change	18.9	22.8	3.8	21.0	23.2	27.9	16.4
US balance	(36.7)	(91.3)	(90.2)	(111.4)	(134.9)	(175.8)	(201.6)

Sources: US International Trade Commission, US Department of Commerce.

Table 4.17 China's merchandise trade with the United States reported by China, 1995 and 2000–5

	1995	2000	2001	2002	2003	2004	2005
US exports	16.1	22.4	26.2	27.2	33.8	44.6	48.7
% change		14.9	17.0	3.8	24.3	31.9	9.3
US imports	24.7	52.1	54.3	70.0	92.5	125.0	162.9
% change		24.3	4.2	28.9	32.1	35.1	30.3
Trade total	40.8	46.7	80.5	97.2	126.3	169.6	211.6
% change		14.5	72.4	20.8	29.9	34.3	30.7
US balance	(8.6)	(29.7)	(28.1)	(42.8)	(58.7)	(80.4)	(114.2)

Sources: National Bureau of Statistics of China.

Table 4.18 US exports to China by the annual growth rate (1995–2004) and export value
for 2004 (amounts in US$ billion)

Goods category	Annual growth rate (%)			
	Overall (1995–2004)	*First five years (1995–9)*	*Second five years (2000–4)*	*Export value (2004)*
Machinery, electronics, and high-tech apparatus	15	9	19	12.8
Chemicals, plastics, and minerals	10	6	20	5.8
Animal and plant products	14	(10)	20	3.4
Aircraft, vehicles, and other transportation	5	20	6	2.6
Base metals and articles of base metals	23	2	23	2.6
Textiles, apparel, leather, and footwear	11	(20)	45	2.6
Wood and paper products	17	20	22	1.6
Miscellaneous manufacturing and special provision products	4	0	10	0.5
Prepared foods, beverages, spirits, and tobacco	18	26	20	0.4
Glassware, precious metals and stones, and jewelry	15	14	8	0.3
Total	13	6	19	32.7

Source: GAO (2005) study of US Census Bureau trade statistics.

Note
Data were adjusted for inflation and expressed in 2004 constant dollars.

origin, as tariffs and quota often depend on region of origin." As a result,
Mainland China overstates its merchandise exports to Hong Kong and understates
its exports to other countries. For the same reason, other countries may also
overstate their exports to Hong Kong, but understate their exports to
China. Consequently, the true size of the US–China deficit may be difficult to
estimate.

Over the decade from 1995 to 2004, US goods exported to China have grown
much faster than overall US goods exported according to the GAO (2005) report.
According to the report, "U.S. exports to China tripled in value and grew at an
annual rate of 13 percent versus 2 percent annually for overall U.S. exports, from
1995 to 2004, adjusted for inflation." Table 4.18 shows US exports to China by
annual growth rate (1995–2004) and export value for 2004 by goods category. We
can observe that the 19 percent growth rate for 2000–4 was much faster than that
for the five years from 1995 to 1999. Machinery, electronics, and high-tech
apparatus ($12.8 billion) accounted for about 39 percent of US export value
in 2004. Other important goods categories included chemicals, plastics, and
minerals ($5.8 billion), and animal and plant products ($3.4 billion).

The two-way trade between China and the US will continue to grow in the next few years because of the following factors:

- US direct investment in China in manufacturing and service sectors will continue to grow as China continues to reduce its trade barriers and provide greater market access to banking, insurance, securities, and other industries. Increases in US direct investment will lead to greater demand for US capital goods, intermediate goods, services, and technology.
- China has also committed to liberalize wholesaling and retailing services for most products, including imported goods. In addition, China has opened the logistical chain of services such as maintenance, repair, storage, warehousing, packaging, advertising, trucking and air express services, and marketing. These measures should expand US–China trade in services.
- American consumers will continue to buy a wide range of goods from China. These include computers, electronics, clothing, footwear, toys, furniture, and machine tools. For example, Wal-Mart's direct and indirect procurements in China totaled $18 billion in 2004. Other chain stores such as Home Depot, Target, and Kmart also purchased a large variety of merchandise from China.
- As the living conditions and income level of Chinese consumers improve, many Chinese will buy more American products including machinery and equipment, aircraft, computer software, and automobiles. For example, sales of Ford automobiles in China grew 46 percent to 82,225 units in 2005. During the same year, General Motors (GM) also sold 665,390 vehicles in China, up 35 percent from 2004 (Browne, 2006a).

Investment climate and major regulations in Hong Kong

Hong Kong became a special administrative region after it reverted to China on July 1, 1997. Article 2 of the Basic Law of the Hong Kong Special Administrative Region (HKSAR) authorized Hong Kong "to exercise a high degree of autonomy and enjoy executive, legislative and independent judicial power, including that of final adjudication, in accordance with the provisions" of the Basic Law. Article 5 of the same Law stated further that "The socialist system and policies shall not be practiced in the HKSAR, and previous capitalist system and way of life shall remain unchanged for 50 years" beginning July 1, 1997.

Hong Kong is also a free port with a free market economy. Hong Kong has retained its position as the world's freest economy for the twelfth consecutive year according to a ranking of economic freedom produced by the Heritage Foundation based in Washington, DC. Singapore is the second and Ireland the third most free economy in the 2006 ranking.

Hong Kong relies on its container port and tourism for prosperity and economic growth. The port is vital to Hong Kong and Southern China because Hong Kong is a major hub port in the global supply chain and is "served by 80 international shipping lines with over 450 container liner services per week to over

Table 4.19 Major economic indicators of Hong Kong, 2001–5

Item	2001	2002	2003	2004	2005 estimate
GDP growth rate (%)	0.5	2.3	3.3	7.5	7.0
Inflation rate (change in consumer price index) (%)	−1.6	−3.0	−2.5	1.1	1.5
Fiscal balance/GDP (%)	−5.0	−4.9	−4.0	−3.1	−2.5
Merchandise export growth rate (%)	−5.8	4.9	12.1	6.8	7.3
Merchandise import growth rate (%)	−5.5	3.1	12.2	9.0	6.4
Current account balance/GDP (%)	61.0	8.5	11.0	6.8	8.5
Inward direct investment inflow (US$ billion)	23.7	9.7	13.6	34.0	NA
Outward direct investment outflow (US$ billion)	11.3	17.4	5.5	45.7	NA

Source: Hong Kong Census and Statistics Department.

Note
NA = Not available.

500 destinations worldwide" (HKPDC, 2006). On tourism, according to a recent Hong Kong Government statistic, more than 23 million tourists visited Hong Kong in 2005. About 55 percent of those tourists came from Mainland China.

Table 4.19 shows some major economic indicators of Hong Kong from 2001 to 2005. Hong Kong's economy suffered severely during the Asian financial crisis between July 1997 and the end of 1998. In 2001 and 2002, the Island's economy slowed further due to global economic recession. In early 2003, the outbreak of Severe Acute Respiratory Syndrome (SARS) in Guangdong Province and Hong Kong had a negative impact on Hong Kong's economy. Apartment prices bottomed out in August 2003 after a plunge of more than 50 percent from the 1997 peak. In the third quarter of 2003, Hong Kong rebounded and the economy grew at an annual rate of 3.3 percent in 2003.

Hong Kong's recovery that began in late 2003 was due to the following factors:

- The SARS outbreak faded.
- China's economy is growing rapidly and Hong Kong's economy is closely integrated with China. A survey conducted by the Federation of Hong Kong Industries in 2003 indicated that about 10 million Chinese workers were employed in Guangdong Province by industrial ventures with Hong Kong interests.
- The US economy and the European economies began to expand again in 2003.
- The signing of CEPA I between Hong Kong and China in June 2003.
- Beginning in July 2003, Mainland Chinese from many cities were allowed to tour Hong Kong individually. This scheme brought in millions of tourists from China and expanded consumer spending significantly in Hong Kong.

Hong Kong's economy remained strong in 2004 and 2005. Between August 2003 and August 2004, housing prices rebounded by more than 50 percent.

Inward direct investment continued to expand in 2005. The Census and Statistics Department reported FDI inflows of $26.7 billion during the first three quarters of 2005. During the same year, the Hong Kong investment promotion agency assisted 232 overseas Mainland and Taiwan businesses to set up or expand operations in Hong Kong. These projects were expected to create over 7,900 jobs.

Moreover, foreign investment is always welcome and there is no discrimination against foreign investors. Hong Kong has several laws governing mergers and acquisitions (Baker and McKenzie, 2004):

- The common law of contract (which is heavily based on the English common law of contract) as interpreted by the courts of Hong Kong.
- Specific Hong Kong legislation or regulations which apply depending upon the nature of the transaction and the relevant industry involved.
- Where publicly listed companies are involved, regulations such as the *Rules Governing the Listing of Securities on the Stock Exchange of Hong Kong Limited*, the *Code on Takeovers and Mergers*, and decisions of the Securities and Futures Commission, as well as certain specific legislation.

To promote competition, the Hong Kong Government allows the free play of market forces and keeps Government intervention to the minimum. That is the reason why there are no restrictions on trade, on capital inflow, and no exchange control.

Hong Kong's taxation is very simple and transparent for the following reasons:

- a flat tax system: the current profit tax is 17.5 percent for corporations and 16 percent for noncorporate taxpayers;
- only income and profits derived from Hong Kong are subject to tax; salary tax is charged on Hong Kong-sourced salaries;
- no taxes on capital gains, dividends, or interest;
- no estate duty on estates of citizens dying on or after July 15, 2005.

Major economic indicators and new regulations in Taiwan

In earlier sections, we provided a brief economic profile of Taiwan in Table 4.1, Taiwan's merchandise trade statistics with China and Hong Kong in Table 4.12, US direct investment position in Taiwan was included in Table 4.13, and Taiwan investment position in the United States was reported in Table 4.14. In Figure 4.1, we also reported Taiwan's imports by sources, and Taiwan's exports by destination. We noted that China, Hong Kong, Japan, and the United States are Taiwan's major trading partners.

In Table 4.20, we summarized some major economic indicators of Taiwan from 2001 to 2005. Like Hong Kong, Taiwan's economy was in deep recession in 2001. Their GDP growth rate was a negative 2.18 percent in that year. The year 2002 witnessed a slow recovery of Taiwan's economy. Taiwan's GDP growth rates were not as robust as those in Mainland China or in Hong Kong for 2004 and 2005, but Taiwan's economy was still growing at a moderate rate. The inflation rate

Table 4.20 Major economic indicators of Taiwan, 2001–5

Item	2001	2002	2003	2004	2005 estimate
GDP growth rate (%)	−2.18	3.59	3.31	5.7	3.70
Inflation rate (change in consumer price index) (%)	−0.01	−0.20	−0.30	1.4	2.30
Merchandise export growth rate (%)	−17.2	6.3	10.4	20.7	8.8
Average unemployment rate (%)	4.57	5.17	4.99	4.44	4.13
Average exchange rate (NT$/US$)	33.8	34.6	34.4	33.8	NA
Average prime interest rate (%)	7.38	7.1	3.43	3.41	NA
Approved overseas Chinese and foreign investment (US$ billion)	5.1	3.3	3.6	4.0	4.2
Approved outward investment (US$ billion)	4.4	3.4	4.0	3.4	7.9[a]

Source: Ministry of Economic Affairs, Taiwan.

Notes
a January to November 2005.
NA = Not available

(consumer price index) was under control from 2001 to 2005. Merchandise exports went up sharply (20.7 percent) in 2004, but the rate of increase was down to about 8.8 percent in 2005.

However, as we mentioned earlier, Taiwan's trade with Hong Kong and China continued to grow at a double-digit rate.

Unemployment rates from 2001 to 2005 averaged around 4.66 percent. The average rate for 2005 was about 4.13 percent. The amounts of approved inward direct investment for 2001 to 2005 were small compared to those invested in Hong Kong and China. In 2005, Taiwan attracted only $4.2 billion of overseas Chinese and foreign investment. Approved outward investment was about $3.4 billion in 2004. In 2005, approved outward investment went up sharply to $7.9 billion for the first 11 months of the year. This included $5.6 billion invested in Mainland China.

Taiwan has a Statute for Investment by Foreign Nationals that was last amended on November 9, 1997. Most foreign investments require the approval of the Investment Commission of Ministry of Economic Affairs. The statute defines investments to include the following:

- holding shares issued by a Taiwanese company, or contributing to the capital of a company in Taiwan;
- establishing a branch office, a proprietary business or a partnership in Taiwan;
- providing loan(s) to the invested Taiwanese business for a period exceeding one year.

Taiwan also has regulations governing the approval of investment or technical cooperation in Mainland China. Investment in Mainland China by any national, legal entity, organization, or other institution in Taiwan should obtain the approval of the Investment Commission. Because the procedure for obtaining this approval may be long and tedious, some companies in Taiwan have chosen to invest in China or Hong Kong through their overseas affiliates.

In Taiwan, merger usually refers to a "statutory merger" where two or more companies are consolidated into one company, and acquisition refers to the purchase by one firm of either the shares or assets of the target company. There are four pieces of legislation that have significant impact on M&A activities in Taiwan: (1) The Business Merger and Acquisition Act; (2) The Financial Holding Company Act; (3) The Merger Law of Financial Institutions; and (4) The Fair Trade Law.

The Business Merger and Acquisition Act was promulgated in February 2002. According to statistics published by the Ministry of Economic Affairs (MOEA, 2005), 288 domestic M&A cases were completed in 2002, 2003, and 2004 with a total value of about $4.5 billion. In April 2004, the Business Mergers and Acquisition Act was amended and promulgated on May 5, 2004. Under the new Act, the type of company with which a parent may merge has been expanded to include limited companies. Other amendments were also introduced in the new Act of 2004.

The Financial Holding Company Act of 2001 allows a financial holding company (FHC) to invest in and own 100 percent of banks, securities companies, and insurance firms. The purpose of the Act is to encourage consolidation of fragmented financial and banking industries in Taiwan. A foreign company may be qualified as a FHC if the requirements are met. To cope with the global trend toward financial convergence and consolidation, Taiwan also promulgated the Merger Law of Financial Institutions to encourage mergers to improve economies of scale and operating efficiency. By 2004, about 14 FHCs had been formed and 51 M&A deals had taken place among banking and financial institutions. On July 1, 2004, a new Financial Service Commission (FSC) was established to serve as a cabinet-level supervision authority that integrates various supervisory agencies monitoring the operations of the banking sector, equity markets, and the insurance industry.

Taiwan's Fair Trade Law requires the approval of the Fair Trade Commission before some "combinations" can take place. A combination is defined in Article 6 of the Business Merger and Acquisition Act to include the following (Baker and McKenzie, 2005):

- mergers;
- acquisitions of more than one-third of the voting stock of, or interest in, another company;
- a transfer or lease of all or a major portion of an enterprise's business or property;
- joint operation of business with an enterprise or operation of business entrusted by another enterprise;
- the exercise of effective control over the operation or personnel employed by another enterprise.

An enterprise includes a foreign enterprise for the purpose of the Act.

Tax incentives and new regulations in Mainland China

Throughout this chapter, we have discussed many aspects of the Chinese economy and its investment and trade relations with Hong Kong, Taiwan, and the United States. In this section, we will summarize some tax incentives provided by China and important regulations and changes that may have significant impact on China's M&A activities.

China has adopted preferential income tax policies toward foreign invested enterprises (FIE). The enterprise income tax rate for FIE in economic zones, high-tech industrial zones, and economic and technological development zones is 15 percent. FIE in the coastal opening areas and provincial capital cities will pay the enterprise income tax rate of 24 percent. Tax reduction and exemption policies are granted for new FIE as follows:

- A new foreign invested enterprises can enjoy income tax exemption in the first two years after making profits and income tax reduction by half in the following three years.
- A foreign invested high-tech enterprise will enjoy income tax exemption in the first two years after making profits and income tax reduction by half in the following six years.
- In addition to the above preferential treatments, an export-oriented enterprise will enjoy income tax reduction by half as long as the volume of its annual exports accounts for more than 70 percent of its sales revenue.

In 2005, investment projects listed below are the items strongly recommended by the Chinese Government:

- items of new agricultural technology and agricultural development as well as industrial projects of energy, transportation, and vital raw materials;
- high-tech projects;
- export-oriented projects;
- projects of renewable resources and prevention of environmental pollution;
- projects that will benefit western and central regions of China.

China became a WTO member on December 11, 2001. In keeping with WTO commandments, China has changed many laws and regulations, and has opened its domestic market further to foreign investors. To encourage more M&A activities, restrictions on prohibitions against foreign acquisitions of many types of industries or companies (including SOEs) have been lifted.

According to the Baker and McKenzie (2005) Guide to M&A in China, there are six ways for a foreign investor to acquire or increase an equity interest in a Chinese target company:

- direct acquisition of all or part of the nonlisted equity interest of a Chinese target company;

- acquisition of a Chinese target company through the offshore purchase of some or all of the shares of the Chinese company's foreign parent(s);
- direct purchase of some or all of the business and assets of the Chinese target company through an existing FIE or a new FIE;
- acquisition of a SOE or state-owned interest in companies;
- mergers by absorption when the absorbed company is dissolved and its registered capital and assets are merged into the surviving company;
- merger by new establishment in which the pre-merger companies are dissolved and a new company is established to control the capital and assets.

Under current Chinese law, cross-border merger between a foreign company and a Chinese target is still not allowed. The only permissible mergers are between FIEs and FIEs, or between FIEs and domestic companies. In November 2005, there were about 280,000 foreign-invested enterprises in China.

Beginning in April 2003, the Chinese Government introduced an antitrust review under the Provisional Regulations for the Acquisition of Domestic Enterprises. According to the regulations, the foreign purchaser in an offshore acquisition is required to submit the acquisition plan to the Ministry of Commerce (MOFCOM) and the State Administration for Industry and Commerce (SAIC) if certain thresholds are met.

In February 2006, the Chinese Government was still drafting its Anti-Monopoly Law. Under the proposed law, the Government would review acquisitions for their impact on competition in the domestic market (Batson, 2005). In the July 2005 draft of the law, any global transaction with a value of more than 200 million Yuan (or $25 million) and in which one party has at least 1.5 billion Yuan ($186 million) in sales or assets in China is subject to the notification requirement. No one knows how such a process would impact international M&A activity in China.

The M&A transactions in China may create some foreign exchange transactions involving Chinese currency RMB and a foreign currency. All types of foreign exchange transactions are subject to Government control and the Chinese currency is not freely convertible in the international market. The following four types of transactions are regulated by the State Administration of Foreign Exchange (SAFE): (1) inward remittance; (2) settlement of foreign exchange; (3) sale of foreign exchange; and (4) outward remittance.

Another new development in China that should help foreign investors is China's plan to substantially adopt international accounting standards beginning in 2007. Companies listed on the Shanghai and Shenzen exchanges will be required to adopt international financial reporting standards for their financial reports (Areddy, 2006). China's MOF is expected to publish details of the new accounting standards in 2006.

In the last five years, many multinational companies have purchased Chinese companies as a key element of their business strategies in China. The purchasers include General Motors, Ford Motor, Eastman Kodak, eBay, Anheuser-Busch, Amazon.com, and many others. We will discuss the details of major M&A deals in China in Chapter 5.

According to the Asia-Pacific M&A bulletin published by Pricewaterhouse-Coopers (2005), "the total value of announced M&A deals in China for the first half of 2005 increased by 22% compared to the same period in 2004. The total number of M&A deals, however, declined over the same period from 947 to 804 in total." Leading industries for M&A deals in China were energy, utilities and mining, financial services, logistics, and telecommunications. An important development is the significant growth of China's overseas investment. By the end of 2004, China's overseas investment position had reached $37 billion. About half of China's overseas investment is in neighboring Asian countries.

Summary and conclusions

In this chapter, we have provided an economic profile of the three regions of Greater China: Hong Kong, Taiwan, and Mainland China. Trade and investment between the three regions were examined. We noted that the economies of those three regions were growing rapidly in 2004 and 2005. Trade volume and investment relations between the three regions are expanding and will continue to increase in volume and scope in the next few years. In other words, the economic integration among the three regions will intensify in the future.

We also reviewed US trade and investment relations with the three regions of Greater China. The US trade with the three regions of Greater China grew at a double-digit rate in 2004 and 2005. The United States is now the largest trading partner of China and the US trade deficit within China reached an all time record of $201.6 billion in 2005. While US DI position in Greater China was still small in 2005 compared with those in Europe, Canada, and Japan, there are signs that many US multinational companies are acquiring interests in Chinese firms. Sales of US affiliates in China are growing more rapidly than US exports to China.

In this chapter, we also reviewed some major regulation and administrative changes impacting M&A activity in Hong Kong, Taiwan, and Mainland China. We noted that all three regions have introduced new laws and regulations over the last five years. Most of those changes are designed to encourage more M&A activity in industries that require consolidation to improve efficiency and economy of scale. The banking and financial service industry in Taiwan is a good example.

In the next few years, we expect M&A activities in Hong Kong, Taiwan, and China to expand further. The rate of expansion will be the fastest in Mainland China because of the following reasons:

- The Chinese economy is still expanding at a rate of more than 9 percent per year.
- Many multinational companies from Europe, North America, Japan, and other Asian countries will continue to invest in China and Hong Kong.
- China has a large pool of inexpensive but skilled labor. China's domestic market is huge and consumer spending is increasing.

- China will continue to restructure and privatize many SOEs and they are aggressively looking for domestic and foreign investors.
- Many large Chinese multinationals plan to expand their overseas investment to secure such resources as oil, natural gas, and basic materials.

In conclusion, the three regions of Greater China have enormous potential to create new M&A opportunities and challenges for potential investors from both inside and outside Greater China.

5 Mergers and acquisitions in Greater China

As explained in Chapter 4, the economic environments of Hong Kong, Taiwan, and Mainland China have changed significantly over the last two decades. China's economy has been growing at an annual rate of more than 9 percent in recent years. The trade and investment flows among the three regions of China have also been expanded. Economic integration among these three regions will continue in the future. Therefore, it is appropriate to discuss the M&A in China, Hong Kong, and Taiwan in one chapter.

In Chapter 5, we will first provide an overview of M&A deals and transaction values in China, Hong Kong, and Taiwan. Then, we will discuss the nationality of target and acquiring firms and acquisition methods used in the three regions. Lists of twenty largest M&A in China, Hong Kong, and Taiwan will be provided. Investment in China's banks by foreign banks will be discussed. We will also compare the M&A practices among the three regions of Greater China. The economic impact of M&A and FDI in Greater China and future prospects will also be examined.

An overview of M&A in Greater China

Table 5.1 shows the announced M&A deals in China, Hong Kong, and Taiwan from 1990 to 2004. Over the last 15 years, the number of deals has expanded significantly in all three regions. For example, China had only four M&A deals that were of $1 million or higher in 1990. The number increased rapidly and surpassed one thousand for the first time in 2003. In 2004, China had 1,373 deals of $1 million or higher. During the same period, Hong Kong's M&A deals have increased from 105 in 1990 to 714 in 2004. Taiwan's M&A number increased from 22 deals in 1990 to 108 in 2004. Altogether, the three regions of Greater China had 11,088 deals during the 15-year period.

Announced M&A transaction values for China, Hong Kong, and Taiwan are shown in Table 5.2. China's M&A value increased steadily from $48 million in 1990 to a peak of $47.6 billion in 2000. The M&A value dropped by 70 percent to $14.1 billion in 2001 due to global economic recession. From 2002 to 2004, M&A in China averaged about $30 billion per year.

Table 5.1 Announced M&A deals in Greater China[a], 1990–2004

Year	Greater China total	China	Hong Kong	Taiwan
1990	131	4	105	22
1991	248	17	212	19
1992	219	28	175	16
1993	370	69	288	13
1994	396	89	288	19
1995	318	76	208	34
1996	424	102	289	33
1997	605	192	382	31
1998	592	201	340	51
1999	698	195	432	71
2000	1,103	249	753	101
2001	857	305	465	87
2002	1,249	579	575	95
2003	1,683	1,008	575	100
2004	2,195	1,373	714	108
1990–2004 total	11,088	4,487	5,801	800
Averages				
1990–4	273	41	214	18
1995–9	527	153	330	44
2000–4	1,417	702	616	98

Source: Thomson Financial.

Note

a Only transactions of US$1 million or higher are included.

Hong Kong's M&A value increased rapidly in the second half of the 1990s to reach $103.9 billion in 2000. Then, the value dropped by about 60 percent to $42.7 billion in 2001. The M&A value continued to decline in 2002 and 2003 before recovering a bit in 2004. The severe decline in 2003 may be due to the SARS outbreak in that year.

The M&A transaction value in Taiwan did not change much during the 1990s. In 2000, it increased suddenly to $15.6 billion, and then dropped to $12.1 billion in 2001. M&A transaction value went up in 2000 because there were several mega deals in that year. These included the $6.4 billion acquisition of Worldwide Semiconductor by Taiwan Semiconductor Manufacturer Company (TSMC) and the $1.95 billion purchase of TSMC–ACER by the TSMC. M&A value went up to $20.2 billion in 2002 because of several large transactions and decreased to $9.4 billion in 2003. In 2004, the M&A value in Taiwan was only $3.3 billion.

From Table 5.2, we can observe that the focus of M&A in Greater China has shifted from Hong Kong and Taiwan to Mainland China. This trend should

Table 5.2 Announced M&A transaction value in Greater China[a], 1990–2004 (amounts in US$ million)

Year	Greater China total	China	Hong Kong	Taiwan
1990	10,377	48	7,982	2,347
1991	14,527	839	10,019	3,669
1992	12,024	1,487	9,461	1,076
1993	22,291	3,281	16,863	2,147
1994	13,597	2,376	9,477	1,744
1995	11,408	1,537	7,643	2,228
1996	24,974	4,121	19,858	995
1997	43,706	11,170	30,699	1,837
1998	34,627	9,266	21,804	3,557
1999	55,674	16,600	34,167	4,907
2000	167,107	47,602	103,882	15,623
2001	68,947	14,132	42,700	12,115
2002	80,020	29,749	30,086	20,185
2003	59,564	31,801	18,333	9,430
2004	56,399	29,376	23,753	3,270
1990–2004 total	675,242	203,385	386,727	85,130
Averages				
1990–4	14,563	1,606	10,760	2,197
1995–9	34,078	8,539	22,834	2,705
2000–4	86,407	30,532	43,750	12,125

Source: Thomson Financial.

Note
a Only transactions of US$1 million or higher are included.

continue in the future as China expands its trade and investment relations with the rest of the world.

Target and acquiring firms of M&A in China

Table 5.3 shows the M&A transaction value in China by the nationality or region of the target firms from 1990 to 2004. During that period, there were 4,487 deals with a total value of $203.4 billion. The average value per deal was $45.3 million.

The M&A value subtotal for target firms from Mainland China amounted to $186.3 billion (or 92 percent) while the subtotal for target firms from other countries and regions was $17.0 billion or 8 percent. There were 197 deals involving acquisitions of target firms in Hong Kong with M&A value of $5.3 billion. During the 1990–2004 period, Mainland Chinese firms have also acquired two companies in the United Kingdom, 18 firms in the United States, 14 companies in Australia, and 23 companies in Singapore.

Table 5.3 M&A transaction value in China by the nationality or region of the target firms, 1990–2004

Nationality/region	Transaction value (US$ million)	% of total	No. of deals	% of total	Average value per deal (US$ milion)
China	186,345	92	4,167	93	44.7
Hong Kong	5,259	3	197	5	26.7
United Kingdom	1,920	1	2	—	960.0
Kazakhstan	1,757	1	5	—	351.4
South Korea	1,726	1	5	—	345.2
Indonesia	1,293	1	4	—	323.3
Australia	1,157	—	14	—	82.6
Thailand	660	—	2	—	330.0
Singapore	603	—	23	1	26.2
United States	378	—	18	—	21.0
Other countries	2,287	1	50	1	45.7
Total	203,385	100	4,487	100	45.3

Source: Thomson Financial.

Table 5.4 M&A transaction value in China by the nationality or region of the acquiring firms, 1990–2004

Nationality/region	Transaction value (US$ million)	% of total	No. of deals	% of total	Average value per deal (US$ million)
China	90,094	44	2,933	65	30.7
Hong Kong	79,949	39	776	17	103.0
United States	11,136	6	171	4	65.1
United Kingdom	3,880	2	59	1	65.8
Japan	3,089	2	71	2	43.5
Singapore	2,829	1	118	3	24.0
Australia	1,022	1	21	—	48.7
Taiwan	480	—	22	—	21.8
Other countries	9,150	4	258	7	35.5
Unknown	1,755	1	58	1	30.3
Total	203,384	100	4,487	100	45.3

Source: Thomson Financial.

Table 5.4 shows the M&A transaction value in China by nationality or region of the acquiring firms from 1990 to 2004. In 2,933 deals (65 percent), the acquiring firms were Chinese companies, accounting for 44 percent of the total M&A value or $90.0 billion. On the other hand, for 35 percent or 1,554 deals, the acquirers were from Hong Kong or other countries. These 1,554 deals created M&A value of $113.3 billion.

Table 5.4 also shows that there were 171 deals valued at $11.1 billion that involved US acquirers. British companies acquired Chinese targets in 59 deals that were worth $3.9 billion. Singaporean firms also acquired Chinese target firms in 118 deals with a total value of $2.8 billion. Taiwanese acquirers were involved in 22 deals worth $480 million.

The 20 announced largest M&A in China for the 1990–2004 period are shown in Table 5.5. The largest deal was a $34.0 billion acquisition of Beijing Mobile (China) by China Telecom Hong Kong Ltd registered in Hong Kong. China Telecom Hong Kong may be a company listed in Hong Kong, but it is really a subsidiary of China Telecom in China. China Telecom Hong Kong Ltd was also involved in two other deals to acquire Fujian Mobile, Henan Mobile (China) and Jiangsu Mobile Communication (China). These are typical examples of so called "round tripping" of mainland capital in Hong Kong: "Mainland capital that flows to Hong Kong and then back to the mainland in order to capture the benefits to foreign investor" (Sung, 2005). This type of investment inflates both Mainland China's investment in Hong Kong and Hong Kong's investment in the mainland. The exact amount of such round tripping is unknown.

The second largest deal was a $10.3 billion acquisition of CH Mobile HK (BVI)–Mobile by China Mobile–Hong Kong Ltd. We can observe that 19 of the 20 target companies are Chinese companies. MG Rover Group (UK) was the only target company that was acquired by an investor group from China in a $1.9 billion deal. Interestingly, seven of the 20 target companies are in the telecommunications industry.

A review of the acquirer list in Table 5.5 indicates seven of the 20 acquirers were Hong Kong companies or subsidiaries of Mainland companies listed in Hong Kong. Another seven acquirers were companies in China (e.g. Sinopec Corporation, Baoshan Iron & Steel Co.). Procter & Gamble Co. (U.S.) was involved in a $2.0 billion acquisition of Procter & Gamble-Hutchison Ltd (China). HSBC Holdings PLC from the U.K acquired BoCOMM (China) in 2004 in a $1.7 billion deal. Nissan Motor (Japan) acquired Dong Feng Motor (China) in a $1.0 billion deal.

Together, these top 20 deals related to China had a total M&A value of $88.0 billion, which accounted for 43 percent of the total M&A value related to Mainland China from 1990 to 2004. In order to be listed among the top 20 deals in China, an M&A transaction must have a minimum value of $750 million. But, there are many high-profile M&A transactions with values less than $750 million each. Table 5.6 shows a list of M&A with US acquirers. We can see that many well-known US companies such as Anheueser-Busch, Amazon.com, American International Group (AIG), Citibank, FedEx, General Motors, eBay, General Electric, and UPS were involved in acquiring Chinese companies in recent years.

In recent years, many foreign banks have also invested in China's banks to gain access to the large consumer loan and credit card markets in China. A list of such investment is provided in Table 5.7. We can observe that many banks from the United States, Britain, Hong Kong, Singapore, Australia, and Canada were involved in this wave of investment in China's banks.

Table 5.5 Twenty announced largest M&A in China, 1990–2004

Announced date	Effective date	Target name and nationality	Acquirer and nationality	Amount (US$ million)
10/4/2000	1/13/2000	Beijing Mobile (China)	China Telecom Hong Kong Ltd (HK)	34,008
5/16/2002	7/1/2002	C H Mobile HK (BVI) – Mobile (China)	China Mobile – Hong Kong Ltd (HK)	10,335
7/14/2003	12/31/2003	China Telecom – Fixed Line Asset (China)	China Telecom Corp. Ltd. (China)	9,676
10/4/1999	12/10/1999	Fujian Mobile, Henan Mobile (China)	China Telecom Hong Kong Ltd (HK)	6,398
9/15/2000	10/1/2000	Sinopec Corp. (China)	Investor Group (China)	3,642
4/28/1998	6/15/1998	Jiangsu Mobile Communication (China)	China Telecom Hong Kong Ltd (HK)	2,900
11/21/2002	12/31/2002	Unicom New Century (BVI) Ltd (China)	China Unicom Ltd (HK)	2,721
12/16/1999	12/22/2000	G H Water Supply (Holdings) Ltd (China)	Guangdong Investment Ltd (HK)	2,328
11/16/2001	11/16/2001	Shanghai Baosteel Corp. – Steel (China)	Baoshan Iron & Steel Co. Ltd (China)	2,204
5/11/2004	6/30/2004	Procter & Gamble – Hutchison Ltd (China)	Procter & Gamble Co. (US)	2,000
8/23/2004	2/23/2005	MG Rover Group Ltd (UK)	Investor Group (China)	1,908
8/24/2004	8/18/2004	BoCOMM (China)	HSBC Holdings PLC (HSBC) (UK)	1,749
11/4/2002	11/4/2002	China Unicom (BVI) Ltd (China)	China United Telecom Corp. Ltd (China)	1,359
7/20/1999	8/16/1999	Enron Oil & Gas Prop (China)	Enron Corp. (US)	1,230
4/20/2001	12/31/2001	Sinopec Star Petroleum Co. (China)	Sinopec Corp. (China)	1,103
8/4/1997	8/4/1997	Argyle Centre Phase I (China)	Honnex Development (China)	1,070
9/18/2002	6/9/2003	Dong Feng Motor Corp. (China)	Nissan Motor Co. Ltd. (Japan)	1,032
12/2/1997	12/31/1997	Shanghai Shidongkou No. 2 – Power (China)	Huaneng Power International Inc. (China)	788
8/15/1997	8/20/1997	Shanghai Investment and Trust (China)	Temasek Holdings (Pte.) Ltd (Singapore)	762
10/22/2001	10/22/2001	Avansys Power Co. Ltd (China)	Emerson Electric Co. (US)	750

Source: Thomson Financial.

Table 5.6 Some high profile acquisitions of Chinese companies by US acquirers, 2002–4

Year completed	US acquirer	Chinese target	Amount (US$ million)
2006	FedEx Corporation	DTW Group	400.0
2005	United Parcel Service (UPS)	Sinotrans	100.0
2004	Anheuser–Busch Cos., Inc.	Harbin Brewery Group Ltd	600.0
2004	Amazon.com, Inc.	Joyo.com Ltd	75.0
2003	American International Group, Inc.	PICC Property and Casualty Co. Ltd	257.0
2003	Anheuser–Busch Cos., Inc.	Qingdao Brewery Co. Ltd	182.0
2003	Yahoo! Inc.	3721 Network Software Co.Ltd	120.0
2003	General Motors Corp., Shanghai Automotive Industry Corp.	Shandong Bodyshop Corp.	108.4
2003	Eastman Kodak Co.	China Lucky Film Group Corp.	100.0
2003	Morgan Stanley (and two other investors)	China Mengniu Dairy Co.	26.0
2002	General Motors Corp.	SAIC-Wuling Automobile	30.0
2002	eBay Inc.	EachNet Inc.	30.0
2002	H. J. Heinz Co.	Guangzhou Meiweiyuan Foodstuffs Co., Ltd	NA
2002	GE Plastics	Zhongshan Plastech Sunsheet Co. Ltd.	NA

Source: Compile by the authors from various sources.

Note
NA = Not available.

From the Chinese Government's point of view, foreign investments in China's banks may accomplish the following objectives:

• to wean the banks off government support;
• to promote reform in corporate governance;
• to make Chinese banks more competitive by listing them outside Mainland China.

In recent months, many Chinese banks also asked large investment banks to handle their initial public offerings (IPO). For example, in 2005, China Construction Bank raised $9.2 billion in the world's largest IPO for 2005. The deal helped Morgan Stanley earn about $130 million in fees (Linebaugh, 2006a). In February 2006, Goldman Sachs, Merrill Lynch and four other international investment banks were asked to compete for a role in managing the $10 billion IPO of China's largest bank, Industrial and Commercial Bank of China. In March 2006, Goldman Sachs and UBS were working on Bank of China's IPO which may raise about $6 billion.

Table 5.7 Foreign banking investment in China, 2001–5

Chinese Bank	Foreign investor(s)	% shares held	Date
Bank of Shanghai	HSBC/IFC/Shanghai Comm. Bank	8/7/3	Dec. 2001
Nanjing Comm. Bank	IFC	15	Feb. 2002
Shanghai Pudong Dev. Bank	Citigroup	4.6	Dec. 2003
Fujian Asia Bank	HSBC/Ping An Insurance	50/50	Dec. 2003
Bank of Communications	HSBC	19.9	June 2004
Industrial Bank	Hang Seng Bank/GIC/IFC	16/5/4	April 2004
Minsheng Bank	IFC/Asia Financial Holding	1.08/4.55	Jan. 2005
Xi'an City Comm. Bank	IFC/Scotia Bank	12.5/12.4	Oct. 2004
Shenzhen Dev. Bank	Newbridge Capital	17.9	Dec. 2004
China Minsheng Bank	Temasek Group of Singapore	5	Jan. 2005
China Construction Bank	Bank of America	9	June 2005
China Construction Bank	Temasek Group of Singapore	5.1	July 2005
Bank of China	Royal Bank of Scotland consortium	10	Aug. 2005
Jinan City Comm. Bank	Commonwealth Bank of Australia	11	TBA
Bohai Bank	Standard Charted	19.99	TBA
Bank of Beijing	ING Group/IFC	19.9/5	TBA
Hangzhou City Commercial Bank	Commonwealth Bank of Australia	20	TBA
Industrial and Commercial Bank of China	Goldman Sachs, Allianz, Amex and others	10	TBA

Sources: Moody's CFO Asia and other sources.

Note
TBA = To be announced.

Target and acquiring firms of M&A in Hong kong

Table 5.8 shows the M&A transaction value in Hong Kong by the nationality or region of the target firms from 1990 to 2004. In 4,245 or 73 percent of all M&A deals, the target firms were companies registered in Hong Kong. These 4,245 deals had a total M&A value of $253.7 billion, or 66 percent of all transaction value. Mainland Chinese firms were targets in 776 deals with M&A value of about $79.9 billion.

Interestingly, many M&A in Hong Kong were also involved buying US firms (109 deals with values of $8.8 billion) and UK firms (65 deals with values of $8.1 billion). In addition, there were 77 deals for buying Australian firms and 106 deals for acquiring Singaporean companies. Taiwanese targets were involved in 38 deals worth about $1.5 billion. The average value per deal varies substantially by the nationality of target firms.

A summary of acquiring firms by nationality (or region) is shown in Table 5.9. For 4,593 deals (79 percent), the acquirers are firms registered in Hong Kong.

Table 5.8 M&A transaction value in Hong Kong by the nationality or region of the target firms[a], 1990–2004

Nationality/region	Transaction value (US$ million)	% of total	No. of deals	% of total	Average value per deal (US$ million)
Hong Kong	253,679	66	4,245	73	59.8
China	79,949	21	776	13	103.0
United States	8,753	2	109	2	80.3
United Kingdom	8,114	2	65	1	124.8
Australia	6,901	2	77	1	89.6
Singapore	4,111	1	106	2	38.8
Thailand	3,114	1	35	1	88.9
Philippines	2,938	1	31	1	94.8
South Korea	2,431	1	31	1	78.4
Taiwan	1,529	—	38	1	40.2
Indonesia	1,560	1	27	—	57.8
Canada	1,585	1	29	1	54.7
Bermuda	1,531	—	5	—	306.2
Netherlands	1,456	—	4	—	364.0
India	1,347	—	24	—	56.1
Malaysia	1,227	—	39	1	31.5
Brazil	1,000	—	1	—	1,000.0
Other countries	5,522	1	159	3	34.7
Total	386,747	100	5,801	100	66.7

Source: Thomson Financial.

Note
a Only transactions of US$1 million or higher are included.

Table 5.9 M&A transaction value in Hong Kong by the nationality or region of the acquiring firms[a], 1990–2004

Nationality / region	Transaction value (US$ million)	% of total	No. of deals	% of total
Hong Kong	320,789	83	4,593	79
Singapore	12,889	3	174	3
United States	9,991	3	156	3
United Kingdom	7,556	2	94	2
Australia	6,094	2	35	—
China	5,259	1	197	3
Japan	4,458	1	88	2
Taiwan	1,838	—	30	—
Other countries	13,657	4	342	6
Unknown	4,215	1	92	2
Total	386,746	100	5,801	100

Source: Thomson Financial.

Note
a Only transactions of US$1 million or higher are included.

Acquiring firms from Singapore were involved in 174 deals worth $12.9 billion. US firms were acquirers in 156 deals worth about $10 billion. British acquirers were involved in 94 deals with a total value of $7.6 billion. Mainland Chinese firms spent about $5.3 billion to acquire Hong Kong firms in 197 deals. Taiwanese acquirers were involved in 30 deals worth $1.8 billion.

The 20 largest deals in Hong Kong from 1990 to 2004 are listed in Table 5.10. We can observe that the largest deal was the acquisition of Cable & Wireless HKT (HK) by Pacific Century Cyber Works Ltd in Hong Kong. This mega deal was worth $37.4 billion and was completed in 2000.

A review of the top 20 deals shows that half of them are related to the telecommunications industry, three related to banking, and five related to utilities. The list also includes a high profile acquisition of IBM Personal Computing by Lenovo Group Ltd listed in Hong Kong.

By comparing Table 5.10 with Table 5.5, we can find several deals involving Mainland Chinese companies as targets appear in both tables. These include the acquisitions of Beijing Mobile, CH Mobile HK (BVI)–Mobile, Fujian Mobile, Henan Mobile, Jiangsu Mobile Communication, and Unicom New Century (BVI) Ltd by acquirers registered in Hong Kong. The total M&A value of the top 20 deals in Hong Kong from 1990 to 2004 was about $28.3 billion, accounting for 33 percent of all M&A value during that period.

Target and acquiring firms of M&A in Taiwan

M&A transaction value in Taiwan by the nationality or region of the target firms and acquiring firms are shown in Tables 5.11 and 5.12. Both tables indicate there were 800 deals in Taiwan from 1990 to 2004, considerably less than the 4,487 deals recorded in China, or 5,801 deals recorded in Hong Kong during the same period. Seventy-seven percent of the 800 deals involved Taiwanese companies as targets with a total M&A value of $72.8 billion.

There were 67 deals with $5.5 billion value where US firms were targets. Hong Kong companies were targets in 30 deals that were worth about $1.8 billion. Interestingly, Mainland Chinese firms were targets in 22 deals that were worth $480 million.

Table 5.12 indicates Taiwanese acquirers were involved in 72.0 percent of the 800 deals or 85 percent of the total M&A value that was worth $72.0 billion. US firms were acquirers in 51 deals with a total value of $3.9 billion. Hong Kong companies were involved as acquirers in 38 deals that were worth $1.5 billion. British firms were acquirers in 15 deals that were worth $842 million. Interestingly, Mainland China firms were acquirers in three deals that were worth $170 million.

The 20 largest deals in Taiwan are listed in Table 5.13. We can observe that all of the 20 target firms in Table 5.13 are Taiwanese companies. Only two of the largest 20 acquirers were foreign companies. These were ABN-AMRO Holding NV (Netherlands) acquiring Bank America–Asia Retail (Taiwan), and Citigroup Inc. (US) buying Fubon Securities (Taiwan).

Table 5.10 Twenty largest M&A deals in Hong Kong, 1990–2004

Announced date	Effective date	Target name and nationality	Acquirer and nationality	Amount (US$ million)
2/29/2000	8/17/2000	Cable & Wireless HKT (HK)	Pacific Century Cyber Works Ltd (HK)	37,442
10/4/2000	11/13/2000	Beijing Mobile (China)	China Telecom Hong Kong Ltd (HK)	34,008
5/16/2002	7/1/2002	C H Mobile HK (BVI) – Mobile (China)	China Mobile (Hong Kong) Ltd (HK)	10,335
1/4/1999	12/1/1999	Fujian Mobile, Henan Mobile (China)	China Telecom Hong Kong Ltd (HK)	6,398
4/11/2001	9/3/2001	Dao Heng Bank Group (GUOCO) (HK)	DBS Group Holdings Ltd (Singapore)	5,680
9/3/1998	9/3/1998	HSBC Holdings PLC (HSBS) (UK)	Hong Kong Monetary Authority (HK)	4,689
4/28/1998	6/15/1998	Jiangsu Mobile Communications (China)	China Telecom Hong Kong Ltd (HK)	2,900
11/21/2002	12/31/2002	Unicom New Century (BVI) Ltd (China)	China Unicom Ltd (HK)	2,721
1/6/1997	3/27/1997	Cheung Kong Infrastructure (HK)	Hutchison Whampoa Ltd (HK)	2,647
1/6/1997	3/20/1997	Hong Kong Electric (Holdings) Ltd (HK)	Cheung Kong Infrastructure (HK)	2,423
12/16/1999	12/22/2000	G H Water Supply (Holdings) Ltd (China)	Guangdong Investment Ltd (HK)	2,328
10/9/1996	1/29/1997	Consolidated Electric Power (HK)	Southern Electric (US)	2,288
12/12/1999	1/31/2000	ETSA Utilities, ETSA Power (Australia)	Investor Group (HK)	2,223
1/28/1997	3/7/1997	China Light & Power Co. Ltd (HK)	CITIC Pacific Ltd (HK)	2,100
4/11/2001	1/10/2003	DBS Diamond Holdings Ltd (HK)	DBS Bank (Singapore)	1,965
12/07/2004	5/2/2005	IBM Corp. – Personal Computing (US)	Lenovo Group Ltd (HK)	1,750
4/12/2000	2/7/2001	Pacific Century Cyber-wireless (HK)	Telstra Corp. Ltd (Australia)	1,680
2/9/1998	2/15/1998	HK Telecomm (HK)	China Telecom Hong Kong Ltd (HK)	1,660
8/26/1999	9/15/1999	Pacific Convergence Corp. (HK)	Pacific Century Cyber Works Ltd (HK)	1,610
5/9/1997	6/10/1997	HK Telecom (HK)	China Everbright Holding Co. Ltd (HK)	1,472

Source: Thomson Financial.

Table 5.11 M&A transaction value in Taiwan by the nationality or region of the target firms[a], 1990–2004

Nationality/region	Transaction value (US$ million)	% of total	No. of deals	% of total	Average value per deal (US$ million)
Taiwan	72,831	86	612	77	119.0
United States	5,464	6	67	8	81.6
Hong Kong	1,838	2	30	4	61.3
Netherlands	941	1	2	—	470.5
Singapore	883	1	14	2	63.1
Malaysia	625	1	2	—	312.5
China	480	1	22	3	21.8
Japan	437	1	10	1	43.7
Thailand	383	—	10	1	38.3
Australia	286	—	7	1	40.9
Italy	227	—	1	—	227.0
Other countries	735	1	23	3	31.9
Total	85,130	100	800	100	106.4

Source: Thomson Financial.

Note
a Only transactions of US$1 million or higher are included.

Table 5.12 M&A transaction value in Taiwan by the nationality or region of the acquiring firms[a], 1990–2004

Nationality/region	Transaction value (US$ million)	% of total	No. of deals	% of total	Average value per deal (US$ million)
Taiwan	72,017	85	578	72	124.6
United States	3,888	5	51	6	76.2
Hong Kong	1,529	2	38	5	40.2
Japan	1,120	1	36	5	31.1
Singapore	895	1	29	4	30.9
United Kingdom	842	1	15	2	56.1
Australia	423	—	3	—	141.0
China	170	—	3	—	56.7
Other countries	2,762	3	30	4	92.1
Unknown	1,486	2	17	2	87.4
Total	85,130	100	800	100	106.4

Source: Thomson Financial.

Note
a Only transactions or US$1 million or higher are included.

Table 5.13 Twenty largest M&A deals in Taiwan, 1990–2004

Announced date	Effective date	Target name and nationality	Acquirer and nationality	Amount (US$ million)
1/7/2000	6/30/2000	Worldwide Semiconductor (Taiwan)	Taiwan Semiconductor Manufacturer Co. (Taiwan)	6,448
8/12/2002	12/18/2002	UWCCB (Taiwan)	Cathay Financial Holding Co. Ltd (Taiwan)	2,933
8/7/2002	12/23/2002	Taipei Bank Co. Ltd (Taiwan)	Fubon Financial Holding Co. Ltd (Taiwan)	2,347
12/27/2002	8/15/2003	South China Insurance Co. Ltd (Taiwan)	Nua Nan Financial Holding Co. Ltd (Taiwan)	2,337
5/7/2002	12/30/2002	ICBC (Taiwan)	CTB Financial Holding Co. (Taiwan)	2,114
12/30/1999	6/30/2000	TSMC–ACER (Taiwan)	Taiwan Semiconductor Manufacturer Co. (Taiwan)	1,954
12/16/2002	12/17/2002	Chunghwa Telecom Co. Ltd (Taiwan)	Investors Group (Taiwan)	1,875
7/02/2003	9/30/2003	Grand Commercial Bank (Taiwan)	Chinatrust Financial Holding Co. Ltd (Taiwan)	1,729
12/27/2002	2/26/2003	Jye Tai Precision Industrial (Taiwan)	Jye Tai Precision Industrial (Taiwan)	1,594
12/10/1998	5/20/1999	Bank America–Asian Retail (Taiwan)	ABN–AMRO Holding NV (Netherlands)	1,300
8/21/2001	3/27/2002	Acer Inc. (Taiwan)	Acer Sertek Inc. (Taiwan)	1,258
2/3/1993	8/25/1997	Chiao Tung Bank (Taiwan)	Investors Group (Taiwan)	1,166
9/12/2001	12/19/2001	Fubon Securities Co. Ltd. (Taiwan)	Fubon Insurance Co. Ltd (Taiwan)	1,027
9/12/2001	12/19/2001	Fubon Commercial Bank Co. Ltd (Taiwan)	Fubon Insurance Co. Ltd (Taiwan)	967
3/13/2001	9/1/2001	Unipa Optoelectronics Corp. (Taiwan)	Acer Display Technology Inc. (Taiwan)	962
7/17/2003	4/29/2004	K G Telecommunications Co. Ltd (Taiwan)	Far Eastone Telecom Co. Ltd. (Taiwan)	880
3/28/1995	3/28/1995	China Steel Corp. (Taiwan)	Investors Group (Taiwan)	822
9/29/1993	3/9/1995	China Steel Crop. (Taiwan)	Investors Group (Taiwan)	821
6/5/1991	6/28/1992	China Steel Corp. (Taiwan)	Investors Group (Taiwan)	801
5/5/2000	12/31/2000	Fubon Securities, Fubon (Taiwan)	Citigroup Inc. (US)	750

Source: Thomson Financial.

The largest M&A deal in Taiwan from 1990 to 2004 was the acquisition of Worldwide Semiconductor by TSMC that was worth $6.4 billion. TSMC also acquired TSMC-ACER (Taiwan) in another $2.0 billion deal.

Some target companies were involved in more than one deal as shown in Table 5.13. Parts of Fubon Securities was sold to Citigroup in 2000, and sold to Fubon Insurance in 2001. China Steel shares were sold to three different investor groups in 1992 and 1995.

Table 5.13 also shows that nine target firms were in the banking industry and four targets were in the high-tech industry. Another two targets (Chunghwa Telecom and KG Telecommunications) are in the telecommunications industry. Total M&A value for the largest 20 deals in Taiwan was about $34.1 billion, accounting for 40 percent of all M&A during the 1990–2004 period.

Acquisition methods in Greater China

Table 5.14 shows the M&A transaction value in China by acquisition methods. Two-thirds of the cases involved asset acquisition. Fifteen percent of the cases were acquisitions of partial interests. Acquisitions of majority interests were involved in 10 percent of the deals and merger was used in 5 percent of the cases. It appears that merger had the largest value per deal ($96.1 million) while acquisition of remaining interest has the lowest value per deal of $16.1 million.

The acquisition methods used in M&A in Hong Kong are summarized in Table 5.15. These methods were similar to those used in M&A in China with the exception that asset acquisition was used in 57 percent of the cases. Mergers in Hong Kong have the largest value per deal of $137.9 million while acquisitions of remaining interest have the lowest value per deal of $40.6 million.

Table 5.16 summarizes the acquisition methods used by M&A in Taiwan. Asset acquisition was used in 52 percent of the deals with 32 percent of the M&A

Table 5.14 M&A transaction value in China by acquisition methods, 1990–2004

Transaction type	Transaction value (US$ million)	%	No. of deals	%	Average value per deal (US$ million)
Asset acquisition	132,740	65	2,959	66	44.9
Merger	20,174	10	210	5	96.1
Acquisition of majority interest	17,360	9	430	10	40.4
Acquisition of partial interest	29,956	15	692	15	43.3
Acquisition of remaining interest	3,155	1	196	4	16.1
Total	203,385	100	4,487	100	45.3

Source: Thomson Financial.

Table 5.15 M&A transaction value in Hong Kong by acquisition methods, 1990–2004

Transaction type	Transaction value (US$ million)	%	No. of deals	%	Average value per deal (US$ million)
Asset aquisition	214,911	56	3,289	57	65.3
Merger	66,051	17	479	8	137.9
Acquisition of majority interest	33,861	9	555	10	61.0
Acquisition of partial interest	55,205	14	1,066	18	51.8
Acquisition of remaining interest	16,718	4	412	7	40.6
Total	386,746	100	5,801	100	66.7

Source: Thomson Financial.

Table 5.16 M&A transaction value in Taiwan by acquisition methods, 1990–2004

Transaction type	Transaction value (US$ million)	%	No. of deals	%	Average value per deal (US$ million)
Asset acquisition	27,374	32	416	52	65.8
Merger	31,901	37	74	9	431.1
Acquisition of majority interest	8,811	10	75	9	117.5
Acquisition of partial interest	12,607	15	133	17	94.8
Acquisition of remaining interest	4,438	6	102	13	43.5
Total	85,131	100	800	100	106.4

Source: Thomson Financial.

transaction value. Merger was used in 9 percent of the cases with 37 percent of the value. The value per deal for mergers in Taiwan has the highest value of $431.1 million each. Acquisitions of majority interests and partial interests accounted for 9 percent and 17 percent of the deals respectively. Acquisitions of remaining interests accounted for 13 percent of the deals and have the lowest value per transaction of $43.5 million.

A comparison of acquisition methods used in Mainland China, Hong Kong, and Taiwan from 1990 to 2004 is shown in Table 5.17. In terms of transaction values, 65 percent of China's M&A used asset acquisition, compared to 56 percent in Hong Kong, and 32 percent in Taiwan. In Taiwan, merger was used by 37 percent of the M&A, compared to 10 percent in China, and 17 percent in Hong Kong. On the other hand, the percentages of firms in the three regions using either "acquisition of majority interest" or "acquisition of partial interest" are about the same.

Table 5.17 A comparison of acquisition methods used in China, Hong Kong, and Taiwan, 1990–2004

Acquisition method	China		Hong Kong		Taiwan	
	Transaction value (US$ million)	%	Transaction value (US$ million)	%	Transaction value (US$ million)	%
Asset acquisition	132,740	65	214,911	56	27,374	32
Merger	20,174	10	66,051	17	31,901	37
Acquisition of majority interest	17,360	9	33,861	9	8,811	10
Acquisition of partial interest	29,956	15	55,205	14	12,607	15
Acquisition of remaining interest	3,155	1	16,718	4	4,438	6
Total	203,385	100	386,746	100	85,131	100

Source: Thomson Financial.

Comparison of M&A practices in the three regions of Greater China

Up to now we have discussed many aspects of M&A in Greater China separately by region. In this section, we will compare the M&A practices among the three regions. Table 5.18 compares the extent of domestic M&A versus those of cross-border M&A in Mainland China, Hong Kong, and Taiwan. Taiwan had the highest percentage (70 percent) of domestic mergers (Taiwanese firms acquiring other Taiwanese firms). The domestic M&A ratios for China and Hong Kong were 36 percent and 49 percent, respectively. Similar statistics of Singapore are also provided for reference purpose.

In Mainland China, non-Mainland Chinese firms acquiring Chinese companies accounted for 56 percent of all M&A. In Hong Kong, non-Hong Kong firms acquiring Hong Kong companies only accounted for 17 percent of the M&A. In Taiwan, the equivalent ratio was only 15 percent. One unique feature of Hong Kong M&A is that they have a high ratio (34 percent) for Hong Kong firms buying nonnative companies. Mainland Chinese firms acquiring non-Mainland Chinese companies only accounted for 8 percent of M&A which was worth $17.0 billion during the 1990–2004 period. This may change in the future. In 2005, the Lenovo Group completed its $1.7 billion acquisition of IBM's personal computer business and China National Offshore Oil Corporation (CNOOC) acquired 17 percent of Canadian Oil–Sand company MEG Energy for $124 million. China Petroleum & Chemical (or SINOPEC) also paid $124 million for a 40 percent stake in Northern Lights Oil–Sands project in Alberta, Canada. As explained by Sender (2005), "Corporate China's quest for natural resources and manufacturing know-how, brands, distribution and technology is backed by massive, low-cost

Table 5.18 A comparison of domestic and cross-border M&A in Mainland China, Hong Kong, Taiwan, and Singapore, 1990–2004

Mainland China	M&A value (US$ million)	%	Taiwan	M&A value (US$ million)	%	Hong Kong	M&A value (US$ million)	%	Singapore	M&A value (US$ million)	%
Mainland Chinese firms acquiring other Mainland Chinese firms	73,054	36	Taiwanese firms acquiring other Taiwanese firms	59,718	70	Hong Kong firms acquiring other Hong Kong firms	187,721	49	Singaporean firms acquiring other Singaporean firms	66,854	38
Mainland Chinese firms acquiring non-Mainland Chinese companies	17,040	8	Taiwanese firms acquiring non-Taiwanese companies	12,299	15	Hong Kong firms acquiring non-Hong Kong companies	133,068	34	Singaporean firms acquiring non-Singaporean firms	76,485	43
Non-Mainland Chinese firms acquiring Chinese companies	113,291	56	Non-Taiwanese firms acquiring Taiwanese companies	13,113	15	Non-Hong Kong firms acquiring Hong Kong companies	65,958	17	Non-Singaporean firms acquiring Singaporean companies	33,728	19
Total	203,385	100		85,130	100		386,747	100		177,067	100

Source: Thomson Financial.

credit lines from domestic banks, particularly China Development Bank. Funding isn't a problem."

Table 5.19 compares the industries of target firms by nationality (or region) for M&A in Greater China. For target firms involving Mainland China, only 19 percent of the M&A value were related to manufacturing industries. But, for target firms involving Taiwanese companies, 42 percent of the transaction values were related to manufacturing.

Service industries accounted for 61 percent of the M&A value in China, compared to 42 percent in Hong Kong and 22 percent in Taiwan. On the other hand, financial industries (including banking) accounted for about one-third of the total M&A value in either Hong Kong or Taiwan. In China, the same ratio was only 10 percent.

The economic impact of M&A and FDI in China

As described earlier in this chapter, both M&A deals and transaction values of Greater China have gone up in all three regions over the last 15 years. The pace of increase in China's M&A during the 1990–2004 period was the fastest among the three regions. In the following sections, we will use Mainland China as an example to explain the economic impact of M&A and FDI on China's economic performance.

Table 5.20 summarizes some M&A and economic statistics of China for selected years between 1990 and 2004. The increases in M&A deals and transaction values are parallel to those of contracted FDI and utilized FDI in China except for 2004. Cross-border M&A is an important form of FDI. In a cross-border merger, the assets and operations of two firms belonging to two different countries are combined to establish a new business enterprise with a new legal entity. Cross-border acquisitions may utilize any form of acquisition methods as shown in Table 5.14: asset acquisition, merger, acquisition of majority interest or partial interest. Acquisition of less than 10 percent interest is usually classified as portfolio investment. Cross-border M&A is a quick way to expand production and markets in China and into other neighboring markets.

In 2004, the utilized FDI in China was about $60.6 billion. According to Chinese Government statistics, this FDI was invested in the following five types of enterprises:

	Amount (US$ billion)	%
Wholly foreign-owned enterprises	40.22	66.3
Equity joint ventures	16.39	27.0
Contractual joint ventures	3.11	5.2
Cooperative development	0.11	0.2
Share-based enterprises with foreign investment	0.77	1.3
Total	60.60	100

Table 5.19 M&A in Greater China by the industry of the target firms, 1990–2004 (value in US$ million)

Country or region	Services	Manufacturing	Financial	Natural resources	Retail	Wholesale trade	Others	Total
Mainland China	163,186	50,922	25,601	15,359	3,130	2,154	6,421	266,773
	61%	19%	10%	6%	1%	1%	2%	100%
Hong Kong	109,777	44,731	83,762	1,383	8,989	6,241	5,892	260,775
	42%	17%	32%	1%	4%	2%	2%	100%
Taiwan	16,512	31,568	24,831	143	437	907	131	74,529
	22%	42%	33%	0.5%	1%	1%	0.5%	100%
Others	24,425	20,608	13,404	7,932	3,838	1,604	1,374	73,185
	33%	28%	18%	11%	6%	2%	2%	100%
Total	313,900	147,829	147,598	24,817	16,394	10,906	13,818	675,262
	46%	22%	22%	4%	2%	2%	2%	100%

Source: Thomson Financial.

Table 5.20 M&A and some economic indicators of Mainland China, selected years

Per capital annual disposable	1990	1995	2000	2004	2005
M&A deals	4	76	249	1,373	NA
M&A transaction value (US$ million)	48	1,537	47,602	29,376	NA
Contracted FDI (US$ million)	6,596	91,282	62,380	153,500	NA
Utilized FDI (US$ million)	3,487	37,521	40,715	60,600	60,330
GDP (US$ billion)	225	695	1,067	1,981[a]	2,279
Annual GDP growth rate %	9.7	25.1	8.0	10.1	9.9
Per capital annual disposable income of urban households (US$)	183	518	759	1,096	NA
Merchandise exports (US$ million)	62,091	148,780	249,203	593,400	761,999
Merchandise imports (US$ million)	53,345	132,084	225,094	561,400	660,118

Sources: Thomson Financial, the Ministry of Commerce, and National Bureau of Statistics of China.

Notes

a China's total GDP for 2004 was revised from US$1.7 trillion to US$1.98 trillion by China's Statistics Bureau in December 2005.

NA = Not available.

Some wholly foreign-owned enterprises may be the so-called "greenfield" FDI where new companies or projects were created. Foreign invested enterprises are the driving forces for exports. Statistics published by China's Ministry of Trade indicate that in 2005, exports of foreign invested enterprises totaled $444.2 billion, or 58.3 percent of China's total export value.

In addition to exports, foreign-invested enterprises also produce products and services for the Chinese market. Table 5.21 provides a list of the top 20 foreign invested enterprises by sales for 2004. Total sales of these 20 firms in 2004 were about $68.3 billion. These companies employ thousands of workers, and improve the living standards of millions of Chinese citizens.

In the near future, many foreign investors plan to invest more in China. For example, in the automobile industry, several large automakers including General Motors (GM), Ford and Honda plan to invest $15 billion in China to triple capacity to seven million cars per year by 2008. In 2005, GM sold 665,390 vehicles in China, up 35 percent from 2004 (Browne, 2006a). In the banking industry, HSBC Holding PLC paid $1.75 billion in 2004 for a 19.9 percent stake in Bank of Communications, China's fifth-largest bank. In June 2005, Bank of America Corp. reached a deal to purchase a 9 percent stake in China Construction Bank for $3 billion (Bauerlein and Linebaugh, 2005).

Besides attracting foreign investment, M&A in China has played a positive role in privatizing and revitalizing many inefficient SOEs and rationalizing industrial structure (Dong and Hu, 1995). After a decade of consolidation, China has about 50,000 SOEs that must be restructured and re-capitalized (Woodard and Wang, 2004). In the

Table 5.21 Top 20 foreign-invested enterprises by sales in 2004

Rank	Foreign invested enterprise	Sales value (US$ billion)
1	Shanghai Volkswagen Co., Ltd	6.86
2	Hongfujin Precision Industries (Shenzhen) Co., Ltd	6.63
3	FAW–Volkswagen Co., Ltd	5.93
4	Dafeng Computer (Shanghai) Co., Ltd	5.78
5	Motorola (China) Electronics Co., Ltd	4.67
6	Shanghai General Motors Co., Ltd	4.20
7	Great Wall International Information Products (Shenzhen) Co., Ltd	3.52
8	Shanghai Hewlett–Packard Co., Ltd	3.47
9	CNOOC China Co., Ltd	3.26
10	Dell (China) Co., Ltd	3.05
11	EMB International Trading (Shanghai) Co., Ltd	2.94
12	Huaneng Power International, Inc.	2.84
13	Guangzhou Honda Automobile Co., Ltd	2.70
14	Lenovo (Beijing) Co., Ltd	2.10
15	West Pacific Petrochemical Co., Ltd., Dalian	1.91
16	Maanshan Iron and Steel Co., Ltd	1.90
17	Ocean Crown Logistics (Shanghai) Co., Ltd	1.83
18	Dong Feng Motor Co., Ltd	1.60
19	Nokia (China) Investment Co., Ltd	1.55
20	Seagate Technology International (Wuxi) Co., Ltd	1.54
	Total	68.28

Source: Ministry of Commerce of China.

meantime, China is relaxing its foreign exchange restrictions on the capital account, which should support continued growth of cross-border M&A. In recent months, China has also changed the rules on stock buying by foreign investors. Qualified foreign institutional investors can now buy Chinese shares (or Class A shares), and other yuan-denominated securities including bonds (Linebaugh, 2006b).

Summary and conclusions

This chapter describes the M&A activities in Mainland China, Hong Kong, and Taiwan. We found that M&A activities of Greater China increased almost steadily from 1990 and reached their peak around 2000. The decline in M&A in 2001 was caused by the stock market crash and recession. The SARS outbreak in 2003 also depressed M&A activity in Hong Kong and Taiwan for that year. The year 2004 marked a slow recovery of M&A in China and Hong Kong. Taiwan's M&A activity declined further in 2004.

In Chapter 5, we also compared the target and acquiring firms of M&A among the three regions of Greater China. Taiwan had the highest percentage (74 percent) of domestic mergers while the domestic M&A ratios in China and Hong Kong were 59 percent and 56 percent respectively. In other words, there were more cross-border M&A in Mainland China and Hong Kong than in Taiwan. On the use of acquisition methods in terms of M&A values, 65 percent of China's M&A involved asset acquisition, compared to 56 percent in Hong Kong, and only 32 percent in Taiwan. In Taiwan, merger was used by 37 percent of the M&A, compared to 10 percent in China, and 17 percent in Hong Kong.

The increases in M&A deals and transaction values in China almost parallel those of contracted FDI and utilized FDI in China over the last 15 years. Cross-border M&A and foreign-invested enterprises in China are the driving forces of increased exports and domestic sales. These enterprises have also provided thousands of jobs and have improved the living standards of millions of Chinese citizens. The future prospect of M&A in Greater China is good especially in Mainland China for the following reasons:

- China's economy will continue to grow at a rapid rate;
- China's foreign trade will continue to expand;
- the privatization of China's state-owned enterprises will continue;
- foreign investors will increase their investment in China to produce goods and services for both the Chinese and overseas markets;
- Chinese firms will also expand their overseas direct investment to secure energy resources and take advantage of other global opportunities.

In conclusion, China's booming economy and its expanding trade and investment relations with Hong Kong, Taiwan, Japan, the United States, and the ASEAN countries will create many more investment and M&A opportunities for investors in and outside of Greater China.

6   The economic environment of Southeast Asian countries

Southeast Asia covers a large area of Asia, east of India but south of China and Japan as shown in Figure 6.1. There are more than 10 highly diverse countries rich in natural resources in this region. Ten of those countries are member states of the Association of Southeast Asian Nations (ASEAN): Indonesia, Malaysia, the Philippines, Singapore, Thailand, Brunei, Myanmar (Burma), Cambodia, Laos, and Vietnam. The first five are the founding members that created ASEAN on August 8, 1967, with the Bangkok Declaration. For convenience in this book, those original five are also called the ASEAN Big Five countries. These countries have larger economies and play important roles in international trade and investment. Five other states joining ASEAN later were Brunei (January 7, 1984), Vietnam (July 28, 1995), Laos (July 23, 1997), Myanmar (July 23, 1997), and Cambodia (April 30, 1999). In this book, we call these five states that joined ASEAN after 1967, the Small Five countries. Other countries in this area that are not members of ASEAN include East Timor which became an independent state in May 2002.

The 10 member states of ASEAN cover a total area of about 4.5 million square kilometers. They have a population of about 540 million or 8.6 percent of the world's total population. The nominal GDP of ASEAN, in 2005, was about $700 billion, and the 10 countries had a total trade volume (imports and exports) of about $760 billion in 2005.

In this book, the scope of our analysis of Southeast Asia will be limited to the 10 member states of ASEAN. The following sections will cover a wide range of topics related to ASEAN:

- an economic profile of the Big Five and the Small Five ASEAN countries;
- the 1997 Asian financial crisis;
- foreign direct investment in ASEAN;
- international trade related to ASEAN countries;
- US investment and trade relations with ASEAN;
- investment and M&A related regulations in the Big Five ASEAN countries. Because the Small Five ASEAN countries have a very limited number of M&A deals, we will not cover their investment and M&A regulations.

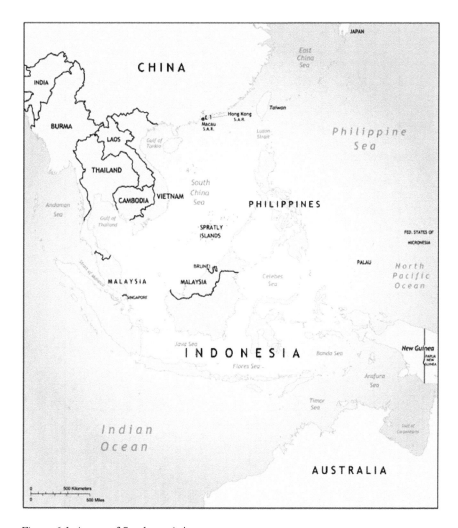

Figure 6.1 A map of Southeast Asia.

Source: The CIA World Factbook (http://www.cia.gov).

Economic profile of the Big Five ASEAN countries

Table 6.1 provides an economic profile of the five founding member states of ASEAN. They vary substantially in size and population. Indonesia is the largest country among the Big Five with a land area of 1.8 million square kilometers, and about 242 million people. Singapore is a small island state with only 683 square kilometers, and 4.4 million people. The Big Five countries also have different languages and religions. In Indonesia and Malaysia, Islam is the dominant religion. A substantial majority of Thais are Buddhists while a large majority of Filipinos

Table 6.1 Economic profile of the Big Five countries of the ASEAN

	Indonesia	Malaysia	Philippines	Singapore	Thailand
Land area (sq.km)	1,826,440	328,550	298,170	682.7	511,770
Population (thousands) (July 2005)	241,974	23,953	87,857	4,426	65,444
Main religion (%)	Islam (88)	Islam (60)	Catholicism (83)	Buddhism/Taoism (51)	Buddhism (95)
GDP at purchasing power parity in 2005 (US$ billions)	899	248	451.3	131.3	545.8
GDP at official exchange rate in 2005 (US$ billions)	245.3	124.1	90.3	113.6	180.9
GDP per capita in 2005 (US$)	3,700	10,400	5,100	26,833	8,300
Exports in 2004 (US$ billions)	69.86	123.5	38.63	174	87.91
Imports in 2004 (US$ billions)	45.07	99.3	37.5	155.2	80.84
Key trading partners	Japan, Singapore, China	US, Japan, Singapore	US, Japan, Netherlands	Malaysia, US, China	US, Japan, China
Principal exports	Oil, gas, electrical products, plywood	Electrical equipment, natural gas, rubber	Machinery and equipment, garments fruits and nuts	Machinery and equipment, chemicals	Textiles, rice, rubber, jewelry
Labor force (millions)	111.5	10.49	35.86	2.18	36.43
Unemployment rate (2004) (%)	9.9	3.6	10.9	5.3	1.5
Inflation rate (2004) (%)	6.1	1.3	5.5	1.7	2.8
Exchange rate (2004) (1 US$ = national currency)	8,985	3.8	56.0	1.7	40.2

Sources: CIA World Factbook, the ASEAN, and other sources.

are Catholics. In Singapore, slightly more than half of the population is Buddhist or Taoist.

Indonesia had the largest GDP of $245.3 billion (at official exchange rate) in 2005, while Singapore had the largest GDP per capita of $26,833 in the same year. Interestingly, Singapore had the largest trade total of about $329 billion in 2004. A large portion of Singaporean trade in 2004 was re-exports. Most of these Big Five countries traded heavily with other Asian countries including Japan, China, and South Korea. The United States is also an important trading partner of the Big Five. Other information including the principal exports, labor force, unemployment rate, inflation and exchange rates is also reported in Table 6.1. Unemployment rates are high in Indonesia (9.9 percent) and the Philippines (10.9 percent). Inflation rates are under control in most of the Big Five countries.

On August 8, 1967, the five original members signed the Bangkok Declaration and founded ASEAN to achieve the following objectives:

- To accelerate the economic growth, social progress and cultural development in the region through joint endeavors in the spirit of equality and partnership in order to strengthen the foundation for a prosperous and peaceful community of Southeast Asian nations.
- To promote regional peace and stability through abiding respect for justice and the rule of law in relationships among countries in the region and adherence to the principles of the United Nations Charter.

In 1995, the ASEAN member states also reaffirmed that "Cooperative peace and shared prosperity shall be the fundamental goals of ASEAN."

On February 24, 1976, the same five countries also signed the Treaty of Amity and Cooperation (TAC) in Southeast Asia, declaring that their relations with one another be guided by the following principles:

- mutual respect for the independence, sovereignty, equality, territorial integrity, and national identity of all nations;
- the right of every State to lead its national existence free from external interference, subversion, or coercion;
- noninterference in the internal affairs of each other;
- settlement of differences of disputes by peaceful manner;
- renunciation of the threat or use of force;
- effective cooperation among themselves.

In January 1992, the ASEAN member states signed the Singapore Declaration with the aim of creating the ASEAN Free Trade Area (AFTA) in 15 years. In 1995, the Fifth ASEAN Summit held in Bangkok adopted the Agenda for Greater Economic Integration that accelerated the timetable for the realization of AFTA. On January 1, 2003, AFTA became fully operational. Reduction of tariff and nontariff barriers had expanded intra-ASEAN trade and trade with other countries including Japan, China, and the United States.

A profile of the Small Five ASEAN countries

Important economic statistics of the ASEAN Small Five are provided in Table 6.2. We can observe that Myanmar has the largest land area among the Small Five while Vietnam had the largest population of 83.5 million in 2005. Vietnam's GDP in 2004 was larger than the other four countries combined. Brunei had the highest GDP per capita because it has large petroleum and natural gas reserves, and a small population.

Four of the ASEAN Small Five have Buddhism as their dominant religion, and three quarters of the population in Brunei follow Islam. With the exception of Vietnam, most of the Small Five countries have very limited international trade. Because they are not playing a significant role in international trade and investment, their M&A deals and transaction values are very small. Details of the M&A activity of all ASEAN countries will be reported in Chapter 7.

Inflation rates are high in Myanmar (17.2 percent), Laos (9.5 percent), and Vietnam (12.3 percent). With the exception of Brunei, most of the currencies of the other four countries are very weak against the US dollar or other hard currencies.

The 1997 Asian financial crisis

A discussion of the economic environment is incomplete without describing the major events and effects of the 1997 Asian financial crisis. In Table 6.3, major events of the Asian financial crisis are reported in chronological order. As shown in Table 6.3, the crisis began with the collapse of the Thai Baht on July 2, 1997, and quickly spread to Malaysia, Indonesia, the Philippines, and South Korea. In 1978, the Asian crisis also indirectly impacted the Russian economy and led to the Russian financial crisis.

The Asian financial crisis that started in July 1997 affected currencies, stock markets, and asset prices across Southeast Asia, Hong Kong, South Korea, and Japan. Japan's economy was severely affected because 40 percent of Japan's exports went to other Asian countries. As a result, Japan's GDP growth slowed substantially to 1.6 percent in 1997 and sank into a recession in 1998.

Table 6.4 summarizes the impact of the Asian financial crisis on the market capitalization of stock exchanges of selected countries. We can observe that the most severely affected was the Jakarta Stock Exchange (Indonesia). Between June 1, 1997, and August 1, 1998, its market capitalization dropped by about 84 percent. Malaysia's Kuala Lumpur Stock Exchange lost about 75 percent of its market capitalization during the same period. Other countries including Thailand, the Philippines, and South Korea also witnessed their market capitalization decline by 49 percent or more. The Asian economic crisis led to political unrest and changes in the governments of many countries including Indonesia, Thailand, South Korea, and Japan. The crisis had impacted the livelihood of millions of citizens in East Asia. It would take many countries in East Asia at least two years to recover from the turmoil and recession created by this financial crisis.

Table 6.2 Economic profile of the Small Five countries of the ASEAN

	Brunei	Burma (Myanmar)	Cambodia	Laos	Vietnam
Land Area (sq. km)	5,270	657,740	176,520	230,800	325,360
Population (thousands) (July 2005)	372	42,910	13,607	6,217	83,536
Main Religion (%)	Islam (75)	Buddhism (89)	Buddhism (95)	Buddhism (90)	Buddhism (70)
GDP at purchasing power parity in 2005 (US$ billions)	6.84	76.2	28.71	11.92	251.8
GDP at official exchange rate in 2005 (US$ billions)	N/A	8.243	4.92	2.598	5.61
GDP per capita in 2005 (US$)	23,600	1,800	2,100	1,900	3,000
Exports in 2004 (US$ billions)	5.1	2.1	2.3	0.37	23.7
Imports in 2004 (US$ billions)	1.4	1.8	3.1	0.58	26.3
Key trading partners	ASEAN, UK, US	China, Thailand	US, Germany, Vietnam	Thailand, Vietnam, China	China, US, Japan
Principal exports	Crude oil, natural gas, refined products	Clothing, gas, wood products, beans	Clothing, timber, rubber, rice	Garments, wood products, coffee, electricity	Crude oil, marine products, rice, coffee
Labor force	158,000	27.01 (millions)	7 (millions)	2.6 (millions)	42.98 (millions)
Unemployment rate (2004) (%)	4.8	4.0	0.8	7.0	5.6
Inflation rate (2004) (%)	1.1	17.2	3.1	12.3	9.5
Exchange rate (2004) (1 US$ = national currency)	1.7	1,293	4,036	10,560	15,704

Sources: CIA World Factbook, the ASEAN, and other sources.

Table 6.3 Major events of the 1997–8 Asian financial crisis

Date	Event
July 1, 1997	Hong Kong became a special administrative region of China
July 2, 1997	Thailand abandoned several months of defense of the baht against speculative attack and allowed its currency to float. At about the same time, speculators turned to Indonesia, Malaysia, and the Philippines and the currency of those three countries were devalued significantly
August 11, 1997	The IMF announced a rescue package of $16 billion for Thailand
August 20, 1997	The IMF approved an additional $3.9 billion aid package for Thailand
October 27, 1997	The Asian financial crisis triggered a substantial decline on the Hong Kong stock market and a record one day loss of 554 points (7.2%) on the New York Stock Exchange
October 31, 1997	The IMF announced a $40 billion bailout package for Indonesia
November 7, 1997	The Seoul stock exchange market value fell by 4%
November 8, 1997	The Seoul stock exchange fell by another 7%
November 24, 1997	Yamaichi Securities, Japan's fourth-largest brokerage firm, collapsed and left about $24 billion in liabilities
December 3, 1997	The IMF announced a record $58 billion rescue plan for South Korea
December 18, 1997	Mr Kim Dae-Jung, an opposition leader, won the presidential election in South Korea
January 2, 1998	The Thai baht reached it lowest point of 56 to the US dollar (compared to 25 to the dollar before the crisis). By this time, the Thai stock market had dropped by about 75% in value
May 21, 1998	President Suharto of Indonesia resigned after ruling Indonesia for 32 years
June 19, 1998	Russia asked for a $10–15 billion aid package from the IMF and other international leaders
July 13, 1998	Japanese Prime Minister Hashimoto resigned and acknowledged responsibility for Japan's financial crisis
July 13, 1998	International lenders granted a $22.6 billion credit to Russia

Source: Compiled by the authors from various sources.

Table 6.4 Market capitalization of stock exchanges in selected East Asian countries on 6/1/97 and 8/1/98 (amounts in US$ billion)

	June 1, 1997 market capitalization	*August 1, 1998 market capitalization*	*% change*
Hong Kong	428.2	229.7	−46.4
Indonesia	76.5	12.5	−83.7
Japan	3,050.6	2,173.0	−28.8
Malaysia	177.1	43.4	−75.5
Philippines	58.8	22.4	−61.8
Singapore	125.1	67.5	−46.1
South Korea	88.0	44.5	−49.4
Thailand	47.9	16.3	−65.9

Source: Compiled from various sources including the stock exchanges of different countries.

Foreign direct investment in ASEAN

Table 6.5 shows FDI in ASEAN by source countries from 2000 to 2004. The statistics are published by the ASEAN Secretariat. We can observe that FDI in ASEAN totaled about $22.7 billion in 2000, and declined to $18.6 billion in 2001 and $13.7 billion in 2002. FDI in ASEAN began to recover in 2003 and expanded to $25.7 billion in 2004.

The EU provided about $6.4 billion of FDI to ASEAN in 2004. The United States also provided $5.1 billion and Japan supplied $2.5 billion of direct investment in the same year. Other countries investing in ASEAN included Taiwan, South Korea, Australia, and China. Intra-ASEAN FDI was about $2.4 billion in 2004.

Table 6.6 shows FDI in ASEAN by host country or region. The annual totals from 2000 to 2004 are similar to those in Table 6.3. We can observe that from 2000 to 2004, Singapore had always been the largest host country of FDI in ASEAN. For example, in 2004, FDI in Singapore accounted for 63 percent (or $16 billion) of the total for all 10 ASEAN countries. Malaysia received $4.6 billion of FDI in the same year. Other ASEAN countries having significant FDI in 2004 were Vietnam, Thailand, and Indonesia.

Some ASEAN countries are investing heavily in China. According to China's Ministry of Commerce statistics, by November 2005, ASEAN's cumulative actual investment in China totaled $38.2 billion, involving 26,659 projects. Most of ASEAN's investment came from Singapore, Malaysia, Thailand, and the Philippines. In contrast, China's investment in ASEAN is still relatively small. By November 2005, China's actual investment in ASEAN totaled $1.14 billion according to the Ministry of Commerce.

Table 6.5 FDIs in ASEAN by source country, 2000–4 (amounts in US$ million)

	2000	2001	2002	2003	2004
ASEAN	763.1	2,495.4	3,634.4	2,301.8	2,432.7
Rest of the world	21,909.1	16,088.7	10,070.3	16,145.2	19,371.1
Hong Kong	1,128.9	(431.9)	204.5	100.1	344.9
South Korea	(45.0)	(264.8)	92.4	632.0	896.5
Taiwan	375.9	2,524.7	270.7	826.9	1,186.6
China	(133.4)	147.3	(80.9)	188.7	225.9
Japan	455.0	1,606.3	3,366.2	2,317.7	2,538.2
European Union	13,840.1	6,053.6	5,087.5	6,674.7	6,357.7
Canada	(397.6)	(555.4)	(191.7)	(10.7)	92.1
USA	7,311.6	4,569.4	357.6	1,395.3	5,051.9
Australia	(302.8)	(95.1)	202.6	181.1	392.5
New Zealand	43.1	14.7	53.7	88.5	(1.9)
Other	(366.7)	2,519.9	707.7	3,750.9	2,286.7
Total	22,672.2	18,584.1	13,704.7	18,447.0	25,654.2

Source: The ASEAN Secretariat.

Table 6.6 FDIs in ASEAN by host country, 2000–4 (amounts in US$ million)

	2000	2001	2002	2003	2004
Big Five					
Indonesia	(4,550.0)	(3,278.5)	144.7	(595.6)	1,023.4
Malaysia	3,787.6	553.9	3,203.4	2,473.2	4,623.9
Philippines	1,345.0	982.0	1,111.0	319.0	469.0
Singapore	16,485.4	14,121.7	5,821.3	9,330.6	16,059.1
Thailand	3,350.3	3,886.0	947.0	1,952.0	1,414.0
Subtotal for Big Five	20,418.3	16,265.1	11,227.4	13,479.2	23,589.4
Small Five					
Brunei	549.2	526.4	1,035.3	3,123.0	161.2
Cambodia	148.5	149.4	145.1	84.0	131.4
Laos	34.0	23.9	25.4	19.5	16.9
Myanmar (Burma)	208.0	192.0	191.4	291.2	145.1
Vietnam	1,288.7	1,300.3	1,200.1	1,450.1	1,610.1
Subtotal for Small Five	2,228.4	2,192.0	2,597.3	4,967.8	2,064.7
Total for ASEAN-10	22,646.7	18,457.1	13,824.7	18,447.0	25,654.1

Source: The ASEAN Secretariat.

International trade of the ASEAN countries

Many of the ASEAN countries, especially the Big Five, are heavily involved in international trade. Table 6.7 provides statistics on merchandise exports of the 10 ASEAN countries from 2000 to 2004. We can observe that the merchandise exports of most ASEAN countries expanded rapidly in 2003 and 2004. For example, Singapore exported $197.3 billion of goods in 2004, an increase of 24.5 percent over 2003. In 2005, Singapore's exports expanded to $229.8 billion. Malaysia exported $126.6 billion of goods in 2004 which represented a 20.9 percent increase over 2003. Thailand, Indonesia, the Philippines, and Vietnam also recorded significant increases in their merchandise exports in 2004.

Merchandise imports of all ASEAN countries are reported in Table 6.8. Singapore imported $166.1 billion of goods in 2004, an increase of 27.5 percent from 2003. In 2005, Singapore's imports expanded further to $200.2 billion. Other countries including Malaysia, Thailand, the Philippines, and Indonesia also recorded double-digit increases in imports in 2004.

One key factor for the expansion of trade among ASEAN is the AFTA that became operational on January 1, 2003. According to the ASEAN Secretariat, by 2004, more than 99 percent of the products in the Common Effective Preferential Tariff inclusion list of ASEAN-6 (Brunei, Indonesia, Malaysia, the Philippines, Singapore, and Thailand) had been brought down to the 0–5 percent tariff range. Vietnam has until 2006 to bring down its tariffs of products on the inclusion list to no more than 5 percent duties. Laos and Myanmar have until 2008 and Cambodia until 2010 to do the same thing.

In November 2002, at the Eighth Summit of ASEAN, China, and the ASEAN countries signed a framework agreement that committed them to establish a

Table 6.7 Merchandise exports of the ASEAN countries on balance of payments basis, 2000–4 (amounts in US$ billion)

Country	2000	2001	2002	2003	2004
Big Five					
Indonesia	65.4	57.4	59.2	64.1	72.2
Malaysia	98.4	88.0	94.3	104.7	126.6
Philippines	37.3	31.2	34.4	35.3	38.7
Singapore	139.7	124.5	137.4	158.4	197.3
Thailand	67.9	63.1	66.1	78.1	95.0
Subtotal for Big Five	408.7	364.2	391.4	440.6	529.8
Small Five					
Brunei	3.9	3.6	3.7	4.4	5.1
Cambodia	1.4	1.6	1.8	2.0	2.5
Laos	0.3	0.3	0.3	0.3	0.4
Myanmar (Burma)	1.6	2.4	2.5	2.7	3.0
Vietnam	14.4	15.0	16.7	20.2	26.5
Subtotal for Small Five	21.6	22.9	25.0	29.6	37.5
Total for ASEAN-10	430.3	387.1	416.4	470.2	567.3

Source: The ASEAN.

Table 6.8 Merchandise imports of the ASEAN countries on balance of payments basis, 2000–4 (amounts in US$ billion)

Country	2000	2001	2002	2003	2004
Big Five					
Indonesia	40.4	34.7	35.7	39.5	50.6
Malaysia	77.6	69.6	75.4	79.0	99.1
Philippines	33.5	32.0	34.0	40.8	45.1
Singapore	127.5	109.8	117.5	130.3	166.1
Thailand	62.4	60.6	63.4	74.3	93.7
Subtotal for Big Five	341.4	306.7	326.0	363.9	454.6
Small Five					
Brunei	1.0	1.1	1.5	1.3	1.4
Cambodia	1.9	2.1	2.3	2.6	3.2
Laos	0.5	0.5	0.4	0.5	0.7
Myanmar (Burma)	2.2	2.4	2.1	1.9	2.0
Vietnam	15.3	14.5	17.8	22.7	28.8
Subtotal for Small Five	20.9	20.6	24.1	29.0	36.1
Total for ASEAN-10	362.3	327.3	350.1	392.9	490.7

Source: The ASEAN.

China-ASEAN Free Trade Area by 2010. The China-ASEAN Free Trade Area will create the world's largest trading bloc with a combined market of about two billion people. In 2005, the two-way trade between China and the ASEAN was more than $120 billion. This two-way trade is expected to reach $200 billion in 2010.

Another significant development is the signing of the US–Singapore FTA that became effective on January 1, 2004. This FTA should encourage other developed ASEAN countries to negotiate bilateral FTA with the United States.

Japan is an important trading partner of ASEAN. Southeast Asia provides Japanese manufacturers with both a production base and a market. Japan signed an FTA with Singapore on January 13, 2002, which became effective on November 30, 2002. The key components of this FTA involve liberalization and facilitation of trade through reduction of tariff and nontariff barriers. On December 13, 2005, Japan and Malaysia also signed a comprehensive EPA to liberalize and facilitate trade in goods and services, and to mutually improve investment opportunities and ensure protection for investments and investment activities. As of March 2006, Japan was negotiating bilateral FTAs with Indonesia and Thailand.

US investment and trade relations with ASEAN

The United States has substantial trade and investment relationships with the Big Five ASEAN countries. Table 6.9 provides statistics on the US direct investment positions in ASEAN by country for the years 2000–4. We can observe that most US DIs (99.5 percent) were mainly in the Big Five countries. As a matter of fact, about 70 percent of all of the US direct investment positions (or $56.9 billion) were in Singapore in 2004. During the same year, the US direct investment position in Malaysia was $8.7 billion, in Thailand $7.7 billion, and in the Philippines $6.3 billion.

Table 6.9 US DI positions in the ASEAN countries, 2000–4 (amounts in US$ million)

	2000	2001	2002	2003	2004
Big Five					
Indonesia	8,904	10,511	(D)	(D)	(D)
Malaysia	7,910	7,489	7,101	7,270	8,690
Philippines	3,638	5,436	5,964	5,790	6,338
Singapore	24,133	40,764	50,955	50,343	56,900
Thailand	5,824	6,176	7,774	7,098	7,747
Subtotal for Big Five	50,409	70,376	71,794	70,501	79,675
Small Five					
Brunei	(2)	(17)	(33)	(28)	(23)
Cambodia	1	1	1	1	1
Laos	a	a	a	a	a
Myanmar (Burma)	(D)	(D)	(D)	(D)	(D)
Vietnam	141	172	181	218	241
Subtotal for Small Five	140	156	149	191	219
Total for ASEAN-10	50,549	70,532	71,943	70,692	79,894

Source: US Bureau of Economic Analysis.

Notes
a Less than $500,000 (+/−).
(D) Suppressed to avoid disclosure of data of individual companies.

Table 6.10 provides statistics on the US imports from and exports to the 10 ASEAN countries from 2001 to 2005. Again, we can observe that the bulk of the US trade was trade with the Big Five countries. Malaysia was the largest ASEAN trading partner with the United States. Malaysia's exports to the United States totaled $33.7 billion in 2005, and US exports to Malaysia were $10.5 billion during the same year. Singapore was the second largest ASEAN trading partner with the United States. In 2005, the United States exported $20.6 billion of goods to Singapore, and imported $15.1 billion from Singapore. The US trade with Thailand, Indonesia, and the Philippines was also significant in 2005. As a whole, US trade with the 10 ASEAN countries amounted to $148.5 billion in 2005.

There have been continuing dialogues between ASEAN representatives and the United States at the senior officials' level since 1977. The most recent one was the meeting between the ASEAN foreign ministers and the US Secretary of State in New York on September 12, 2005.

In recent years, the United States has also signed some bilateral agreements with individual ASEAN countries. For example, in 2003, the United States and Singapore signed a FTA that became effective on January 1, 2004. On that day, Singapore guaranteed zero tariffs immediately on all US products, and most US tariffs on Singaporean goods were also eliminated with the remaining tariffs phased out over a period of 3 to 10 years. In addition, Singapore will accord substantial market access to US firms in service industries including but not limited to the following:

- financial services including banking, insurance, securities, and related services
- computer and related services
- direct selling
- telecommunications services
- audiovisual services
- construction and engineering
- tourism
- advertising
- express delivery
- professional services (architects, engineers, accountants, etc.)
- distribution services, such as wholesaling, retailing, and franchising
- adult education and training services
- environmental services and
- energy services.

US companies also have the right to own equity stakes in entities that may be created if Singapore chooses to privatize certain government-owned services.

In October 2002, the United States and Thailand signed the US–Thailand Trade and Investment Framework Agreement (TIFA) and in the year 2005, the two countries pursued a vigorous timetable for US–Thailand FTA negotiations. In May 2004, the United States and Malaysia also signed the US–Malaysia TIFA.

Table 6.10 US imports from and exports to the ASEAN countries, 2000–4 (amounts in US$ million)

Countries	2001 Imports	2001 Exports	2002 Imports	2002 Exports	2003 Imports	2003 Exports	2004 Imports	2004 Exports	2005 Imports	2005 Exports
Big Five										
Indonesia	10,103.5	2,520.5	9,643.4	2,555.8	9,515.1	2,516.4	10,810.5	2,671.4	12,016.5	3,045.3
Malaysia	22,340.3	9,357.7	24,008.9	10,343.6	25,440.2	10,914.1	28,178.9	10,921.2	33,703.2	10,450.9
Philippines	11,325.5	7,660.0	10,979.8	7,276.1	10,059.0	7,987.3	9,136.7	7,087.0	9,248.2	6,892.8
Singapore	15,000.0	17,651.8	14,802.3	16,217.8	15,137.7	16,560.2	15,370.4	19,608.5	15,117.7	20,646.4
Thailand	14,727.0	5,989.4	14,792.9	4,860.2	15,178.5	5,835.3	17,578.9	6,368.4	19,892.4	7,233.1
Subtotal for Big Five	73,496.3	43,179.4	74,227.3	41,253.5	75,330.5	43,813.3	81,075.4	46,656.5	89,978.0	48,268.5
Small Five										
Brunei	398.8	103.8	287.2	46.5	422.5	37.5	405.8	47.9	562.7	49.7
Cambodia	962.5	29.6	1,071.1	29.3	1,262.1	57.9	1,497.4	58.9	1,766.6	69.5
Laos	3.7	3.6	2.7	4.1	4.2	4.7	3.4	5.9	4.2	9.8
Myanmar (Burma)	469.9	11.4	356.4	10.3	275.7	6.9	0.0	11.7	0.1	5.5
Vietnam	1,053.2	460.4	2,394.8	580.0	4,554.8	1,323.8	5,275.3	1,164.3	6,630.1	1,191.8
Subtotal for Small Five	2,888.1	608.8	4,112.2	670.2	6,519.3	1,430.8	7,181.9	1,288.7	8,963.7	1,326.3
Total for ASEAN-10	76,384.4	43,788.2	78,339.5	41,923.7	81,849.8	45,244.1	88,257.3	47,945.2	98,941.7	49,594.8

Source: US Census Bureau.

The two governments used TIFA to address trade issues and the necessary conditions for movement toward an FTA.

Investment and M&A regulations in the Big Five ASEAN countries

Indonesia

Indonesia is the largest archipelago in the world. The country's five main islands are Java, Sumatra, Sulawesi, Kalimantan, and Irian Jaya (or western new Guinea). In addition, Indonesia has more than 17,000 islands of which only 6,000 are inhabited. Indonesia also has a very diverse culture with 300 socio-linguistic groups, each with a distinct culture and heritage. Less than 20 percent of Indonesians speak the national language (Bahasa Indonesia) at home. English is now the most widely spoken foreign language.

Indonesia was a Dutch colony for more than 300 years from the early seventeenth century until 1942 when the Japanese occupied the country during the Second World War. Two days after the Japanese forces surrendered on August 17, 1945, a unilateral declaration of independence was made.

Because the Dutch ruled Indonesia for more than 300 years, much of Indonesian Law is based on old and outdated Dutch Law such as the Indonesian Commercial Law which is based on the Dutch Commercial Code of 1847. Since the mid-1980s, the country has made significant changes to its regulatory framework to encourage foreign investment and economic growth. In early 2006, the Indonesian Government began preparing a unified law on investment that will eventually replace the current Domestic Capital Investment Law and Foreign Investment Law. In the near future, the Government will also introduce amendments to the Company Law, the Bankruptcy Law, and other legislation.

The Indonesian Government welcomes foreign investment and has coordinated foreign and domestic capital investment through the Investment Coordination Board. The Board works closely with the Ministry of Trade, Ministry of Industry, and Ministry of Mining and Energy to coordinate foreign investment policy. Investors are permitted to invest in any sector of the economy except a small number of industries included in the "Negative list." Current tax law provides tax incentives to investors who invest in certain industries and certain regions. These incentives include:

- investment allowances
- accelerated depreciation and amortization
- expanded loss compensation but not more than 10 years
- ten percent tax rate on dividends paid to foreign taxpayers, except to prevailing tax conventions maintaining a lower tax rate.

According to the 2005 Baker and McKenzie Guide to Mergers and Acquisitions in Indonesia, "the Company Law and Government Regulation No. 27 of 1998 (the M&A Regulations)" set out a statutory framework for combination of business through limited liability companies. When a proposed merger or acquisition involves a publicly traded company, the companies must comply with the general requirements of the Capital Markets Law. Mergers and acquisitions in the banking sector are required to comply with the Banking Law and related regulations. Most matters related to M&A activity must also be reported to the Investment Coordination Board.

Indonesia has an Anti-Monopoly Law which established the presumption of a monopoly if a business has more than 50 percent of the market share. The law prohibits such practices as price fixing, price discrimination, or boycotts of other businesses. A Competition Supervisory Commission was established under the Anti-Monopoly Law to examine and approve mergers, acquisitions, and consolidations which may have the potential of violating the Anti-Monopoly Law.

There are no exchange controls in Indonesia. Foreign investors can move funds freely in and out of the country. Bank Indonesia is responsible for setting the exchange rate for translating the approved foreign investment into share capital denominated in Indonesian rupiah.

According to the 2005 PricewaterhouseCoopers assessment, "the outlook of M&A activity in Indonesia is one of cautious optimism across various industry sectors, including the financial services, energy, and infrastructure sectors." Bank Indonesia (the Central Bank) recently announced a plan to consolidate the Indonesia banking industry that had 134 banks in 2005. Bank Indonesia is urging the 52 smaller banks with capital under US$ 11 million (or Rp 100 billion) to merge with larger banks.

The US exports to Indonesia in 2005 totaled $3.0 billion while US imports from Indonesia were $12.0 billion during the same year. US FDI position in Indonesia was about $133 million in 2004. Most of US DIs are concentrated in the energy and mining industries. In 2005, Philip Morris agreed to purchase Hanjaya Mandala Sampoerna Tbk for $5 billion. This is one of the biggest M&A deals in Indonesia in recent years.

Malaysia

Malaysia is also a diverse country with more than 60 ethnic or culturally differentiated groups. Malays are the largest group and account for about 64 percent of the population. The rest are Chinese (27 percent), Indians (8 percent) and others.

In 1826, Singapore, Malacca and Penang were combined as the British Colony of the Straits Settlements. For 115 years, Malaysia was under the British rule until Japanese forces occupied Singapore and Malaya in 1941. The Japanese occupation ended in 1945 and British rule resumed until the summer of 1963. On September 16, 1963, the British colonies of Singapore, Sarawak, and Sabah joined together and formed the Federation of Malaysia. About two years later, Singapore left the Federation on August 9, 1965, and formed the independent Republic of Singapore.

Malaysia welcomes FDI, especially those in export-oriented manufacturing and high-tech industries. However, Malaysia also wanted to increase Malaysian and Bumiputera (ethnic Malay and other indigenous people) participation in the economy. The country has adopted a national development policy (NDP) that promotes the ownership of property and assets reflecting the following equity composition: at least 30 percent by Bumiputeras, 40 percent by other Malaysians and a maximum of 30 percent by foreigners. Recently, the Malaysian Government has introduced new policies that emphasize the following key components:

- developing Malaysia into a knowledge-based society;
- generating endogenously-driven growth through strengthening domestic investment and developing indigenous capability, while continuing to attract FDI in strategic areas;
- increasing the dynamism of the agriculture, manufacturing, and services sectors through greater infusion of knowledge;
- achieving effective Bumiputera participation as well as equity ownership of at least 30 percent by 2010;
- reorienting human resource development to support a knowledge-based society.

To develop Malaysia into a knowledge-based society, the Government is actively attracting foreign investment in the information technology industry, especially in the Multimedia Super Corridor (MSC), a project to transform a 15-by-40 kilometer area near Kuala Lumpur into a high-tech region. Foreigners who invest in the MSC will receive many tax and regulatory exemptions in exchange for a commitment of technology transfer. In September 2004, Malaysian Prime Minister also pledged that MSC status would soon be available to the other two industrial areas: the Bayan Lepas Industrial Area in Penang and the Kulim High Technology Park in Kedah.

All investment proposals, domestic and foreign, are reviewed by the Malaysian Industrial Development Authority (MIDA). The MIDA determines whether a project is consistent with the long-term economic plan (the Ninth Malaysian Plan for 2006–10) and other government policies. Investment regulations are explained in the Promotion of Investment Act of 1986 and the Industrial Coordination Act of 1975. Control of foreign ownership is done through legal and nonlegal or administrative means.

The administrative control is done by Foreign Investment Committees (FICs) through two sets of FIC Guidelines:

- guideline on the acquisition of interest, mergers, and takeovers by local and foreign interest;
- guideline on the acquisition of properties by local and foreign interests.

According to the first guideline, all proposed acquisitions, mergers, takeovers, and joint ventures require the approval of the FIC. The second guideline imposed conditions on acquisitions of properties by foreigners. Certain exemptions are available for companies that have the MSC status.

Some exchange control measures have been imposed by the Malaysian Government. For example, residents can pay nonresidents in either Ringgit (the Malaysian currency) or in a foreign currency up to RM 50,000. For amounts in excess of RM 50,000, a bank statistical form must be completed. Also residents are allowed to export foreign currency only up to the equivalent of RM 10,000. Nonresidents are allowed to export foreign currency up to the amount brought into Malaysia. However, there is no restriction on repatriation of capital, profits, dividends, interests, and fees on rentals by foreign direct investors. Companies with the MSC status may continue to be exempted from all exchange control rules.

The United States is Malaysia's largest trading partner and largest foreign investor. In 2005, Malaysia exported $33.7 billion worth of goods to the United States and imported $10.5 billion from the United States. At the end of 2004, the US direct investment position was about $8.7 billion according to data reported by the US Bureau of Economic Analysis. US companies with significant investment in Malaysia include Exxon/Mobil, ConocoPhillips, Dow Chemical, Texas Instruments, Intel, National Semiconductor, and Dell Company. Most Japanese consumer electronic companies including Sony, Panasonic, Matsushita, and Hitachi also have investments in Malaysia.

Philippines

The Philippines have more than 7,000 islands that are divided into three geographical regions: Luzon, that contains the capital city of Manila, the Visayas, and Mindanao. The Philippines was a Spanish colony from the late sixteenth century until 1898. In 1898, the Philippines were ceded to the United States following the Spanish–American War. The country gained its independence from the United States on July 4, 1946.

Because Spain ruled the Philippines for about 300 years, more than 80 percent of Filipinos are Catholics. The United States also left a strong legacy in the Philippines. The legal and political systems of the Philippines are similar to those of the United States and English is the language of business, government, and education.

Foreign investments are encouraged and a wide range of investment incentives is available. The legislation governing foreign investments is the Foreign Investment Act. The Board of Investments, a unit of the Department of Trade and Industry, is the leading agency for investment promotion. The Board of Investments prepares an annual Investment Priorities Plan that includes a list of investment areas and activities that are eligible for investment incentives. The 2005 Plan provided a list of preferred investment activities (or areas) as follows:

- agribusiness
- healthcare and wellness products and services
- information and communication technology
- electronics

- motor vehicle products
- energy
- infrastructure
- tourism
- shipbuilding/shipping
- jewelry, and
- fashion garments.

The Board of Investments also published negative lists for foreign investment. One list of limited activities is foreign ownership of certain businesses by mandate of the constitution and specific laws. For example, no foreign equity is allowed in mass media except recording. Practices of all professions including engineering, medicine, and allied professions are limited to Filipino citizens. Another list of limited foreign ownership concerns security, defense, and protection of small- and medium-scale enterprises. Foreigners are not allowed to own land in the country according to the 1987 Constitution. But foreign companies investing in the Philippines can lease land for 50 years, and can renew the lease once for another 25 years.

The Philippines do not have any specific M&A legislation. M&A are normally governed by the Corporation Code, the Securities Regulation Code, and the Civil Code. While the most common form of M&A activity is acquisitions, the Philippines also accept the concept of merger or consolidation. Acquisitions are done in one of two methods: acquiring shares from shareholders of the target firm or acquiring assets from the target company. A share acquisition involves the transfer of stock from shareholders of the target firm to the buyer. An asset acquisition involves the transfer of various types of assets and liabilities to the buyer. Each type of asset and liability may need different legal treatment and documentation. Banking M&A deals are subject to the approval of the Central Bank.

The Philippines do not have a comprehensive Anti-Monopoly Law, but the Civil Code allows the recovery of damages from unfair trade practices. Foreign exchange may be legally sold and purchased outside the banking system. Foreign investments may also be registered with the Central Bank if inward remittance is done through the Philippine banking system.

All Board of Investments registered companies may be eligible for the following and other incentives:

- income tax holiday;
- additional tax deduction for wages;
- tax and duty exemption on imported breeding stocks and genetic materials and/or tax credits on local purchases;
- tax and duty exemption on importation of required supplies/spare parts for consigned equipment;
- tax credit for taxes and duties paid on imported raw materials used in processing of export products;
- employment of foreign nationals in supervisory, technical, and advisory positions.

In addition, the Philippines have more than 100 special economic zones (SEZs) to attract foreign investors into the country. The Special Economic Zone Act grants preferential tax treatment to enterprises located in SEZs.

In 2005, the two-way trade between the Philippines and the United States amounted to about $16.1 billion. The US DI position in the Philippines was about $6.3 billion at the end of 2004. Large US banks and manufacturers investing in the Philippines include Citibank, Intel, Procter and Gamble. Philip Morris, and Texas Instruments. As of February 2006, the Philippines had signed bilateral investment agreements and tax treaties with the United States and many other countries.

Singapore

Singapore is a very small country located at the tip of the Malaysian peninsula, near the southeastern end of the straits of Malacca. The main island of Singapore has an area of only 574 square kilometers. In 1867, Singapore became part of the British Straits Settlement that also includes Penang and Malacca. From February 15, 1942 to August 1945, Singapore was occupied by Japanese forces during the Second World War. After the war in 1946, Singapore was made into a separate crown colony of Britain. In 1959, self-government with a fully elected parliament was established in Singapore. On September 16, 1963, Singapore joined Malaya to form the Federation of Malaysia. On August 9, 1965, Singapore separated from Malaysia and became a democratic and independent republic.

As a small country with limited natural resources, Singapore must rely on trade and international investment to survive. Singapore's strategic location has also helped it to become one of the most important seaports and shipping centers in Asia. In 2005, Singapore was the world's busiest port in terms of shipping tonnage. Today, Singapore is also a thriving international financial center, a leader in both petroleum refining and the manufacture of computer components.

Singapore has a free-enterprise system and an investment promotion strategy that attracts major investment in high value-added manufacturing and service activities. Singapore's legal system and public policies are friendly to foreign investors. The country also provides generous tax and other incentives to eligible investors.

The goals of Singapore's investment incentives are to develop Singapore into a global financial center, an international business center, an international air and sea cargo center, a location for regional and global operational headquarters of multinational companies, and an exporter of value-added services. The Economic Development Board (EDB) is Singapore's investment promotion agency. Incentives administered by the EDB include the following:

- Pioneer status: new manufacturing and service investments with high-tech skills can enjoy a corporate income tax holiday up to 15 years.
- A development and expansion incentive that replaces the post-pioneer incentive. Firms that engage in new projects, expand or upgrade operations

which result in significant economic spin-offs are eligible for a concessionary tax rate for up to 10 years or longer.

- An investment allowance incentive: companies engaged in qualifying activities are eligible for exemption of taxable income equal to a specified proportion (up to 50 percent) of new fixed investment.
- A double deduction for research and development expenses: This incentive applies to manufacturing and service activities engaged in research and development. Double deduction is allowed for qualifying R&D expenses against taxable income.

In addition, there are many incentives offered by the Monetary Authority of Singapore (MAS), the International Enterprise Singapore, and the Media Development Authority. Tax concessions including tax holidays and reduced tax rates play an important role in attracting foreign investment. The governing statutes are the Income Tax Act and the Economic Expansion Incentives Act.

There are no exchange control restrictions in Singapore. Investors can repatriate capital, loans, and income to the home country. Dividends, interest, royalties, and service fees may be repatriated after paying applicable withholding taxes.

Singapore's taxes are on a territorial basis. Only income derived in Singapore, or income derived overseas but received in Singapore, are subject to tax. Table 6.11 provides an outline of corporate taxes. We can observe that the

Table 6.11 Singapore's corporate tax structure

Key features	
Corporate income tax	20%[a]
Capital gains tax	None
Withholding tax[b]	
Dividends	None[c]
Interest	15%
Royalties	10%
Branch remittance tax	None
Net operating losses (years)	
Carry forward	Unlimited
Carry back	Companies can carry back losses of up to $100,000 from one year back (with effect from year of assessment 2006)

Source: The Economic Development Board of Singapore.

Notes

a The tax rate of 20% is effective from the year of assessment 2005. It applies to both Singapore-incorporated subsidiaries as well as to branches of foreign companies. It applies equally to resident and nonresident companies.

b Withholding taxes at the corporate income tax rate also apply to certain other payments to nonresidents, such as technical assistance fees and management fees.

c A one-tier corporate taxation system took effect on January 1, 2003. It replaced the imputation system of taxing dividends, where taxes paid by a company can be imputed or passed on to shareholders.

corporate income tax rate is 20 percent and there is no capital gains tax. On the other hand, Singapore imposes a 5 percent Goods and Services Tax (GST) on the supply of goods and services in Singapore and on the importation of goods into Singapore. Relief from GST on imports may be granted under certain conditions. The governing statutes for tax concessions are the Income Tax Act and the Economic Expansion Incentives Act.

On M&A legislation, the Singapore Parliament passed the Companies (Amendment) Bill 2005 on May 16, 2005. This bill (the Amendment Act) became effective in January 2006. The Amendment Act introduced a more efficient statutory form of merger and amalgamation. According to the Baker and McKenzie (2005) Guide for Mergers and Acquisitions in Singapore, the following requirements must be complied with in a corporate merger or an amalgamation:

- an amalgamation proposal setting out the terms of the amalgamation that must be approved by members of each amalgamating company by special resolution;
- the proposal will have to be sent to every secured creditor of the amalgamating company;
- notice of the proposed amalgamation will have to be published in one Chinese and one English daily newspaper.

In the case of share acquisition, profits derived from the disposal trading stock are taxable at the normal corporate income tax rate (20 percent). In addition, the buyer must pay a stamp duty at 0.2 percent of the purchase price for the shares or their market value, whichever is higher.

The leading foreign investors in Singapore are US Firms. At the end of 2004, the US direct investment position in Singapore amounted to $56.9 billion. According to the US Embassy in Singapore, currently there are over 1,500 US firms in Singapore. The United States is also a major trading partner of Singapore. In 2005, the United States imported $15.1 billion of goods from Singapore, and exported $20.6 billion of merchandise to Singapore. Singapore has bilateral investment agreements and FTA with the United States. Singapore also has tax treaties with many other countries, but not with the United States.

In addition, Singapore also has free trade agreements with other ASEAN Big Five countries (Malaysia, Indonesia, Thailand, and the Philippines), as well as with Japan, South Korea, and New Zealand. In 2005, Singapore also signed a Trans-Pacific Strategic Economic Partnership agreement with New Zealand, Chile, and Brunei.

Thailand

Thailand is bordered on the west by Myanmar (Burma), on the east by Cambodia, on the North by Laos, and on the south by Malaysia. Thailand has a relatively homogeneous population. More than 85 percent of the population speak a dialect of Thai and share a common culture. About 12 percent of Thai are Chinese, but the Sino-Thai community is closely integrated. Malay-speaking Muslims account for about 2.3 percent of the population. Buddhism is the official religion and is the religion of about 95 percent of the people.

Thailand is a constitutional monarchy with the King as chief of state and the Prime Minister as head of government. Thailand is the only country that has avoided European colonization. It was occupied briefly by Japanese forces during Second World War, until Japan's defeat in 1945.

Thailand's economy is dependent on exports that account for about 60 percent of its GDP. Before the Asian financial crisis, the Thai economy's average growth rate was about 9.4 percent for the decade from 1986 to 1996. The country was severely impacted by the Asian financial crisis in 1997 and 1998. More recently, Thailand's GDP was growing at a rate of 6.9 percent in 2003 and 6.1 percent in 2004.

The Thai Government welcomes foreign investment. The Board of Investment (BOI) is responsible for investment promotion. The structure, role, and policies of the BOI follow the guidelines contained in the Investment Promotion Act of 1977, later amended in 1991. Foreign investors who are willing to meet certain requirements can apply for special investment privileges through the BOI. The Board has six regional offices in Thailand and four overseas offices in New York, Frankfurt, Tokyo, and Paris.

The BOI divides all provinces of Thailand into three investment zones as follows:

- Zone 1 includes six central provinces with high income and good infrastructure: Bangkok, Samut Prakan, Samut Sakhon, Pathum Thani, Nonthaburi, and Nakhon Pathom.
- Zone 2 includes thirteen provinces: Samut, Songkhram, Ratchaburi, Kanchanaburi, Suphanburi, Ang Thong, Ayutthaya, Saraburi, Nakhon Nayok, Chachoengsao, Chon Buri, Rayong, and Phuket.
- Zone 3 includes the remaining 58 provinces with low income and less developed infrastructure.

The BOI provides two major types of tax incentives to promote industries and companies:

- exemption or reduction of tariffs on imported machinery and equipment, as well as raw materials for the promoted activity;
- exemption from income tax on net profits and dividends.

The extent of these incentives varies according to the location of the company. A list of Thailand's general tax incentives is shown in Table 6.12. Additional tax incentives for projects located in less developed Zone 3 are shown in Table 6.13.

In addition, the following nontax incentives may be granted to eligible companies:

- Guarantees against

    - nationalization
    - competition of new state enterprises

- state monopolies
- price controls and
- tax-free imports by the public sector.

- Permission to

    - own land;
    - bring in foreign nationals to undertake investment feasibility studies;
    - bring in foreign technicians and experts to work on the promoted project.

- Protection measures

    - imposition of a surcharge on competing imported products of up to 50 percent of CIF value for a period of one year at a time;
    - imposition of an import ban on competing products;
    - implementation of other tax relief measures as appropriate.

Table 6.12 A summary of general tax incentives provided by Thailand

Customs duty exemption

The general rules for granting import duty exemptions on the import of machinery and raw materials by eligible companies are outlined in the tables:

Import duty on machinery

Zone 1	50% reduction
Zone 2	50% reduction
Zone 3	100% reduction

Import duty on raw materials

Zone 1	1-year exemption
Zone 2	1-year exemption
Zone 3	5-year exemption

Income tax exemption

In general, the duration of income tax exemption granted to eligible companies depends on the project's location. The period of tax exemption generally starts from the date of the first sale. The exemptions are shown in the table below:

Corporate income tax exemption

	Inside industrial estate	*Outside industrial estate*
Zone 1	3 years	Not exempt
Zone 2	5 years	3 years
Zone 3	8 years	8 years

Source: The Board of Investment of Thailand.

Table 6.13 Additional government incentives for projects located in Zone 3 of Thailand

Projects located in the following 40 provinces (Krabi, Kamphaeng Phet, Khon Kaen, Chanthaburi, Chai Nat, Chalyaphum, Chumphon, Chiang rai, Chiang Mai, Trang, Trat, Tak, Nakhon Ratchasima, Nakhon Si Thammarat, Nakhon Sawan, Prachuab Khiri Khan, Prachin Buri, Phangnga, Phattalung, Pichit, Phitsanulok, Phetchaburi, Phetchabun, Mukdahan, Mae Hong Son, Ranong, Lop Buri, Lamphang, Lamphun, Loei, Songkhla, Sa Kaew, Sing Buri, Sukhothai, Surat Thani, Nong Khai, Udon Thani, Uttaradit, Uthai Thani, and Ubon Ratchathani) shall be granted additional tax and duty privileges, as follows:

Additional incentives for locating in these 40 provinces of Zone 3

	Inside industrial estate	*Outside industrial estate*
50% reduction of income tax for an additional 5 year period	Yes	No
Double deduction of water, electricity, transport costs for 10 years	Yes	No
25% deduction of infrastructure installation or construction costs	No	Yes

Projects located in the 18 least-developed provinces (Kalasin, Nakhon Phanom, Narathiwat, Nan, Buri Ram, Pattani, Phayao, Phrae, Maha Sarakham, Yasothon, Yala, Roi Et, Si Sa Ket, Sakhon Nakhon, Sathun, Surin, Nong Bualamphu, and Amnat Charoen) shall be granted the following tax and duty privileges:

Additional incentives for locating in the 18 least-developed provinces of Zone 3

	Inside industrial estate	*Outside industrial estate*
50% reduction of income tax for an additional 5 year period	Yes	Yes
Double deduction of water, electricity, transport costs for 10 years	Yes	Yes
25% deduction of infrastructure installation or construction costs	Yes	Yes

Source: The Board of Investment of Thailand.

In 2006, the BOI placed priority on promotion of projects in the following sectors: agriculture and agricultural products, direct involvement in technological and human resource development, public utilities and infrastructure, environmental protection and conservation, and other targeted industries.

Mergers and acquisitions in Thailand may be concluded in one of the following three categories:

- an amalgamation or a consolidation;
- share acquisition;
- acquisition of assets of the target company.

The consolidation for shares and assets may be in the form of cash, shares in the buying companies, other securities, or a combination of them.

Under the Foreign Business Act (FBA), businesses are divided into three categories:

- *Category (Schedule) one*: Types of business that aliens are not permitted to pursue for special reasons. These businesses include newspaper publishing; radio or television station broadcasting; raising animals; and dealing in land.
- *Category (Schedule) two*: Businesses concerning national security or safety with an adverse effect on Thai art and culture, customs, or native manufacture/handicrafts or with a negative impact on natural resources and the environment. These businesses include the production, disposal (sales) and overhaul of firearms, ammunition, gunpowder and explosives; raising silkworms and producing Thai silk threads, and weaving and printing patterns on Thai silk textiles.
- *Category (Schedule) three*: Businesses that Thailand companies are not ready to compete in undertakings with aliens. This includes rice milling and production of flour from rice and farm plants; accounting and legal services; and some brokerage and agency services.

Thailand is a member of the WTO and ASEAN. It has close economic ties with other ASEAN countries. Japan is Thailand's largest trading partner and the United States is the second largest. In 2005, the United States merchandise imports from Thailand totaled $19.9 billion, and merchandise exports amounted to $7.2 billion. Thailand's largest foreign investors are the United States, Japan, Singapore, and the European Union. The US direct investment position in Thailand was about $7.7 billion at the end of 2004. In March 2006, Thailand was negotiating an FTA with the United States.

Summary and conclusions

This chapter has provided an economic profile of the 10 member countries of ASEAN. We noted that all of them have different languages, religions, and cultures. Their economic performances of the past decade have also varied significantly. In general, the ASEAN Big Five countries (Indonesia, Malaysia, the Philippines, Singapore, and Thailand) are doing better than the Small Five countries (Brunei, Myanmar, Cambodia, Laos, and Vietnam). However, in recent years, Vietnam has improved its international trade and expanded its economy. The other four small

ASEAN countries are less developed, but have plenty of opportunities to expand their trade and investment.

The Asian financial crisis in 1997 and 1998 created economic turmoil and political unrest in many South Asian countries. Many of them learned important lessons from the crisis and they welcomed foreign investors with significant tax and nontax incentives. In addition, these countries are promoting international trade and have taken economic measures to expand their economies. Singapore has concluded FTAs with Australia, Japan, South Korea, New Zealand, Chile, and the United States. Other large ASEAN countries are also negotiating FTAs with Japan and the United States.

The US trade and investment relations with the ASEAN Big Five countries have been expanding significantly in recent years. US imports from the Big Five countries totaled $89.9 billion in 2005, and US exports to those countries amounted to $48.3 billion during the same year. The US DI position in the ASEAN Big Five amounted to $79.7 billion at the end of 2004, 70 percent of which was in Singapore.

Many ASEAN countries are improving their investment climate to attract foreign investors. While generous tax and nontax investment incentives are provided in Singapore, Thailand, Malaysia, Indonesia, and the Philippines, the nature and extent of incentives given by those five countries vary significantly.

All the ASEAN Big Five countries are changing their M&A and related regulations. As those countries expand their economy and trade, foreign investors should be able to find many investment opportunities. M&A activity in the Big Five ASEAN countries is expected to grow significantly in the next few years. Details of the M&A activity in Southeast Asia will be reported in the next chapter.

7 Mergers and acquisitions in Southeast Asia

Southeast Asia is one of the fastest growing regions in the world. The growth rates among some Southeast Asian countries in the 1970s and 1980s were unprecedented among developing countries. The high level of economic growth accompanied by substantial reforms and policies made Southeast Asia an attractive investment region. M&A in Southeast Asia continued to grow in popularity as a means of corporate investment expansion in the early 1990s. But in July 1997, some Southeast Asian countries were confronted with a financial crisis that started with the collapse of the Thai baht. Later, as described in Chapter 7, the Malaysian ringgit and the Indonesian rupiah also lost much of their values against the US dollar and Japanese yen. Other countries including Singapore and the Philippines also suffered from the same financial crisis in 1997. It took several years for these countries to recover from the financial crisis and the severe recession that followed.

In this chapter we will discuss M&A activities in Southeast Asia from 1990 to 2004. Because most of the M&A activities occurred in the original five member countries of the ASEAN: Indonesia, Malaysia, Singapore, Philippines, and Thailand, our discussion in the chapter will focus on these five countries. We will cover the following aspects of M&A activities:

- recent trends of M&A activities;
- M&A transactions by the nationality of target firms;
- home countries of the acquiring firms and the twenty largest M&A firms in each of the Big Five ASEAN member countries;
- comparison of M&A practices of those Big Five countries and their acquisition methods.

Recent trends in M&A in Southeast Asia

In the last 15 years, M&A activity in the ASEAN countries has increased significantly. Table 7.1 shows the number of M&A deals announced in the ASEAN countries from 1990 to 2004. The total number of M&A deals expanded from 152 in 1990 to 870 in 1996. The number of deals declined in 1997 and 1998 due to the financial crisis in Southeast Asia. The increase that began in the 1990s

Table 7.1 Announced M&A deals in the ASEAN countries,[a] 1990–2004

Year	The ASEAN total	Indonesia	Malaysia	Singapore	Philippines	Thailand	Other five ASEAN countries[b]
1990	152	11	54	75	4	7	1
1991	301	22	174	80	9	15	1
1992	193	13	82	66	10	21	1
1993	418	28	190	145	24	26	5
1994	567	30	273	187	33	41	3
1995	780	48	389	179	69	91	4
1996	870	82	451	192	78	51	16
1997	787	78	390	203	47	65	4
1998	639	37	270	159	47	119	7
1999	818	47	273	282	96	111	9
2000	897	58	327	304	77	119	12
2001	775	69	263	266	52	111	14
2002	780	63	324	242	33	107	11
2003	824	48	376	246	33	104	17
2004	1,020	69	385	328	55	171	12
Total	9,821	703	4,221	2,954	667	1,159	117
Averages							
1990–4	326	21	155	111	16	22	2
1995–9	778	58	355	203	67	87	8
2000–4	859	61	335	277	50	122	13

Source: Thomson Financial.

Notes
a Only transactions of US$1 million or higher are included.
b Includes Myanmar, Vietnam, Laos, Brunei, and Cambodia.

reached its peak of 897 in 2000 before dropping to 775 in 2001. Then the number increased gradually and surpassed 1,000 for the first time in 2004. M&A deals in Malaysia have increased from 54 in 1990 to 385 in 2004. During the same period, Singapore's M&A number increased from 75 deals in 1990 to 328 deals in 2004. It is interesting to note that the most significant increase occurred in only five countries: Indonesia, Malaysia, Singapore, Philippines, and Thailand. Altogether, the ASEAN countries had 9,821 deals during the last 15 years with the Big Five countries accounting for 99 percent, or 9,704, of the deals.

Table 7.2 presents the changes in the announced M&A values in the ASEAN countries for the same period. The total value of M&A as a whole reached a record level of $46.5 billion in 1997 as compared to $15.3 billion in 1990. The M&A value dropped by 31 percent to $32.2 billion in 1998 due to the financial crisis in the region. From 2000 to 2004, M&A total transaction value averaged $44.3 billion per year. This upward trend in total M&A value is expected to continue for the next few years as a result of the process of industrial and corporate restructuring set in motion by the financial crisis years of 1997–9. Malaysia's M&A value increased steadily from $3.7 billion in 1990 to a peak of $25.4 billion in 1996. In the first two years of the financial crisis, the M&A value

Table 7.2 Announced M&A transaction value in the ASEAN countries,[a] 1990–2004 (amounts in US$ million)

Year	ASEAN total value	Indonesia	Malaysia	Singapore	Philippines	Thailand	Other five ASEAN countries[b]
1990	15,299	2,955	3,684	8,032	125	373	130
1991	11,641	1,038	7,708	2,335	289	261	10
1992	8,977	1,963	2,495	1,738	1,305	1,470	6
1993	26,955	745	19,388	4,350	1,523	723	226
1994	24,607	2,702	14,765	4,551	1,329	1,207	53
1995	32,489	4,017	15,607	6,552	3,276	2,997	40
1996	41,121	4,949	25,439	5,477	3,188	1,665	403
1997	46,517	7,393	20,341	11,131	4,527	2,776	349
1998	32,244	2,893	12,539	6,845	3,510	6,439	18
1999	59,363	6,051	15,330	22,723	8,646	6,505	108
2000	48,904	3,573	16,634	20,869	2,570	5,167	91
2001	68,692	6,910	10,815	42,699	4,099	3,624	545
2002	26,383	6,374	8,664	7,179	1,843	1,613	710
2003	36,032	4,691	15,503	10,292	1,936	2,390	220
2004	41,692	3,039	8,018	22,294	3,307	4,910	124
Total	520,916	59,293	197,930	177,067	41,473	42,120	3,033
Averages							
1990–4	17,495	1,881	9,608	4,201	914	807	85
1995–9	42,346	5,061	17,815	10,546	4,629	4,076	184
2000–4	44,340	4,917	11,927	20,667	2,751	3,541	338

Source: Thomson Financial.

Notes
a Only transactions of US$1 million or higher are included.
b Includes Myanmar, Vietnam, Laos, Brunei, and Cambodia.

dropped by 20 percent in 1997 followed by a 38 percent decline in value to $12.5 billion in 1998 before recovering a little in 1999.

M&A value in Singapore did not change much in the first half of the 1990s. In 1997, it increased suddenly to $11.1 billion, and then dropped by 39 percent to $6.8 billion in 1998. M&A transaction value increased by 232 percent in 1999 and then peaked at $42.7 billion in 2001 because of three mega deals in that year. These include the $5.7 billion acquisition of Dao Heng Bank Group (Guoco) by Singapore DBS Group Holding Ltd and the $5.5 billion purchase of Overseas Union Bank Ltd by UOB. In 2004, the M&A value in Singapore was $22.3 billion. Indonesia's M&A value increased rapidly from $745 million in 1993 to a peak of $7.4 billion in 1997. The M&A value dropped by 61 percent to $2.9 billion in 1998 due to the financial crisis and economic slowdown. From 2000 to 2004, M&A in Indonesia averaged $4.9 billion per year. The Philippines' M&A value increased steadily in the first half of the 1990s to a peak of $4.5 billion in 1997. Then the value dropped by 22 percent to $3.5 billion in 1998 before achieving its peak of $8.6 billion in 1999. In 2004, the M&A value in the Philippines was only $3.3 billion. Thailand is the only country to experience a growth in M&A value during the crisis years of 1997–9. The M&A value increased by 134 percent from $2.7 billion in 1997 to a peak of $6.5 billion in 1999. From 2002 to 2004, M&A in Thailand averaged about $3.5 billion.

From Table 7.2, we can observe that the share of M&A value in the five major countries increased steadily but at a varying rate from 1990 to 1997. In 1998 all the major countries except Thailand experienced a large drop in M&A value that reflected the different degrees to which each country was affected by the financial crisis years of 1997–9. The drop in M&A value ranged from a low of 22 percent in the Philippines to a high of 61 percent in Indonesia because of the different level of economic development, the extent of privatization and foreign direct investment regulations, and/or the type of macro- and micro-economic policies implemented in each country.

As an exception in 1997, the Thai government started to promote M&A through establishing a program to match potential foreign investors with finan-cially strapped Thai firms. The matching program helped Thailand to experience an increase in its M&A values in 1998 and 1999.

M&A transactions by the nationality of the target firms

Table 7.3 shows the M&A transaction value by nationality (or region) of the target firms from 1990 to 2004. During that period, there were 9,821 M&A transactions with a total value of $520.9 billion. The average value per deal was $53.0 million. The M&A value subtotal for target firms from the ASEAN countries amounted to $425.9 billion (or 82 percent) while the subtotal for target firms from non-ASEAN countries was $95.0 billion (or 18 percent). The average value per deal with target firms from the ASEAN countries was about $50.2 million, substan-tially lower than the average value of $71.1 million for M&A deals with target firms from non-ASEAN countries.

Table 7.3 also shows that Indonesia had the highest average M&A value per deal of $85.5 million, as compared to $61.3 million for the Philippines, $54.6 million for Laos, and $54.1 million for Singapore. It is interesting to note that Malaysia accounted for over 39 percent of the total deals and 33 percent of the M&A transaction value of target firms in ASEAN countries in 1990–2004. Singapore and Thailand accounted for over 21 percent and 11 percent of the total deals and over 22 percent and 7 percent of the transaction value respectively during the same period. Indonesia and the Philippines also had substantial volumes of M&A activity.

Home countries of the acquiring firms

We can observe from Table 7.4 that acquiring firms from the ASEAN countries accounted for 85 percent of the deals and 83 percent of the M&A transaction value during the 1990–2004 period. Acquiring firms from non-ASEAN countries accounted for 15 percent of the deals and 17 percent of the M&A transaction value. Acquiring firms from Malaysia accounted for 41 percent of the M&A deals

Table 7.3 M&A transaction value in ASEAN by the nationality or region of the target firms,[a] 1990–2004

Nationality/region	Transaction value (US$ million)	% of total	No. of deals	% of total	Average value per deal (US$ million)
Brunei	344	0.1	11	0.1	31.3
Cambodia	51	0.0	9	0.1	5.7
Indonesia	56,200	10.8	657	6.7	85.5
Laos	546	0.1	10	0.1	54.6
Malaysia	172,621	33.1	3,856	39.3	44.8
Myanmar (Burma)	—	0.0	—	0.0	0.0
Philippines	39,277	7.5	641	6.5	61.3
Singapore	115,605	22.2	2,135	21.7	54.1
Thailand	40,473	7.8	1,102	11.2	36.7
Vietnam	834	0.2	65	0.7	0.0
Subtotal for the ASEAN countries	425,951	82	8,486	86	50.2
Subtotal for target firms from non-ASEAN countries acquired by companies in the ASEAN region	94,965	18	1,335	14	71.1
Total	520,916	100	9,821	100	53.0

Source: Thomson Financial.

Note
a Only transactions of US$1 million or higher are included.

and 36 percent of the transaction value. Acquiring firms from Singapore were involved in 2,454 deals (or 25 percent) and $151.8 billion (or 29 percent) of the transaction value. A comparison between Tables 7.3 and 7.4 shows that slightly more Malaysian and Singapore firms were involved in M&A transactions as the acquiring firms than as the target firms. On the other hand, significantly more companies from Indonesia, the Philippines, and Thailand were involved as the target firms than as the acquiring companies.

The 20 largest M&A in Southeast Asia

The 20 largest mergers and acquisitions announced in the ASEAN countries during the 1990–2004 period are shown in Table 7.5. The largest deal was the $8.5 billion acquisition of Cable & Wireless Optus Ltd (C&W) (Australian) by SingTel (Singapore) in 2001. The second largest deal ($6.3 billion) was the purchase of ASKO Deutsche Kaufhaus (Germany) by Metro Curtainwall & Cladding (Malaysia) in 1993. The $5.7 billion purchase of Dao Heng Bank Group (Guoco) of Hong Kong by DBS Group Holdings Ltd from Singapore was the third largest deal in the ASEAN countries for the 14 year period. The acquirers in the fourth and fifth largest deals were companies from Singapore. We can observe that in

Table 7.4 M&A transaction value in ASEAN by the nationality of the acquiring firms,[a] 1990–2004

Nationality/region	Transaction value (US$ million)	% of total	No. of deals	% of total
Brunei	758	0	16	0
Cambodia	30	0	7	0
Indonesia	39,926	8	463	5
Laos	44	0	4	0
Malaysia	188,761	36	3,984	41
Myanmar (Burma)	450	0	7	0
Philippines	26,338	5	479	5
Singapore	151,792	29	2,454	25
Thailand	24,832	5	857	9
Vietnam	295	0	34	0
Subtotal for the ASEAN countries	433,226	83	8,305	85
Subtotal for acquiring firms from non-ASEAN countries	87,690	17	1,516	15
Total	520,916	100	9,821	100

Source: Thomson Financial.

Note
a Only transactions of US$1 million or higher are included.

aggregate, 11 of the 20 acquiring firms are from Singapore. The values of these 11 M&A transactions varied from $1.5 billion to $8.5 billion. Another six acquirers were companies in Malaysia (e.g. Malaysia Int'l Shipping Corporation, Petronas, Malakoff Bhd, Hock Hua Bank Bhd. & Malex Industries Bhd.). Coca-Cola Amatil Ltd. (Australia) was involved in a $2.7 billion acquisition of Coca-Cola Bottlers Philippines (Philippines). It is interesting that only one US firm (Solectron Corporation) was involved as an acquirer of a firm from Singapore (Natsteel Electronics Pte. Ltd.). An unnamed investor group from the Philippines acquired Coca-Cola Bottlers Philippines (Philippines) in 2001 in a $1.3 billion deal. Together, these largest 20 deals had a total M&A value of $60.6 billion, which accounted for 12 percent of the total M&A value of the ASEAN countries from 1990 to 2004. A review of the target list in Table 7.5 indicates that five of the twenty targets were companies from Singapore. Another six targets comprised three companies from Malaysia and three from the United States. The remaining nine included companies from Australia, Hong Kong, the Philippines, Germany, New Zealand, and Egypt.

Comparison among the Big Five countries in ASEAN

Understanding the differences in the economies of Malaysia, Singapore, Indonesia, Thailand, and the Philippines will allow us to compare and contrast the

Table 7.5 Twenty largest M&A in the ASEAN countries, 1990–2004

Announced year	Effective year	Target and nationality	Acquirer and nationality	Amount (US$ million)
3/26/2001	9/17/2001	Cable & Wireless Optus Ltd (C&W) (Australia)	SingTel (Singapore)	8,491
12/14/1993	7/19/1996	ASKO Deutsche Kaufhaus, Deutsch (Germany)	Metro Curtainwall & Cladding (Malaysia)	6,325
4/11/2001	9/3/2001	Dao Heng Bank Group (Guoco) (Hong Kong)	DBS Group Holdings Ltd (Singapore)	5,680
6/29/2001	9/24/2001	Overseas Union Bank Ltd (Singapore)	UOB (Singapore)	5,464
6/12/2001	9/24/2001	Keppel Capital Holdings Ltd (Singapore)	Oversea-Chinese Banking Corp. (Singapore)	3,754
4/2/1997	7/1/1997	Coca-Cola Bottlers Philippines (Philippines)	Coca-Cola Amatil Ltd (Australia)	2,739
4/26/2004	7/30/2004	TXU Australia Ltd (Australia)	Singapore Power Pte. Ltd (Singapore)	3,720
7/13/1990	10/29/1993	Singapore Telecom (Singapore)	Group of Investors (Singapore)	2,730
11/22/1999	4/3/2000	DLL Group (United States)	Flextronics International Ltd (Singapore)	2,591
4/30/1998	11/18/1998	Petronas Tankers Sdn Bhd (Malaysia)	Malaysia Int'l Shipping Corp. (Malaysia)	2,464
10/31/2000	1/8/2001	Natsteel Electronics Pte. Ltd (Singapore)	Solectron Corp. (United States)	2,406
4/11/2001	1/10/2003	DBS Diamond Holdings Ltd (Hong Kong)	DBS Bank (Singapore)	1,965
11/1/2004	12/2/2004	US Premium Office Properties (United States)	Investor Group (Singapore)	1,852
4/24/2003	6/27/2003	Egyptian LNG (Egypt)	Petronas (Malaysia)	1,766
2/23/1999	2/28/2001	Tenaga National Bhd-Power (Malaysia)	Malakoff Bhd (Malaysia)	1,650
7/12/2000	11/24/2000	DBS Land Ltd (Singapore)	Pidemco Land Ltd (Singapore)	1,503
2/10/2004	8/5/2004	Chip PAC Inc. (United States)	St. Assembly Test Services Ltd (Singapore)	1,459
6/26/2000	11/9/2000	Public Bank Commercial Banking (Malaysia)	Hock Hua Bank Bhd (Malaysia)	1,423
8/2/1996	8/9/1996	Brierley Investments Ltd (New Zealand)	Malex Industries Bhd (Malaysia)	1,394
2/6/2001	5/30/2001	Coca-Cola Bottlers Philippines (Philippines)	Investor Group (Philippines)	1,269

Source: Thomson Financial.

varied M&A transactions completed in these five important ASEAN countries. In the following we will study the target and acquiring firms of these five countries.

Target and acquiring firms of M&A in Malaysia

Table 7.6 shows the M&A transaction value in Malaysia by the nationality or region of the target firms from 1990 to 2004. In 3,651, or over 86 percent of all M&A deals, the target firms were companies registered in Malaysia. These 3,651 deals had a total M&A value of $160.3 billion, or 81 percent of all transaction value. Singapore firms were targets in 116 deals with M&A value of $7.5 billion and an average value per deal of $64.5 million. The M&A value subtotal for target firms from the ASEAN countries amounted to $172.6 billion (or 90 percent) while the subtotal for target firms from non-ASEAN countries was $24.7 billion (or 10 percent). The average value per deal with target firms from the ASEAN countries was about $45.6 million, about 20 percent less than the average value of $56.7 million for M&A deals with target firms from non-ASEAN countries.

The statistics for the nationality or region of the acquiring firms (1990–2004) are shown in Table 7.7. We can observe that acquiring firms from Malaysia

Table 7.6 M&A transaction value in Malaysia by the nationality or region of the target firms,[a] 1990–2004

Nationality/region	Transaction value (US$ million)	% of total	No. of deals	% of total	Average value per deal (US$ million)
Brunei	5	0.0	1	0.0	5.0
Cambodia	8	0.0	0	0.0	0.0
Indonesia	2,828	1.4	5	0.1	565.6
Laos	—	0.0	0	0.0	0.0
Malaysia	160,295	81.2	3,651	86.5	43.9
Myanmar (Burma)	407	0.2	0	0.0	0.0
Philippines	1,203	0.6	7	0.2	171.9
Singapore	7,483	3.8	116	2.7	64.5
Thailand	379	0.2	6	0.1	63.2
Vietnam	13	0.0	0	0.0	0.0
Subtotal for the ASEAN countries	172,621	87	3,786	90	45.6
Subtotal for target firms from non-ASEAN countries acquired by companies in the ASEAN region	24,679	13	435	10	56.7
Total	197,300	100	4,221	100	46.7

Source: Thomson Financial.

Note

a Only transactions of US$1 million or higher are included.

accounted for 91 percent of the deals (or 3,849 transactions) and 93 percent of the M&A transaction value (or $184.0 billion) during the 1990–2004 period. Acquiring firms from Singapore were involved in 116 deals worth $4.2 billion. Acquiring firms from non-ASEAN countries accounted for 6 percent of the total deals but 5 percent of the M&A transaction value. A comparison between Table 7.6 and Table 7.7 shows that more Malaysian firms were involved in M&A transactions as the acquiring firms than as the target firms.

The 20 largest M&A in Malaysia during the 1990–2004 period are shown in Table 7.8. The largest deal ($6.3 billion) was the purchase of ASKO Deutsche Kaufhaus (a German firm) by Metro Curtainwall & Cladding (Malaysia) effective in 1996. The second largest deal was the $2.5 billion purchase of Petronas Tankers Sdn Bhd (Malaysia) by Malaysia Int'l Shipping Corporation (Malaysia) in 1998. The $1.8 billion purchase of Egyptian LNG (an Egyptian firm) by Petronas from Malaysia was the third largest deal in Malaysia for the time period. Table 7.8 lists the other seventeen largest M&A transactions for the target and acquiring firms. The values of these seventeen M&A transactions varied from $692 million to $1.7 billion. It is interesting to note that all the 20 largest acquiring firms and 16 of the target companies were Malaysian. Total M&A values of the top 20 deals in Malaysia from 1990–2004 was about $27.2 billion accounting for 14 percent of all M&A values during the period.

Table 7.7 M&A transaction value in Malaysia by the nationality or region of the acquiring firms,[a] 1990–2004

Nationality/region	Transaction value (US$ million)	% of total	No. of deals	% of total	Average value per deal (US$ million)
Brunei	119	0.1	1	0.0	119.0
Cambodia	—	0.0	0	0.0	0.0
Indonesia	95	0.0	5	0.1	19.0
Laos	—	0.0	0	0.0	0.0
Malaysia	183,994	93.0	3,849	91.2	47.8
Myanmar (Burma)	—	0.0	0	0.0	0.0
Philippines	203	0.1	7	0.2	29.0
Singapore	4,166	2.1	116	2.7	35.9
Thailand	184	0.1	6	0.1	30.7
Vietnam	—	0.0	0	0.0	0.0
Subtotal for the ASEAN countries	188,761	95	3,984	94	47.4
Subtotal for acquiring firms from non-ASEAN countries	9,169	5	237	6	38.7
Total	197,930	100	4,221	100	46.9

Source: Thomson Financial.

Note

a Only transactions of US$1 million or higher are included.

Table 7.8 Twenty largest M&A in Malaysia, 1990–2004

Date announced	Date effective	Target name/nation	Acquirer name/nation	Value of transaction (US$ million)
12/14/1993	7/19/1996	ASKO Deutsche Kaufhaus, Deutsch (Germany)	Metro Curtainwall & Cladding (Malaysia)	6,325
4/30/1998	11/18/1998	Petronas Tankers Sdn Bhd (Malaysia)	Malaysia Int'l Shipping Corp. (Malaysia)	2,464
4/24/2003	6/27/2003	Egyptian LNG (Egypt)	Petronas (Malaysia)	1,766
2/23/1999	2/28/2001	Tenaga Nasional Bhd-Power (Malaysia)	Malakoff Bhd (Malaysia)	1,650
6/26/2000	11/9/2000	Public Bank-Commercial Banking (Malaysia)	Hock Hua Bank Bhd (Malaysia)	1,423
8/2/1996	8/9/1996	Brierly Investments Ltd (New Zealand)	Malex Industries Bhd (Malaysia)	1,394
2/4/1991	4/30/1991	United Engineering, Faber (Malaysia)	Renong Bhd (Malaysia)	1,114
4/29/2003	7/22/2003	American Eagle Tankers Inc. (Singapore)	Malaysia Int'l Shipping Corp. (Malaysia)	1,100
5/19/1995	4/3/1996	Malaysia National Insurance (Malaysia)	Timah Langat Bhd (Malaysia)	1,034
9/20/1994	4/2/1996	Projek Lebuhraya Utara-Selatan (Malaysia)	UEM Bhd (Malaysia)	1,017
4/3/2003	6/27/2003	Celcom (Malaysia)	Telekom Cellular Sdn Bhd (Malaysia)	970
8/7/1996	6/28/1997	Southern Steel Bhd (Malaysia)	Camerlin Group Bhd (Malaysia)	883
10/25/1996	7/1/1997	Kwong Yik Bank Bhd (Malaysia)	Rashid Hussain Bhd (Malaysia)	854
5/27/1996	10/30/2001	MPI Property Sdn Bhd (Malaysia)	Hong Leong Industries Bhd (Malaysia)	803
4/16/1993	6/30/1994	HICOM (Malaysia)	New Serendah Rubber Co Bhd (Malaysia)	791
7/3/1998	7/3/1998	Guilin Defa Transportation (Malaysia)	Guilin Guifa United Engineer (Malaysia)	752
2/25/1997	6/30/2000	YTL Power Generation Sdn Bhd (Malaysia)	YTL Power International Bhd (Malaysia)	745
11/12/1993	8/10/1994	Consolidated Plantations Bhd (Malaysia)	Sime Darby Bhd (Malaysia)	740
2/28/2000	6/20/2000	Hicom Holdings Bhd (Malaysia)	Diversified Resources Bhd (Malaysia)	714
6/10/1994	10/19/1994	Malaysian Airline System Bhd (Malaysia)	RZ Equities Sdn Bhd (Malaysia)	692

Source: Thomson Financial.

Target and acquiring firms of M&A in Singapore

The M&A transaction values in Singapore (1990–2004) by the nationality or region of the target firms are shown in Table 7.9 while the acquiring firms are shown in Table 7.10. Both tables indicate there were 2,954 deals in Singapore from 1990 to 2004, considerably less than the 4,221 deals recorded in Malaysia (Tables 7.6 and 7.7) during the same period. Sixty-two percent (or 1,819) of the 2,954 total deals involved target companies from Singapore with total M&A value of $101.0 billion. Malaysian companies were targets in 116 deals worth about $4.2 billion. There were 71 deals with $6.5 billion in value targeted in Indonesia.

Table 7.10 indicates that Singaporean acquirers were involved in 79 percent of the 2,954 deals or 81 percent of the total M&A value that were worth $143.3 billion. Malaysian firms were acquirers in 100 deals with a total value of $7.5 billion. Indonesian companies were involved as acquirers in 16 deals that were worth $625 million. The average value per deal varies substantially by the nationality of the acquiring firms.

The 20 largest M&A in Singapore for the 1990–2004 period are shown in Table 7.11. We can observe that only three of the largest 20 acquirers were foreign companies. These were Solectron Corporation (United States) acquiring

Table 7.9 M&A transaction value in Singapore by the nationality or region of the target firms,[a] 1990–2004

Nationality/region	Transaction value (US$ million)	% of total	No. of deals	% of total	Average value per deal (US$ million)
Brunei	8	0.0	3	0.0	2.7
Cambodia	2	0.0	1	0.0	2.0
Indonesia	6,490	3.7	71	2.5	91.4
Laos	—	0.0	0	0.0	0.0
Malaysia	4,166	2.1	116	3.9	35.9
Myanmar (Burma)	43	0.0	5	0.0	8.6
Philippines	1,586	0.8	46	1.5	34.5
Singapore	100,582	57.0	1,819	62.0	55.3
Thailand	2,627	1.3	68	2.1	38.6
Vietnam	101	0.1	6	0.0	16.8
Subtotal for the ASEAN countries	115,605	65	2,135	72	54.1
Subtotal for target firms from non-ASEAN countries acquired by companies in the ASEAN	61,462	35	819	28	75.0
Total	177,067	100	2,954	100	59.9

Source: Thomson Financial.

Note
a Only transactions of US$1 million or higher are included.

Table 7.10 M&A transaction value in Singapore by the nationality or region of the acquiring firms,[a] 1990–2004

Nationality/region	Transaction value (US$ million)	% of total	No. of deals	% of total	Average value per deal (US$ million)
Brunei	8	0.0	8	0.0	8.0
Cambodia	—	0.0	0	0.0	0.0
Indonesia	625	0.8	16	0.4	39.1
Laos	—	0.0	0	0	0.0
Malaysia	7,483	4.0	100	3.5	74.8
Myanmar (Burma)	—	0.0	0	0.0	0.0
Philippines	198	0.1	2	0.0	99.0
Singapore	143,339	81.0	2330	79.0	61.5
Thailand	139	0.1	5	0.1	27.8
Vietnam	—	0.0	0	0.0	0.0
Subtotal for the ASEAN Countries	151,792	86	2,454	83	61.9
Subtotal for acquired firms from non-ASEAN countries	25,275	14	500	17	50.6
Total	177,067	100	2,954	100	59.9

Source: Thomson Financial.

Note
a Only transactions of US$1 million or higher are included.

NatSteel Electronics Pte Ltd (Singapore), Malaysia International Shipping Corporation (Malaysia) buying American Eagle Tankers Inc (Singapore), and Celetica Inc. (Canada) acquiring Omni Industries Ltd (Singapore).

The largest deal was a $8.5 billion acquisition of Cable & Wireless Optus Ltd (C&W) (Australia) by SingTel of Singapore. The second largest deal was a $5.7 billion acquisition of Dao Heng Bank Group (Guoco) (Hong Kong) by DBS Group Holdings Ltd of Singapore. The third largest deal was a $5.5 billion purchase of Overseas Union Bank Ltd (Singapore) by UOB of Singapore. A review of the target list in Table 7.11 indicates that 11 of the 20 targets were companies from Singapore. Total M&A values of the top 20 deals in Singapore from 1990 to 2004 was about $49.7 billion, accounting for 28 percent of all M&A values during the period.

Target and acquiring firms of M&A in Indonesia

Table 7.12 shows the M&A transaction values in Indonesia by the nationality or region of the target firms from 1990 to 2004. In 632 or 90 percent of all M&A deals, the target firms were firms registered in Indonesia. These 632 deals had a total M&A value of $55.4 billion or 93 percent of all transaction values. Singapore firms were targets in 16 deals with M&A value of $625 million and an average value per deal of over $39.1 million. The M&A value subtotal for target firms

Table 7.11 Twenty largest M&A in Singapore, 1990–2004

Date announced	Date effective	Target name/nation	Acquirer name/nation	Value of transaction (US$ million)
3/26/2001	9/17/2001	Cable & Wireless Optus Ltd (C&W) (Australia)	Sing Tel (Singapore)	8,491
4/11/2001	9/03/2001	Dao Heng Bank Group (Guoco) (Hong Kong)	DBS Group Holdings Ltd (Singapore)	5,680
6/29/2001	9/24/2001	Overseas Union Bank Ltd (Singapore)	UOB (Singapore)	5,464
6/12/2001	9/24/2001	Keppel Capital Holdings Ltd (Singapore)	Oversea-Chinese Banking Corp (Singapore)	3,754
4/26/2004	7/30/2004	TXU Australia Ltd (Australia)	Singapore Power Pte. Ltd (Singapore)	3,720
7/13/1990	10/29/1993	Singapore Telecom (Singapore)	Investors Group (Singapore)	2,730
11/22/1999	4/03/2000	DII Group (United States)	Flextronics International Ltd (Singapore)	2,591
10/31/2000	1/08/2001	NatSteel Electronics Pte. Ltd (Singapore)	Solectron Corp. (United States)	2,406
4/11/2001	1/10/2003	DBS Diamond Holdings Ltd (Hong Kong)	DBS Bank (Singapore)	1,965
11/01/2004	12/02/2004	US Premium Office Properties (United States)	Investor Group (Singapore)	1,852
7/12/2000	11/24/2000	DBS Land Ltd (Singapore)	Pidemco Land Ltd (Singapore)	1,503
2/10/2004	8/05/2004	ChipPAC Inc. (United States)	ST Assembly Test Services Ltd (Singapore)	1,459
6/20/2000	6/30/2000	GPU PowerNet Pty Ltd (Australia)	Singapore Power Pte. Ltd (Singapore)	1,264
4/29/2003	7/22/2003	American Eagle Tankers Inc. (Singapore)	Malaysia Intl Shipping Corp. (Malaysia)	1,100
2/24/2004	6/30/2004	Great Eastern Hldgs Ltd (Singapore)	Oversea-Chinese Banking Corp. (Singapore)	1,086
4/09/1990	8/31/1990	Singapore Land Ltd (Singapore)	United Industrial Corp. Ltd (Singapore)	978
7/24/1998	8/06/1998	Post Office Savings Bank (Singapore)	DBS Bank (Singapore)	933
6/15/2001	10/10/2001	Omni Industries Ltd (Singapore)	Celetica Inc (Canada)	926
8/03/2004	9/29/2004	Neptune Orient Lines Ltd (Singapore)	Lentor Investments Pte. Ltd (Singapore)	914
12/20/1999	3/30/2000	Virgin Atlantic Airways Ltd (United Kingdom)	Singapore Airlines Ltd (Singapore)	885

Source: Thomson Financial.

Table 7.12 M&A transaction value in Indonesia by the nationality or region of the target firms,[a] 1990–2004

Nationality/region	Transaction value (US$ million)	% of total	No. of deals	% of total	Average value per deal (US$ million)
Brunei	—	0.0	0	0.0	0.0
Cambodia	—	0.0	0	0.0	0.0
Indonesia	55,427	93.0	632	90.0	87.7
Laos	—	0.0	0	0.0	0.0
Malaysia	95	0.6	5	0.2	19.0
Myanmar (Burma)	—	0.0	0	0.0	0.0
Philippines	7	0.0	1	0.0	7.0
Singapore	625	1.3	16	2.7	39.1
Thailand	46	0.1	3	0.1	15.3
Vietnam	—	0.0	0	0.0	0.0
Subtotal for the ASEAN countries	56,200	95	657	93	85.5
Subtotal for target firms from non-ASEAN countries acquired by companies in the ASEAN	3,093	5	46	7	67.2
Total	59,293	100	703	100	84.3

Source: Thomson Financial.

Note
a Only transactions of US$1 million or higher are included.

from the ASEAN countries amounted to $56.2 billion (or 95 percent) while the subtotal for target firms from the non-ASEAN countries was $3.1 billion (or 5 percent). The average value per deal with target firms from ASEAN countries was about $85.5 million, a great deal higher than the average value of $67.2 million for M&A deals with target firms from non-ASEAN countries.

The statistics for the nationality of the acquiring firms are shown in Table 7.13. Acquiring companies from Indonesia accounted for 50 percent of the M&A transaction value (or $29.6 billion) and 48.5 percent of the deals (or 340 transactions) during the 1990–2004 period. Acquiring firms from Singapore were involved in 71 deals with transaction value worth $6.5 billion and an average value per deal of over $91.4 million. Acquiring firms from non-ASEAN countries accounted for 34 percent of the deals and 33 percent of the M&A transaction value. A comparison between the two tables 7.12 and 7.13 reveals that more Indonesian firms were serving as target firms (632 deals), nearly twice as often as acquirers (340 deals).

The 20 largest deals in Indonesia during the period of 1990–2004 are listed in Table 7.14. The largest deal was the acquisition of East Kalimantan Concession (Indonesia) by Osaka Gas Co. Ltd in Japan. This deal was worth $1.2 billion with an effective date of November 1990.

Table 7.13 M&A transaction value in Indonesia by the nationality or region of the acquiring firms,[a] 1990–2004

Nationality/region	Transaction value (US$ million)	% of total	No. of deals	% of total	Average value per deal (US$ million)
Brunei	130	0.1	1	0.0	130.0
Cambodia	—	0.0	0	0.0	0.0
Indonesia	29,592	50.0	340	48.5	87.0
Laos	—	0.0	0	0.0	0.0
Malaysia	2,828	5.0	43	6.3	65.8
Myanmar (Burma)	—	0.0	0	0.0	0.0
Philippines	—	0.0	0	0.0	0.0
Singapore	6,490	11.0	71	10.7	91.4
Thailand	886	0.9	8	0.5	110.8
Vietnam	—	0.0	0	0.0	0.0
Subtotal for the ASEAN countries	39,926	67.0	463	66.0	86.2
Subtotal for acquiring firms from non-ASEAN countries	19,367	33.0	240	34.0	80.7
Total	59,293	100	703	100	84.3

Source: Thomson Financial.

Note
a   Only transactions of US$1 million or higher are included.

A review of the top 20 deals shows that 12 of them are related to the telecommunication industry, five related to utilities, and three related to food. Total M&A values of the top 20 deals in Indonesia from 1990 to 2004 were about $14.5 billion accounting for 24 percent of all the M&A values during that period.

Target and acquiring firms of M&A in Thailand

Mergers and acquisitions transaction value in Thailand by the nationality or region of the target firms and acquiring firms are shown in Tables 7.15 and 7.16, respectively. Both tables indicate that there were 1,159 deals in Thailand from 1990 to 2004, considerably less than the number of deals recorded in both Malaysia (4,221) and Singapore (2,954) during the same period. Table 7.15 shows that 91 percent (or 1060) of the 1,159 deals involved target firms from Thailand with total M&A value of $38.9 billion. Firms from Indonesia were targets in only eight deals with $886 million in value and the average value per deal of $110.8 million.

Table 7.16 indicates that Thailand acquirers were involved in 66 percent of the 1,159 total deals or 51 percent of the total M&A value that was worth $21.6 billion. Singapore firms were acquirers in 68 deals (or 5.9 percent) with a total value of $2.6 billion. Malaysian companies were involved as acquirers in 20 deals worth

Table 7.14 Twenty largest M&A in Indonesia, 1990–2004

Date announced	Date effective	Target name/nation	Acquirer name/nation	Value of transaction (US$ million)
11/19/1990	11/19/1990	East Kalimantan Concession (Indonesia)	Osaka Gas Co. Ltd (Japan)	1,950
12/23/1999	7/6/2000	Gallo Oil Ltd (United States)	BT Bumi Modern (Indonesia)	1,311
2/18/1994	10/18/1994	Indonesian Satellite Corp. PT (Indonesia)	Investors Group (Unknown)	1,000
2/15/2001	5/17/2001	Telkomsel (Indonesia)	Telkom (Indonesia)	945
2/8/1995	7/14/1995	Bogasari Flour Mills PT (Indonesia)	Indofood Sukses Makmur PT (Indonesia)	835
11/5/2001	12/18/2001	Semen Cibinong PT (Indonesia)	Holcim Ltd (Switzerland)	650
2/20/1997	4/7/1997	Salim Ivomnas Pratama, Intiboga (Indonesia)	Indofood Sukses Makmur PT (Indonesia)	646
12/15/2002	12/20/2002	Indosat (Indonesia)	Singapore Technologies Telemed (Singapore)	635
10/31/2001	12/10/2001	Telkomsel (Indonesia)	SingTel (Singapore)	627
12/11/1996	12/11/1996	Telkom (Indonesia)	Investors Group (Indonesia)	602
1/18/2002	4/19/2002	Repsol YPF SA (Indonesia)	CNOOC Ltd (China)	592
3/9/1995	4/3/1995	Satelit Palapa Indonesia PT (Indonesia)	DeTeMobil (Germany)	585
6/22/1992	7/28/1992	Bogasari Flour Mills PT (Indonesia)	Indocement Tunggal Prakarsa PT (Indonesia)	581
5/12/1997	5/12/1997	Mangistau Oil & Gas (Kazakhstan)	Central Asia Petroleum (Setdco) (Indonesia)	576
3/14/2002	3/28/2002	BCA PT (Indonesia)	Investor Group (Indonesia)	534
3/24/2000	3/30/2000	Astra International Tbk PT (Indonesia)	Investor Group (Multi-national)	506
7/21/2003	10/10/2003	Kaltim Prima Coal PT (Indonesia)	Bumi Resources Tbk PT (Indonesia)	500
7/11/2001	7/11/2001	Tangguh LNG Project Indonesia (Indonesia)	Mitsubishi Corp. (Japan)	482
4/3/2002	7/31/2003	AriaWest International PT (Indonesia)	Telkom (Indonesia)	465
2/20/2002	8/15/2002	Pramindo Ikat Nusantara PT (Indonesia)	Telkom (Indonesia)	458

Source: Thomson Financial.

Table 7.15 M&A transaction value in Thailand by the nationality or region of the target firms,[a] 1990–2004

Nationality/region	Transaction value (US$ million)	% of total	No. of deals	% of total	Average value per deal (US$ million)
Brunei	—	0.0	0	0.0	0.0
Cambodia	—	0.0	0	0.0	0.0
Indonesia	886	2.0	8	0.8	110.8
Laos	44	0.2	4	0.4	11.0
Malaysia	184	0.5	6	0.6	30.7
Myanmar (Burma)	78	0.3	1	0.0	78.0
Philippines	230	0.6	13	1.2	17.7
Singapore	139	0.4	5	0.5	27.8
Thailand	38,892	92.0	1060	91.0	36.7
Vietnam	20	0.0	5	0.5	4.0
Subtotal for the ASEAN countries	40,473	96	1,102	95	36.7
Subtotal for target firms from non-ASEAN countries acquired by companies in the ASEAN	1,647	4	57	5	28.9
Total	42,120	100	1,159	100	36.3

Source: Thomson Financial.

Note
a Only transactions of US$ 1 million or higher are included.

$379 million. The average value per deal varies substantially by the nationality of the acquiring firms from a high of $52.0 million to a low of $15.3 million.

The 20 largest M&A in Thailand for the 1990–2004 period are shown in Table 7.17. We can observe that all of the 20 target firms in Table 7.17 are Thai companies. Interestingly, 5 of the 20 target companies are in the banking industry and three targets were in telecommunications. Another two targets (Shin Digital Co. and Advanced Information Service) are in the high-tech industry. A review of the acquirer list in Table 7.17 indicates that 4 of the 20 acquirers were Thailand firms. Another six acquirers were companies from Hong Kong and Singapore – three each. Together, these top 20 deals in Thailand had a total M&A value of $9.7 billion, which accounted for 23 percent of all M&A during the 1990–2004 period.

Target and acquiring firms of M&A in the Philippines

Table 7.18 shows the M&A transaction value in the Philippines by the nationality or region of the target firms from 1990 to 2004. In 628 (or over 94 percent) of all M&A deals, the target firms were firms registered in the Philippines.

Table 7.16 M&A transaction value in Thailand by the nationality or region of the acquiring firms,[a] 1990–2004

Nationality/region	Transaction value (US$ million)	% of total	No. of deals	% of total	Average value per deal (US$ million)
Brunei	32	0.1	1	0.0	32.0
Cambodia	0	0.0	—	0.0	0.0
Indonesia	46	0.2	3	0.1	15.3
Laos	0	0.0	—	0.0	0.0
Malaysia	379	1.0	20	1.9	19.0
Myanmar (Burma)	0	0.0	—	0.0	0.0
Philippines	156	0.6	3	0.1	52.0
Singapore	2,627	6.1	68	5.9	38.6
Thailand	21,592	51.0	762	66.0	28.3
Vietnam	0	0.0	—	0.0	0.0
Subtotal for the ASEAN countries	24,832	59.0	857	74.0	29.0
Subtotal for acquired firms from non-ASEAN countries	17,288	41.0	302	26.0	58.2
Total	42,120	100	1,159	100	36.3

Source: Thomson Financial.

Note
a Only transactions of US$1 million in or higher are included.

These 628 deals had a total M&A value of $38.7 billion or 93 percent of all transaction value. Malaysian firms were targets in seven deals with an M&A value of $203 million and an average value per deal of $29.0 million. The M&A value subtotal for target firms from the ASEAN countries amounted to $39.3 billion (or 95 percent) while the subtotal for target firms from the non-ASEAN countries was $2.2 billion (or 5 percent). The average value per deal with target firms from ASEAN countries was about $61.3 million, a great deal less than the average value of $84.5 million for M&A deals with target firms from the non-ASEAN countries.

Table 7.19 shows Philippine acquirers were involved in 58 percent of the 667 total deals, or 56 percent of the total M&A value worth $23.3 billion during the 1990–2004 period. Acquiring firms from Singapore were involved in 46 deals with value worth $1.6 billion with an average value per deal over $34.5 million. Malaysian companies were involved as acquirers in 32 deals worth $1.2 billion. Acquiring firms from non-ASEAN countries accounted for 28 percent of the deals but 36 percent of the M&A transaction value. A comparison between the Tables 7.18 and 7.19 reveals that more Filipino companies were being targeted in an M&A transaction than were being acquirers.

The 20 largest M&A announced in the Philippines during the 1990–2004 period are shown in Table 7.20. We can observe that all of the 20 target firms in Table 7.20 are Filipino companies while only 7 of the 20 largest acquirers were

Table 7.17 Twenty largest M&A in Thailand, 1990–2004

Date announced	Date effective	Target name/nation	Acquirer name/nation	Value of transaction (US$ million)
10/8/2003	11/7/2003	Krung Thai Bank PCL (Tha land)	Investors (Non-US) (Unknown)	748
6/27/1995	6/19/1996	Khanom Electricity Generating (Thailand)	EGCO (Thailand)	690
3/2/1998	1/15/1999	Nakornthai Strip Mill PLC (Thailand)	Investor Group (United States)	650
12/18/1998	12/18/1998	Finl Sector Restructuring-BL (Thailand)	Goldman Sachs (Asia) Ltd (China)	645
5/2/1996	5/2/1996	TelecomAsia Corp. PCL (Thailand)	Orient Telecom &Technology (Hong Kong)	556
5/12/2004	7/27/2004	Bank of Asia PCL (Thailand)	UOB (Singapore)	543
5/15/2000	8/31/2000	Total Access Communication PCL (Thailand)	Telenor AS (Norway)	534
1/28/2004	7/2/2004	DBS Thai Danu Bank PCL (Thailand)	Thai Military Bank PCL (Thailand)	513
3/6/1992	3/31/1992	Bangkok Land PLC (Thailand)	STELUX Holdings Ltd (Hong Kong)	498
6/25/1998	6/25/1998	Financial Sector-Tranche ABCD (Thailand)	General Electric Capital Corp. (United States)	497
11/9/2000	11/9/2000	Nong Khae, Samut Prakarn (Thailand)	Tractebel SA (Belgium)	490
3/16/1999	11/25/2003	Thai Airways International PLC (Thailand)	Investors (Non-US) (Unknown)	483
2/11/2004	2/27/2004	Airports of Thailand PCL (Thailand)	Investors (Unknown)	446
7/16/2001	9/12/2001	Shin Digital Co. (Shin Corp) (Thailand)	Advanced Info Service PCL (Thailand)	388
10/7/1999	11/29/1999	Radanasin Bank PCL (Thailand)	UOB (Singapore)	383
5/18/1998	8/7/1998	Lotus Superstore (Thailand)	Tesco PLC (United Kingdom)	350
10/3/2000	10/31/2000	Tawan Mobile Telecom (Thailand)	Hutchison Telecomm Tech (Hong Kong)	331
9/3/1999	9/10/1999	Nakornthon Bank PCL (Thailand)	Standard Chartered Bank PLC (United Kingdom)	319
1/6/1999	1/6/1999	Advanced Info Service PCL (Thailand)	SingTel (Singapore)	318
10/31/1994	4/12/1995	Siam Motors Leasing Co. (Thailand)	SITCA Investment (Thailand)	281

Source: Thomson Financial.

Table 7.18 M&A transaction value in the Philippines by the nationality or region of the target firms,[a] 1990–2004

Nationality/region	Transaction value (US$ million)	% of total	No. of deals	% of total	Average value per deal (US$ million)
Brunei	—	0.0	0	0.0	0.0
Cambodia	—	0.0	—	0.0	0.0
Indonesia	—	0.0	1	0.0	7.0
Laos	—	0.0	0	0.0	0.0
Malaysia	203	0.7	7	1.2	29.0
Myanmar (Burma)	—	0.0	—	0.0	0.0
Philippines	38,670	93.0	628	94.3	61.6
Singapore	198	0.6	2	0.1	99.0
Thailand	156	0.5	3	0.4	52.0
Vietnam	50	0.2	1	0.0	50.0
Subtotal for the ASEAN countries	39,277	95.0	641	96.0	61.3
Subtotal for target firms from non-ASEAN countries acquired by companies in the ASEAN	2,196	5.0	26	4.0	84.5
Total	41,473	100	667	100	62.2

Source: Thomson Financial.

Note
a Only transactions of US$1 million or higher are included.

firms from the Philippines. One company was sold more than once and accounted for the largest and second largest deals. Coca-Cola Bottlers Philippines was sold for $2.7 billion to Coca-Cola Amatil Ltd (Australia) in 1997, and re-sold to a group of investors (Philippines) in 2001 for $1.3 billion. The third largest deal ($1.2 billion) was the acquisition of Far East Bank & Trust Co. (Philippines) by BPI from the Philippines. Total M&A value for the largest 20 deals in the Philippines was about $15.1 billion, accounting for 36 percent of all M&A during the 1990–2004 period.

Acquisition methods in the five countries

Figures 7.1 and 7.2 show the M&A value and number of transactions by acquisition methods in the ASEAN countries for 1990–2004. It is clear that 47 percent of the M&A transaction value and 59 percent of the number of deals were done by asset acquisition with an average value per deal of $46.5 million during that period. Acquisition of remaining interest accounted for 21 percent of the M&A value but only 16 percent of the number of deals with an average value per deal of over $52 million. Merger accounted for 17 percent of the M&A transaction value but only 12 percent of the number of deals. The average value per deal for

Table 7.19 M&A transaction value in the Philippines by the nationality or region of the acquiring firms,[a] 1990–2004

Nationality/region	Transaction Value (US$ million)	% of total	No. of deals	% of total	Average value per deal (US$ million)
Brunei	—	0.0	0	0.0	0.0
Cambodia	—	0.0	0	0.0	0.0
Indonesia	7	0.1	1	0.0	7.0
Laos	—	0.0	0	0.0	0.0
Malaysia	1,203	3.0	32	5.0	37.6
Myanmar (Burma)	—	0.0	0	0.0	0.0
Philippines	23,312	56.0	387	58.0	60.2
Singapore	1,586	4.0	46	7.0	34.5
Thailand	230	0.9	13	2.0	17.7
Vietnam	—	0.0	0	0.0	0.0
Subtotal for the ASEAN countries	26,338	64.0	479	72.0	55.0
Subtotal for acquired firms from non-ASEAN countries	15,135	36.0	188	28.0	80.5
Total	41,473	100	667	100	62.2

Source: Thomson Financial.

Note
a Only transactions of US$1 million or higher are included.

merger was over $109 million, significantly higher than that of any other acquisition method. Other methods include acquisition of majority or partial interest.

Tables 7.21 and 7.22 show the transaction value and number of deals respectively by the acquisition methods in the five major ASEAN countries (Malaysia, Singapore, Indonesia, Thailand, and Philippines) for 1990–2004. We can observe that the acquisition methods used varied among the five countries. For example, "asset acquisition" was used in 52 percent of the M&A transaction value in Singapore, more than 46 percent of the transaction value in Malaysia, 46 percent in Indonesia and 47 percent in Thailand, but only 37 percent of the M&A transaction value in the Philippines. It appears that acquisition of remaining interest had the second largest value per transaction for Singapore ($31.9 billion), Indonesia ($16.9 billion), and Thailand ($12.7 billion) and the third largest value per transaction for both Malaysia ($38.9 billion) and Philippines ($8.9 billion). Interestingly, Table 7.22 shows that acquisition of remaining interest had the second largest number of deals for all the five major countries.

Tables 7.21 and 7.22 respectively indicates that mergers in Malaysia ranked second to asset acquisition with 21 percent (or $41.4 billion) of M&A transaction value and 12 percent (or 526) of the number of deals. Mergers in Singapore have the largest value per deal of $176.5 million, while acquisitions of partial interest have the lowest value per deal of $28.3 million. Acquisitions of majority interest

Table 7.20 Twenty largest M&A in the Philippines, 1990–2004

Date announced	Date effective	Target name/nation	Acquirer name/nation	Value of transaction (US$ million)
4/2/1997	7/1/1997	Coca-Cola Bottlers Philippines (Philippines)	Coca-Cola Amatil Ltd (Australia)	2,739
2/6/2001	5/30/2001	Coca-Cola Bottlers Philippines (Philippines)	Investor Group (Philippines)	1,269
10/21/1999	4/10/2000	Far East Bank & Trust Co. (Philippines)	BPI (Philippines)	1,216
6/4/1999	3/24/2000	Smart Communications Inc. (Philippines)	PLDT (Philippines)	983
6/20/1996	10/7/1996	CityTrust Banking Corp. (Philippines)	BPI (Philippines)	909
4/1/1999	5/12/1999	Philippine Commercial Int'l Bk. (Philippines)	Investor Group (Philippines)	846
12/12/1996	2/5/1997	National Steel Corp. (Wing Tiek) (Philippines)	Hottick Investment Ltd (Hong Kong)	800
8/20/1998	11/13/1998	Nestle Philippines Inc. (Philippines)	Nestle SA (Switzerland)	755
11/25/1998	11/25/1998	PLDT (Philippines)	First Pacific Co. Ltd (Hong Kong)	749
12/2/2004	12/2/2004	NAPOCOR–Masinloc Power Plant (Philippines)	YNN Pacific Consortium Inc. (Australia)	562
1/30/1995	3/2/1995	Shangri-La Hotel Manila, 4 oth (Philippines)	Shangri-La Asia Ltd (Hong Kong)	538
12/14/2001	3/6/2002	San Miguel Corp. (Philippines)	Kirin Brewery Co. Ltd (Japan)	534
12/15/1993	3/4/1994	Petron Corp. (Philippines)	Aramco Overseas Co. (Saudi Arabia)	532
6/24/1994	8/9/1994	Petron Corp. (Philippines)	Investors (Philippines)	405
1/12/1999	2/18/1999	Apo Cement Corp. (JG Summit) (Philippines)	Cia Cementos Mexicanos SA (Mexico)	400
5/28/2001	6/15/2001	ICTSI International Holdings (Philippines)	Hutchison International Ports (Hong Kong)	400
9/10/1999	2/1/2001	Isla Communications (Ayala) (Philippines)	Globe Telecom Inc. (Philippines)	391
6/4/1999	3/24/2000	PLDT (Philippines)	Nippon Telegraph & Tele Corp. (Japan)	386
1/7/1992	3/25/1992	Philippine Airlines Inc. (Philippines)	PR Holdings Inc. (United States)	374
8/16/1995	7/31/1997	Nonoc Mining & Industrial (Philippines)	Pacific Nickel Holdings Ltd (United Kingdom)	333

Source: Thomson Financial.

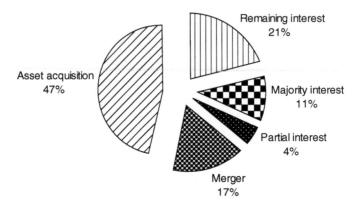

Figure 7.1 Acquisition methods in ASEAN by value of transaction, 1990–2004.
Source: Thomson Financial.

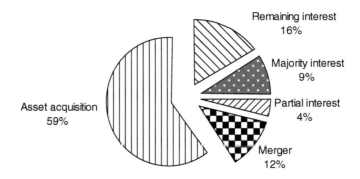

Figure 7.2 Acquisition methods in ASEAN by number of transactions, 1990–2004.
Source: Thomson Financial.

in Indonesia were involved in 14 percent of the 98 deals but only 13 percent of the M&A transaction value, or $7.7 billion. Mergers in Thailand have the largest value per deal of $110.3 million while acquisitions of partial interest have the lowest value per deal of $23.0 million. In Thailand, acquisition of majority interest was used in 12 percent of the transaction value with 11 percent of the deals. In the Philippines, mergers were involved in 26 percent of the transaction value (or $10.8 billion) but only 8 percent of the deals (or 51). The value per deal for mergers has the highest value of $212.3 million each while the acquisition of partial interest has the lowest value per deal of $40.3 million each.

M&A Activities and practices in the five countries

Because the economies of these five countries are different, M&A activities may vary among them. Table 7.23 compares the industries of target firms in the five

Table 7.21 M&A transaction value by acquisition methods used in five ASEAN countries, 1990–2004

Transaction type	Malaysia		Singapore		Indonesia		Thailand		Philippines	
	Transaction value (US$ million)	%	Transaction value (US$ million)	%	Transaction value (US$ million)	%	Transaction value (US$ million)	%	Transaction value (US$ million)	%
Asset Acquisition	92,451	46	91,813	52	27,049	46	19,669	47	15,481	37
Merger	41,372	21	29,826	17	3,393	6	2,758	7	10,828	26
Acquisition of partial interest	3,769	2	7,674	4	4,267	7	1,859	4	1,856	5
Acquisition of majority interest	21,400	11	15,881	9	7,697	13	5,085	12	4,448	11
Acquisition of remaining interest	38,938	20	31,873	18	16,887	28	12,749	30	8,860	21
Total	197,930	100	177,067	100	59,293	100	42,120	100	41,473	100

Source: Thomson Financial.

Table 7.22 M&A number of deals by acquisition methods used in the Big Five ASEAN countries, 1990–2004

Transaction type	Malaysia		Singapore		Indonesia		Thailand		Philippines	
	No. of deals	%	No. of deals	%	No. of deals	%	No. of deals	%	No. of deals	%
Asset acquisition	2,506	59	1,494	51	357	51	572	49	333	50
Merger	526	12	169	6	31	4	25	2	51	8
Acquisition of partial interest	149	4	271	9	56	8	81	8	46	7
Acquisition of majority interest	378	9	292	10	98	14	130	11	73	11
Acquisition of remaining interest	662	16	728	24	161	23	351	30	164	24
Total	4,221	100	2,954	100	703	100	1,159	100	667	100

Source: Thomson Financial.

Table 7.23 M&A in the Big Five ASEAN countries by the industry of the target firms, 1990–2004 (value in US$ millions)

Country	Financial	Manufacturing	Natural resources	Others	Retail	Services	Wholesale trade	Total
Malaysia	42,179	35,231	7,596	5,980	2,770	69,472	1,834	165,062
	26%[a]	21%[a]	5%	4%[a]	2%[a]	42%[a]	1%[a]	100%
Singapore	34,962	21,641	2,072	1,161	3,292	42,738	3,030	108,896
	32%	20%	2%	1%	3%	39%	3%	100%
Indonesia	8,261	21,140	14,262	35	557	21,389	117	65,761
	13%	32%	22%	0%[a]	1%	33%	0%[a]	100%
Philippines	9,008	12,882	2,195	178	179	15,056	2,198	41,696
	22%	31%	5%	0%[a]	0%[a]	36%	5%	100%
Thailand	13,558	9,125	1,631	199	922	16,002	695	42,132
	32%	22%	4%	0%[a]	2%	38%	2%	100%
Other ASEAN countries	136	470	1,031	28	—	552	48	2,265
	6%	21%	46%	1%	0%[a]	24%	2%	100%
Non-ASEAN countries	16,518	15,933	8,110	524	6,969	45,957	1,093	95,104
	17%	17%	9%	1%	7%	48%	1%	100%
Total	124,622	116,422	36,897	8,105	14,689	211,166	9,015	520,916

Source: Thomson Financial.

Note

a Less than 0.5 percent.

countries in addition to providing data for other ASEAN countries and non-ASEAN countries. Service industries accounted for 39 percent of the M&A value in Singapore, compared to 38 percent in Thailand, 36 percent in the Philippines and 33 percent in Indonesia. About 32 percent of the target firms from both Singapore and Thailand were in the financial industry such as banking and insurance, while 32 percent of the target firms in Indonesia and 31 percent of the target firms in the Philippines operated in the manufacturing industry.

For target firms involving Indonesia, only 22 percent of the M&A value was related to natural resources industries. But for target firms involving other ASEAN companies, 46 percent of the transaction values were related to natural resources industries. For non-ASEAN countries, target firms of M&A activity can be found in a variety of industries including services (48 percent), both financial and manufacturing (17 percent), natural resources (9 percent), and retailing (7 percent).

Table 7.24 compares the M&A completed in Malaysia, Singapore, Indonesia, Philippines, and Thailand by the nationality of acquirers. We can observe some similarities and differences among the M&A activity completed in these five countries. For example in Indonesia, the Philippines, Singapore, and Thailand, local firms buying other local firms accounted for about 38 to 49 percent of all the M&A in those four countries. But in Malaysia, M&A transactions between Malaysian firms accounted for 74 percent of all the M&A in Malaysia in 1990–2004. In Indonesia, non-Indonesian firms buying Indonesian companies accounted for 50 percent of the M&A transaction value while in Malaysia, non-Malaysian firms acquiring Malaysian companies only accounted for 7 percent of the M&A value. In the Philippines, non-Filipino firms acquiring Filipino companies, accounted for 44 percent of the M&A transaction value, while in Singapore, non-Singaporean firms buying Singaporean companies only accounted for 19 percent of the M&A value.

On the other hand, many Singaporean firms had spent $76.5 billion (or 43 percent of the total M&A transaction value) in 1990–2004 buying non-Singaporean firms.

Summary and conclusions

This chapter has provided an overview of the M&A activities in Southeast Asia for the last 14 years. Some similarities and differences among the five major countries were also compared and discussed. We noted that both the number of deals and transaction values of M&A in Southeast Asia have expanded significantly from 1990 to the year 2004. This expansion of M&A in Southeast Asia is likely to continue in the future for several reasons. First, many governments are encouraging their banks and finance companies to consolidate. For example, the Central Bank in Malaysia wants the country's 21 commercial banks, 25 finance companies, and 12 merchant banks to consolidate into 6 groups, each with an anchor commercial bank, a finance company and a merchant bank. The trend toward consolidation in banking and other industries may also accelerate in Singapore, Thailand, Indonesia, and the Philippines. Second, many

Table 7.24 Domestic versus cross-border M&A in Malaysia, Singapore, Indonesia, Philippines, and Thailand, 1990–2004 (value in US$ millions)

Malaysia	M&A value	%	Singapore	M&A value	%	Philippines	M&A value	%	Indonesia	M&A value	%	Thailand	M&A value	%
Malaysian firms acquiring other Malaysian firms	146,359	74	Singaporean firms acquiring other Singaporean firms	66,854	38	Filipino firms acquiring other Filipino firms	20,509	49	Indonesian firms acquiring other Indonesian firms	25,726	43	Thai firms acquiring other Thai firms	18,364	43
Malaysian firms acquiring non-Malaysian companies	37,635	19	Singaporean firms acquiring non-Singaporean companies	76,485	43	Filipino firms acquiring Non-Filipino firms	2,803	7	Indonesian firms acquiring non-Indonesian companies	3,866	7	Thai firms acquiring Non-Thai companies	3,228	8
Non-Malaysian firms acquiring Malaysian companies	13,936	7	Non-Singaporean firms acquiring Singaporean companies	33,728	19	Non-Filipino firms acquiring Filipino firms	18,161	44	Non-Indonesian firms acquiring Indonesian companies	29,701	50	Non-Thai firms acquiring Thai companies	20,528	49
Total	197,930	100	Total	177,067	100	Total	41,473	100	Total	59,293	100	Total	42,120	100

Source: Thomson Financial.

Southeast Asian countries are actively recruiting investors from Japan, Europe, and the United States to invest in manufacturing and high-tech industries. These countries, including Malaysia and Singapore, are providing generous tax and investment incentives to attract foreign investors. Third, many multinational companies also plan to increase their investment in Southeast Asia to achieve greater economies of scale, expand their markets, and increase cross-selling of products and services to consumers in different countries. However, potential investors should examine the following issues before expanding their M&A activity in Southeast Asia:

- Does the target company fit into the acquiring firm's strategic goals? Can the acquiring firm integrate the acquisition operationally and financially into existing operations and produce operating and financial synergies?
- Investors should consider the cultural differences between the acquiring company and the target firm. These differences include different national cultures as well as variation in corporate cultures. Cultural differences are the most frequently quoted reasons for failure in cross-border M&A. The acquiring company must develop a strategy for cultural integration before the merger.
- Investors should also study the various risks of the host country where the target company is located. These risks include, but are not limited to, political stability (or instability) of the current government; regulations on mergers, acquisitions, and joint ventures; and foreign exchanges risk.
- Tax implications of the merger and acquisition should also be carefully examined. These may include determining whether the transaction is a taxable or tax-free exchange; the deductibility of interest on borrowing for the host country's tax purposes; tax liability (or credit) for potential gain (or loss) related to the assets of the target company; and the role of tax treaties in the acquisition process.
- If necessary, an investor should hire investment bankers or legal advisors (or public accountants) to assist in determining the value of the target company, selecting the financing alternative, and planning and implementing the integration of the merging entities. The areas that need to be integrated include organization and staffing plans, purchasing and production functions, marketing and distribution strategies, and information systems.

In summary, the trends toward deregulation and consolidation in manufacturing and banking industries in Southeast Asia together with a significant expansion in international business activities in the region will create more M&A in the future. In the past decade, many regional and bilateral FTAs have also been established. Joint ventures and international corporate alliances between many Southeast Asian firms and multinational companies will be expanded in the future. Increased M&A activity in Southeast Asia provides many opportunities as well as challenges to potential investors. An acquiring firm can improve its chances of success by exercising due diligence, selecting the right advisors, and conducting a comprehensive analysis of the target firm and local economy.

8   Cross-national comparisons and general conclusions

In Chapters 2, 4, and 6, we presented some economic information on Japan, China, Taiwan, Hong Kong, and the Big Five ASEAN countries (Indonesia, Malaysia, the Philippines, Singapore, and Thailand). In those chapters, we also provided their international trade and investment statistics and discussed their trade and investment relations with the United States. This last chapter will provide cross-national comparisons in the following areas:

- major economic indicators relevant to M&A activity. These include GDP growth, investment, and expansion of trade in Asia;
- M&A activities that include M&A deals and transaction values;
- target firms, M&A methods, and the largest M&A deal in each country;
- future prospects for M&A activity;
- due diligence and integration issues.

General conclusions will be provided toward the end of the chapter.

Cross-national comparisons of economic growth, investment, and merchandise trade

The levels of M&A activity in many countries are related to economic growth, investment, and trade. In earlier chapters, we presented the GDP figures for Japan, China, Taiwan, Hong Kong, and the Big Five ASEAN countries. In Table 8.1, we compare the annual percentage changes in GDP (at current price) of these countries and the United States. The statistics were obtained from the websites of the IMF, the UNCTAD, and the Ministry of Commerce of China. Some numbers for 2005 and all numbers for 2006 are forecasted percentages.

We can observe that in 2005, all Asian countries listed in Table 8.1 were growing faster than the United States with the exception of Japan, Taiwan, and Thailand. In 2005, the US growth rate in GDP was about 3.5 percent, compared with Japan's 2 percent and Taiwan's 3.4 percent. Thailand's growth rate in 2005 was 3.5 percent. China had the fastest GDP growth rate in Asia from 2003 to 2005, averaging about 10 percent annually. In 2006, Japan's GDP was forecasted to grow another 2 percent and the United States, 3.3 percent. The other

Table 8.1 Annual percentage changes in GDP at current price for selected Asian countries and the United States, 2000–6

Country	2000	2001	2002	2003	2004	2005[a]	2006[a]
Japan	2.4	0.2	(0.3)	1.4	2.7	2.0	2.0
China	8.0	7.5	8.3	10	10.1	9.9	9.2
Taiwan	5.8	2.2	3.9	3.3	5.7	3.4	4.3
Hong Kong	10.2	0.5	1.9	3.2	8.1	6.3	4.5
Indonesia	4.9	3.8	4.4	4.9	5.1	5.8	5.8
Malaysia	8.9	0.3	4.4	5.4	7.1	5.5	6.0
Philippines	4.4	1.8	4.4	4.5	6.0	4.7	4.8
Singapore	9.6	(1.9)	3.2	1.4	8.4	5.7	4.5
Thailand	4.8	2.2	5.3	6.9	6.1	5.5	5.0
United States	3.7	0.8	1.6	2.7	4.2	3.5	3.3

Sources: The IMF, the Ministry of Commerce of China, and the World Bank.

Note

a Some percentage changes for 2005 and all percentage changes for 2006 are forecasted numbers.

eight countries (or regions) are expected to grow including a 4.3 percent growth in Taiwan and a 9.2 percent growth in China.

The inward and outward DI of the selected Asian countries as well as for the United States for 2001–4 are reported in Table 1.12. In recent years, the United States, China, Hong Kong, and Singapore have received substantial inward investment. At the same time, US and Japanese firms were investing substantially overseas. For example, in 2004, outward DI from the United States was $229.3 billion and was $30.9 billion from Japan during the same year. Hong Kong's outward investment surged to $39.8 billion in 2004. Other countries including Singapore and Taiwan were also investing in China and other regions in 2004 and 2005. Recent statistics also show that the US DI in Japan was $11.3 billion in 2004, and its DI in China during 2004 was about $3 billion (Browne 2006).

Table 8.2 provides the statistics of leading merchandise exporters and importers in Asia in 2004. These statistics are available on the WTO website. In recent years, the leading trading nations in Asia include China, Japan, Hong Kong, South Korea, Taiwan, Singapore, and Malaysia. China's exports ($593.3 billion) in 2004 accounted for about 24.8 percent of all exports from Asia. That same year its imports ($561.2 billion) accounted for 25.2 percent of all Asian imports. Recent statistics show that in 2005, China's exports had increased to $762 billion, and its imports expanded by 18 percent to $660 billion. In recent years, China also has shown the highest growth rates in imports and exports among all Asian countries.

In 2004, Japan's merchandise exports totaled $565.8 billion, and imports amounted to $454.5 billion. Hong Kong, South Korea, and Taiwan also recorded substantial growth in their trade in recent years. The ASEAN countries, as a group, exported $551.8 billion and imported $500.1 billion in 2004 according to statistics published by the WTO. The two largest trading nations in ASEAN are

Table 8.2 Leading merchandise exporters and importers in Asia, 2004

	Value (US$ billion) 2004	*Share* 2000	2004	*Annual percentage change* 2000–4	2002	2003	2004
Exporters							
Asia	2,388.4	100.0	100.0	10	8	18	25
China	593.3	15.0	24.8	24	22	35	35
Japan	565.8	28.9	23.7	4	3	13	20
Hong Kong	265.5	10.7	11.1	7	6	13	16
domestic exports	20.0	1.4	0.8	(4)	(10)	7	2
re-exports	245.6	0.0	10.2	8	7	14	17
South Korea	253.8	10.4	10.6	10	8	19	31
Taiwan	182.4	9.1	7.6	5	7	11	21
Singapore	179.6	8.3	7.5	7	3	15	25
domestic exports	98.6	4.7	4.1	6	1	19	24
re-exports	81.0	3.6	3.4	8	5	10	26
Malaysia	126.5	5.9	5.3	7	7	12	21
Thailand	97.4	4.2	4.1	9	5	18	21
Australia	86.4	3.9	3.6	8	3	10	21
India	75.6	2.6	3.2	16	14	16	32
Indonesia	72.3	3.9	3.0	3	3	8	13
Philippines	39.7	2.4	1.7	0	12	1	7
Vietnam	25.6	0.9	1.1	15	11	21	27
Importers							
Asia	2,224.2	100.0	100.0	10	6	19	27
China	561.2	15.0	25.2	26	21	40	36
Japan	454.5	25.3	20.4	5	(3)	14	19
Hong Kong	272.9	12.9	12.4	6	3	12	17
retained imports	27.3	2.3	1.2	(6)	(22)	(1)	13
South Korea	224.5	10.7	10.1	9	8	18	26
Taiwan	168.4	9.3	7.6	5	5	13	32
Singapore	163.9	9.0	7.4	5	0	10	28
retained imports	82.8	5.0	3.7	2	(4)	9	30
Australia	109.4	4.8	4.9	11	14	23	23
Malaysia	105.3	5.5	4.7	6	8	5	26
India	97.3	3.4	4.4	17	12	26	37
Thailand	95.4	4.1	4.3	11	4	17	26
Indonesia	54.9	2.9	2.5	6	2	10	30
Philippines	42.3	2.5	1.9	3	6	6	7
Vietnam	31.1	1.0	1.4	19	22	28	23

Source: The World Trade Organization (WTO).

Singapore and Malaysia. Together, they accounted for 55 percent of ASEAN's exports and 54 percent of imports into the ASEAN in 2004.

What is the role of the United States in trade with major Asian countries? We can find some answers from Table 8.3 which shows the top 10 trading partners of the United States in 2005. In the table, we can see that the two partners of NAFTA (Canada and Mexico) were still the two top trading partners of

Table 8.3 Top 10 trading partners of the United States in 2005 (amounts in US$ billion)

Rank	Country	2005 exports	2005 imports	2005 trade total	% of total trade
	Total, all countries	904.30	1,671.40	2,351.30	100.0
	Total, top 10 countries	583.80	1,121.70	1,705.60	66.3
1	Canada	211.30	287.90	499.20	19.4
2	Mexico	120.00	170.20	290.20	11.3
3	China	41.80	243.50	285.30	11.1
4	Japan	55.40	138.10	193.50	7.5
5	Germany	34.10	84.80	119.00	4.6
6	United Kingdom	38.60	51.10	89.70	3.5
7	South Korea	27.70	43.80	71.40	2.8
8	Taiwan	22.00	34.80	56.90	2.2
9	France	22.40	33.80	56.20	2.2
10	Malaysia	10.50	33.70	44.20	1.7

Source: US Census Bureau.

the United States in 2005. About 30 percent of US foreign trade is trade with Canada and Mexico. Not far behind is China with a total trade of $285.3 billion with the United States. China's trade with the United States accounted for 11.1 percent of US merchandise trade. As a matter of fact, during the last quarter of 2005, China was the second largest trading partner of the United States, according to statistics published by the US Census Bureau. Other Asian countries listed among the US top ten trading partners and their trade volumes with the United States are Japan ($193.5 billion), South Korea ($71.4 billion), Taiwan ($56.9 billion), and Malaysia ($44.2 billion). The US trade deficit with China in 2005 was a record $201.7 billion. This has prompted new calls from some US Senators and Congressmen for the US Government to press China to allow its currency to appreciate further (Hiebert, 2006). Some senators in the US Senate have a proposal to impose a 27.5 percent across the board tariff on Chinese goods if China fails to strengthen its currency (Hitt and Hiebert, 2006). The United States also traded heavily with other ASEAN countries including Singapore, Thailand, Indonesia, and the Philippines.

Comparisons of M&A deals and transaction values

Table 8.4 compares M&A deals and transaction values of nine Asian countries or regions and the United States for 2004 and for the period from 1990 to 2004. From 1990 to 2004, the world's M&A deals totaled 170,549 with a total transaction value of $26,729 billion. During that period, the United States had 76,944 deals or 45.1 percent of the world's total. The US total M&A transaction value for that period was $14,815 billion, or 55.4 percent of the world's total.

The nine Asian countries listed in Table 8.4 had a total of 28,526 deals or 16.7 percent of the world's total from 1990 to 2004. For the same period, total M&A transaction value of these nine Asian countries was $2,197 billion, or

Table 8.4 A comparison of M&A deals and transaction values among selected countries, 2004 and 1990–2004[a]

Country	1990–2004		2004		
	No. of deals	M&A value (US$ million)	No. of deals	M&A value (US$ million)	Average value per deal (2004) (US$ million)
Japan	7,734	1,003,624	1,225	138,521	113
China	4,487	203,385	1,373	29,376	21
Taiwan	800	85,130	108	3,270	30
Hong Kong	5,801	386,727	714	23,753	33
Indonesia	703	59,293	69	3,039	44
Malaysia	4,221	197,930	385	8,018	21
Philippines	667	41,473	55	3,307	60
Singapore	2,954	177,067	328	22,294	68
Thailand	1,159	42,120	171	4,910	29
United States	76,944	14,815,408	4,120	1,183,179	287
World total	170,549	26,728,550	13,260	2,319,331	175

Source: Thomson Financial.

Note

a Only transactions of US$1 million or higher are included.

8.2 percent of the world's total. During this 15 years period, Japan had the largest M&A transaction value ($1,004 billion) among the Asian countries, followed by Hong Kong ($387 billion), China ($203 billion), and Malaysia ($198 billion).

For the year of 2004 alone, the US share of M&A deals was 31.1 percent (or 4,120 deals). The US share of M&A transaction value for 2004 was 51 percent (or $1,183 billion). In 2004, Japan still had the largest M&A transaction value among all Asian countries, with a transaction value of about $138.5 billion. China has the largest number of deals (1,373) with a transaction value of about $29.4 billion. Other countries or regions having significant M&A transaction value in 2004 included Hong Kong ($23.8 billion) and Singapore ($22.3 billion).

In 2004, the average value per deal in the United States was $287 million. In Japan, the average M&A deal was worth $113 million, followed by Singapore ($68 million) and the Philippines ($60 million). The average value per deal in China in 2004 was about $21 million.

Domestic versus cross-border M&A activity

Table 8.5 shows the extent of domestic versus cross-border mergers among nine Asian countries from 1990 to 2004. The last two columns of that table (domestic firms buying foreign firms, and foreign companies buying domestic firms) are normally considered as cross-border M&A activity. Malaysia had the largest percentage of domestic M&A activity (74 percent), followed by Japan (72 percent), and Taiwan (70 percent).

Table 8.5 Domestic versus cross-border M&A activity: a nine country comparison[a], 1990–2004 (US$ million and percentages)

Country	Domestic M&A		Domestic firms buying foreign firms		Foreign companies buying domestic firms	
	Value	%	Value	%	Value	%
Japan	726,181	72	137,735	14	139,707	14
China	73,054	36	17,040	8	113,290	56
Taiwan	59,718	70	12,299	15	13,113	15
Hong Kong	187,721	49	133,068	34	65,958	17
Indonesia	25,726	43	3,866	7	29,701	50
Malaysia	146,359	74	37,635	19	13,936	17
Philippines	20,509	49	2,803	7	18,161	44
Singapore	66,854	38	76,485	43	33,728	19
Thailand	18,364	43	3,228	8	20,528	49

Source: Thomson Financial.

Note
a Only transactions of US$1 million or higher are included.

Interestingly, China had the lowest percentage of domestic M&A activity (36 percent), and foreign companies buying Chinese firms accounted for 56 percent (or $113 billion) of Chinese M&A activity. Singapore's domestic M&A ratio (38 percent) is also quite low; but Singaporean firms buying non-Singaporean firms accounted for 43 percent (or $76 billion) of total M&A activity from 1990 to 2004.

Other countries having large percentages of cross-border M&A activity include Thailand (57 percent), Indonesia (57 percent), Hong Kong (51 percent), and the Philippines (51 percent). In terms of transaction value, Japan had the highest cross-border M&A value of $277 billion among the Asian countries. Other countries or regions having large cross-border transaction values included Hong Kong ($199 billion), China ($130 billion), Singapore ($110 billion), and Malaysia ($51 billion).

Industrial distribution of the target firms

Table 8.6 compares the industries of the target firms of M&A in the nine Asian countries during the 1990–2004 period. In only three countries did manufacturing target companies account for more than 30 percent of the M&A totals: Taiwan (42 percent), Indonesia (32 percent), and the Philippines (31 percent). Service companies accounted for 61 percent of the target firms in China, and 42 percent each of the target companies in Hong Kong and Malaysia. More than one-third of the target companies in Singapore, Thailand, and the Philippines were also service companies. This reflects the importance of service industries in M&A activity in Asia.

Table 8.6 M&A by the industry of the target firms in selected Asian countries (percentages), 1990–2004

Country or region of the target firm	Manufacturing (%)	Service (%)	Financial (%)	Others (%)	Total (%)
Japan	28	29	34	9	100
Mainland China	19	61	10	10	100
Taiwan	42	22	33	3	100
Hong Kong	17	42	32	9	100
Indonesia	32	33	13	22[a]	100
Malaysia	21	42	26	11	100
Philippines	31	36	22	11	100
Singapore	20	39	32	9	100
Thailand	22	38	32	8	100

Source: Thomson Financial.

Note
a Mainly in natural resources.

Financial industries (e.g. banking and insurance) also played an important role in M&A activity in Asia. For example, in Japan, Taiwan, Hong Kong, Singapore, and Thailand, about one-third of the target companies were from financial industries. This phenomenon reflects the need for consolidation in financial industries from 1990 to 2004. This trend may continue for the next few years as many Asian countries continue to privatize and consolidate their banking industries. Indonesia has a unique situation where close to 22 percent of the M&A activity had target companies in the natural resource industries including oil and gas, and mining.

M&A methods and the largest M&A in each country

Table 8.7 shows the five M&A methods used in the nine Asian countries from 1990 to 2004. The last three methods (acquisitions of partial interest, majority interest, and remaining interest) can be classified as share purchases if share transactions are involved.

In three countries or regions, a majority of the M&A activity from 1990 to 2004 involved asset acquisitions: China (65 percent), Hong Kong (56 percent), and Singapore (52 percent). It was also the most popular method used in Thailand (47 percent), Malaysia (46 percent), and Indonesia (46 percent). Asset acquisition was used in about one-third of the cases in Japan, Taiwan, and the Philippines.

Acquisition of partial interest was used between 14 and 17 percent of the cases in Japan, China, Taiwan, and Hong Kong. Acquisition of the remaining interest was used in 18 to 30 percent of the cases in Thailand, Indonesia, the Philippines, Malaysia, and Singapore. Acquisition of majority interest was used in 9 to 13 percent of the cases for the countries listed. Merger was a popular method and used often in Japan (33 percent), Taiwan (37 percent), the Philippines (26 percent), and Malaysia (21 percent).

Table 8.7 M&A methods used by the acquiring firms in selected Asian countries by transaction values, 1990–2004 (in percentages of transaction values)

Country or region of the acquiring firm	Asset acquisition (%)	Merger (%)	Acquisition of partial interest (%)	Acquisition of majority interest (%)	Acquisition of remaining interest (%)	Total (%)
Japan	33	33	17	11	6	100
Mainland China	65	10	15	9	1	100
Taiwan	32	37	15	10	6	100
Hong Kong	56	17	14	9	4	100
Indonesia	46	6	7	13	28	100
Malaysia	46	21	2	11	20	100
Philippines	37	26	5	11	21	100
Singapore	52	17	4	9	18	100
Thailand	47	7	4	12	30	100

Source: Thomson Financial.

Table 8.8 shows the largest M&A deals in each of the nine Asian countries and the United States from 1990 to 2004. During that period, the largest US deal was the acquisition of Time Warner by America Online (AOL) for $164.7 billion, effective in 2001. This deal is also ranked as the second largest M&A deal in the world from 1990 to 2004. The world's largest deal during that period was the acquisition of Mannesmann AG (Germany) by Vodafone AirTouch PLC (UK) in the year 2000. The other largest 20 deals in the world are listed in Table 1.5.

In Japan, the largest M&A deal from 1990 to 2004 was the acquisition of Sakura Bank by Sumitomo Bank in 2001. The deal was worth $45.5 billion and was the largest deal in Asia between 1990 and 2004. Hong Kong's largest deal was the purchase of Cable & Wireless HKT by Pacific Century CyberWorks in 2000 for $37.4 billion. The largest deal in China was the acquisition of Beijing Mobile (China) by China Telecom Hong Kong in 2000 for $34 billion. Singapore's largest deal was the acquisition of Cable & Wireless Optus Ltd (Australia) by Sing Tel (Singapore) in 2001 for $8.5 billion. Taiwan's largest deal was the purchase of Worldwide Semiconductor by Taiwan Semiconductor in 2000 for $6.46 billion. Malaysia's largest deal was the acquisition of ASKO Deutshe Kaufhaus Deutsch (Germany) by Metro Curtainwall & Cladding (Malaysia) in 1996 for $6.3 billion.

It is interesting to note that six of the ten largest deals listed in Table 8.8 were concluded in either 2000 or 2001, at the peak of the last global merger wave. Only four of the ten deals involve manufacturing companies, the rest are in the service or financial industries. Interestingly, the merger of AOL and Time Warner was listed by Bruner (2005) as one of the ten largest M&A deals that failed because nearly $200 billion in market value evaporated in the months following the conclusion of the deal. In April 2002, AOL Time Warner adopted new accounting rules that required a $54 billion charge to earnings due to the impairment of

Table 8.8 Largest M&A deals in each of the selected Asian countries and the United States, 1990–2004

Country or region	Date announced	Effective date	Target and nationality	Acquirer and nationality	Amount (US$ million)
Japan	10/13/1999	4/1/2001	Sakura Bank (Japan)	Sumitomo Bank (Japan)	45,494
China	10/4/2000	1/13/2000	Beijing Mobile (China)	China Telecom Hong Kong (HK)	34,008
Taiwan	1/7/2000	6/30/2000	Worldwide Semiconductor (Taiwan)	Taiwan Semiconductor (Taiwan)	6,448
Hong Kong	2/29/2000	8/17/2000	Cable & Wireless HKT (HK)	Pacific Century CyberWorks (HK)	37,442
Indonesia	11/19/1990	11/19/1990	East Kalimantan Concession (Indonesia)	Osaka Gas Co. (Japan)	1,950
Malaysia	12/14/1993	7/19/1996	ASKO Deutshe Kaufhaus Deutsch (Germany)	Metro Curtainwall & Cladding (Malaysia)	6,325
Philippines	4/2/1997	7/1/1997	Coca-Cola Bottlers Philippines (Philippines)	Coca-Cola Amatil Ltd (Australia)	2,739
Singapore	3/26/2001	9/12/2001	Cable & Wireless Optus Ltd (Australia)	Sing Tel (Singapore)	8,491
Thailand	10/8/2003	11/7/2003	Krung Thai Bank (Thailand)	Investors Group	748
United States	1/10/2000	1/12/2001	Time Warner (US)	America Online (US)	164,700

Source: Thomson Financial.

goodwill. This amount was the largest charge against earnings in US corporate history.

Future prospects for M&A activity in Asia

In this book, we have presented information on the economic environments and M&A activity and practices in nine Asian countries. Comparisons of M&A practices among these countries and with the United States are also provided. After studying M&A in Asia and other regions for about five years, we find that prospects for M&A activity in the next few years are extremely good because of the following factors:

- Globalization and the expansion of international trade and expansion will continue especially in Asia. Statistics on international trade and investment have been provided in this and other chapters.
- The speed of technological change and outsourcing will accelerate which will reduce the costs of communication, production, transportation, and other costs associated with conducting international business.
- Deregulation and privatization of state owned enterprises will continue in China, Taiwan, Malaysia, the Philippines, and many other Asian countries.
- The general economic environment in Asia will continue to support economic growth and expansion in trade and investment. Favorable factors include booming stock markets, low inflation, low interest rates, and growing economies.
- More bilateral and regional FTAs will be concluded and implemented in the future. These FTAs will improve the investment climate of many Asian countries.
- Most countries in Asia have learned some painful lessons from the financial crisis that took place in 1997 and 1998. They are improving their accounting rules and practices, corporate governance, and government oversight.

When we combine the aforementioned factors, it is safe to predict that M&A activity in Asia will grow in the next few years. Preliminary statistics from Thomson Financial show that total worldwide M&A transaction value for 2005 was more than $2.7 trillion, an increase of about 17 percent over 2004. Thomson also reported that the number of deals worldwide expanded by 38 percent in 2005.

In Europe, companies spent $1.09 trillion on 10,457 deals, compared with $691.8 billion on 8,818 deals in 2004 according to the research firm Dealogic's preliminary report (Wall Street Journal, 2006). The value of cross-border transactions within Europe also expanded by 99 percent to reach $322.8 billion in 2005.

Due diligence and integration issues for M&A in Asia

In the past, authors such as Bruner (2004), Weston and Weaver (2001), and Sudarsanam (2003) have emphasized the importance of due diligence in

M&A. The concept of due diligence has many dimensions according to Bruner (2004):

> Due diligence is research, its purpose in M&A is to support the valuation process, arm negotiators, test the accuracy of representations and warranties contained in the merger agreement, fulfill disclosure requirements to investors, and inform the planners of post-merger integration. Due diligence is conducted in a wide variety of corporate finance settings, and is usually connected with the performance of a professional or fiduciary duty. It is the opposite of negligence.

Weaknesses in the due diligence process may cause an M&A to fail. In addition, buyers in M&A may find "ignorance of knowable risks to be a weak basis for a lawsuit seeking damages from sellers" according to Bruner (2004).

A due diligence process should focus at least on the following issues:

- Legal issues: These include examining documents of asset ownership and associated liabilities; actual or potential legal liabilities; and whether the target company is in compliance with government regulations.
- Financial and tax issues: These include examining accounting records and reports to determine whether the target companies are in compliance with generally accepted accounting principles. In addition, the target company's compliance with tax laws and regulations should be examined.
- Marketing issues: These include strengths and weaknesses of products and services provided by the target company and their domestic and foreign competition.
- Cross-border issues: These include foreign currency exchange risks, foreign laws and regulations, investment promotional agency and investment incentives, foreign banking and credit agencies, accounting principles, and local tax rules.
- Cultural and ethical issues: These cover cultural differences between the acquirer and target companies and how to deal with these differences; the degree of compliance with the acquirer's ethical guidelines; and the exposure to liabilities and legal proceedings on unethical conduct such as patent and copyright violations, price fixing, and others.

Culture is important in intercultural business communication as explained by Chaney and Martin (2000):

> Whereas communication is a process, culture is the structure through which the communication is formulated and interpreted. Culture deals with the way people live. When cultures interact, adaptation has to take place in order for the cultures to communicate effectively. In dealing with intercultural business communication, awareness of the symbols of each culture, how they are the same, and how they are different, is important.

Another important M&A issue is integration planning and post-merger integration. Integration is probably the most important issue after a deal is signed between the acquirer and a seller in a cross-border M&A. The areas that need to be integrated include the following: (1) organization and staffing plans; (2) product strategies; (3) purchasing and supply chain management strategies; (4) production strategies and plans; (5) marketing strategies and sales forces; (6) information systems; (7) finance and accounting systems; and (8) human resource management systems. Integration plans of the earlier and other areas should be formulated by various management teams and assisted by experienced consulting firms. The integration teams should also work closely with the teams that conducted the due diligence process. After the integration plan is approved for implementation, it should be communicated, and explained to employees impacted by the plan.

One way to avoid failures is to study failed cross-border mergers and joint ventures, and discover why they failed. For example, in the 1998 merger between Daimler-Benz and Chrysler, the "Daimler Chrysler post-merger integration project was ultimately built around a list of a dozen or so major tasks, derived from a list of almost 100 potential pitfalls in the post-merger integration process" (Habeck *et al.* 2000). This list was developed from studying 50 failures in cross-border mergers and joint ventures.

For specific due diligence and integration issues related to M&A activity in an Asian country, the M&A partners can study a guide such as the Baker and McKenzie *Guide to Mergers and Acquisitions* by countries or other similar publications. Alternatively, the M&A partners may hire an M&A attorney or investment bank to assist with the due diligence and integration processes.

General conclusions

The economic and political environments of many Asian countries have changed substantially over the last decade. They will continue to change in the next decade. Many changes such as deregulation, privatization, and new free trade agreements will have a very positive impact on M&A activity in Asia. Several other general conclusions can be drawn from the study:

- Mergers and acquisitions, if implemented correctly, should lead to further expansion of trade and international investment which in turn would create more M&A opportunities in the future.
- Performing due diligence is a necessary process for domestic M&A. Due diligence is an absolutely essential step for cross-border M&A. An examination of all legal and nonlegal aspects of all potential partners must be conducted to avoid failure. An assessment of the macroeconomic and microeconomic factors, and risk management strategies should be done before investing in an Asian country.
- Cultural components and priorities such as rules, norms, and practices, the work ethic, social structure, education, religion, popular beliefs, and leadership

styles must be examined before approaching the potential partners. These cultural considerations should be continually monitored throughout the M&A negotiation and implementation processes.

- The hot spots for M&A activity in Asia for the next five years are in Japan, China, Singapore, and Hong Kong. Many Japanese executives are now more receptive to the idea of cross-border M&A activity than they had been in the past. The Government of Japan has also reformed its investment and M&A related regulations to welcome foreign investment. As China's rapid economic expansion continues, it will need foreign investment to modernize its state-owned enterprises and to develop many of its noncoastal provinces. Singapore has signed bilateral and regional FTAs with the United States and many other countries. Singapore also provides very generous tax and nontax incentives. Hong Kong is a gateway to the Pearl River Delta of China. Hong Kong has a modern airport, sea transport facilities, and an efficient government. In addition, Hong Kong's tax rates are the lowest among all Asian countries. Firms located in Hong Kong may export goods and services to China free of customs duties.

In summary, the trends toward deregulation, consolidation in banking and manufacturing industries, and a significant expansion of investment and trade will create more M&A activity in Asia. Increased M&A activity in Asia will provide many opportunities and challenges for potential investors in Japan, Greater China, and Southeast Asia. A firm can improve its chances of success in M&A by exercising due diligence, selecting the right advisors, and conducting a thorough analysis of the target company, the related industries, and the local economy. Investment projects, if properly selected, should improve the economy of a host country and create more jobs, and encourage more investment for that country.

Bibliography

Agami, Obdel M. 2002. The Role that Foreign Acquisitions of Asian Companies Played in the Recovery of the Asian Financial Crisis. *Multinational Business Review* (Spring): 11–20.

Areddy, James T. 2005. China to Relax Foreign Quotas. *Wall Street Journal* (July 12): C12.

——. 2006. Adding Up Chinese Data. *Wall Street Journal* (February 27): C10.

Ash, Robert F. and Y. Y. Kueh. 1993. Economic Integration Within Greater China: Trade and Investment Flows Between China, Hong Kong, and Taiwan. *China Quarterly* (December): 711–45.

Azhar, Saeed and Kevin Lim. 2006. Singapore Economy Outstrips Forecasts, Asia Rivals. *Wall Street Journal* (January 4): A9.

Baker & McKenzie International. 2004a. *The 2004/2005 Guide to Mergers and Acquisitions in Hong Kong*. Hong Kong: Baker & McKenzie.

——. 2004b. *The 2004/2005 Guide to Mergers and Acquisitions in Taiwan*. Taipei: Baker & McKenzie.

Baker & McKenzie International and Hadiputranto, Hadinoto & Partners. 2004. *The 2004/2005 Guide to Mergers and Acquisitions in Indonesia*. Jakarta: Hadiputranto, Hadinoto & Partners.

Baker & McKenzie International and Quisumbing Torres. 2005. *The 2005 Guide to Mergers and Acquisitions in the Philippines*. Manila: Quisumbing Torres.

Baker & McKenzie International and Tokyo Aoyama Aoki Law Office. 2005. *The 2005 Guide to Mergers and Acquisitions in Japan*. Tokyo: Aoyama Aoki Law Office.

Baker & McKenzie International and Wong & Leow. 2005. *The 2005/2006 Guide to Mergers and Acquisitions in Singapore*. Singapore: Wong & Leow.

Baker & McKenzie International and Wong & Partners. 2005. *The 2005/2006 Guide to Mergers and Acquisitions in Malaysia*. Kuala Lumpur: Wong & Partners.

Bauerlein, Valerie and Kate Linebaugh. 2005. Bank of America Chairman Sees Extended China Banking Growth. *Wall Street Journal* (June 20): C4.

Berman, Dennis K. and Mark Heinzl. 2005. Canada, Welcome China's Cash. *Wall Street Journal* (July 15): C1, C12.

Browne, Andrew. 2006a. GM's China Sales Hit Record in '05, Increasing by 35%. *Wall Street Journal* (January 6): A14.

——. 2006b China Drew Over $60 Billion in Foreign Investment in 2005. *Wall Street Journal* (January 14): A2.

——. 2006c. As Congress Blusters About Trade With China, U.S. Companies Play Coy Over Profits. *Wall Street Journal* (February 13): A2.

Bruner, Robert F. 2004. *Applied Mergers and Acquisitions.* Hoboken, NJ: John Wiley & Sons.

———. 2005. *Deals from Hell, M&A Lessons That Rise Above the Ashes.* New York: John Wiley & Sons.

Chan, John L. 2003. *China Streetsmart.* Singapore: Pearson and Prentice Hall.

Chaney, Lillian H. and Jeanette S. Martin. 2000. *Intercultural Business Communication.* Upper Saddle River, NJ: Prentice Hall.

Chen, Chunlai and Christopher Findlay. 2003. A Review of Cross-border Mergers and Acquisitions in APEC. *Asian-Pacific Economic Literature* 17(2): 14–38.

Cheung, Gordon W. and Irene Han-Siu Chow. 1999. Subcultures in Greater China: A Comparison of Managerial Values in People's Republic of China, Hong Kong, and Taiwan. *Asia Pacific Journal of Management* (December): 369–87.

Church, Peter. 2003. *A Short History of South-East Asia.* Singapore: John Wiley & Sons (Asia).

Dean, Jason. 2006. China is Set to Spend Billions on Wireless Upgrade. *Wall Street Journal* (February 27): A1, A10.

Delios, Andrew and Kulwart Singh. 2005. *Strategy for Success in Asia.* Singapore: John Wiley & Sons (Asia).

Dong, Jie Lin and Jie Hue. 1995. *Mergers and Acquisitions in China.* Economic Review (November): 15–29.

Eiteman, David K., Arthur I. Stonehill, and Michel H. Moffett. 2004. *Multinational Business Finance.* Boston, MA: Pearson/Addison Wesley (February 11–12): A6.

Fairclough, Gordon. 2006. China Auto Sales Jump Over 70% As Incomes Rise. *Wall Street Journal* (February 11–12): A6.

Farzad, Rober. 2005. Sweet Times for Deal Makers. *Business Week* (December): 114, 116.

Fishman, Ted C. 2005. *China Inc.* New York: Scribner.

Fung, K. C., Lawrence J. Lan, and Joseph S. Lee. 2004. *U.S. Direct Investment in China.* Washington, DC: The AEI Press.

Gaugham, Patrick A. 2002. *Mergers, Acquisitions, and Corporate Restructurings.* New York: John Wiley & Sons.

Gilson, R. J. and B. S. Black. 1995. *The Law and Finance of Corporate Acquisitions.* New York: Foundation Press.

Gitelson, Gene, John W. Bing, and Lionel Laroche. 2001. The Impact of Culture on Mergers and Acquisitions. *CMA Management* (March): 41–4. http://www.itapintl.com/mergersandacquisitions.htm

Habeck, Max M., Fritz Kröger, and Michael R. Träm. 2000. *After the Merger.* London: Pearson Education.

Harvard Business Review. 2004. *Harvard Business Review on Doing Business in China.* Boston, MA: Harvard Business School Publishing.

Hiebert, Murray. 2006. Steep Increases in Chinese Exports May Add to Trade-Policy Tensions. *Wall Street Journal* (February 14): A4.

Hitt, Greg and Muray Hiebert. 2006. U.S. Trade Deficit Ballooned to a Record in 2005. *Wall Street Journal* (February 11–12): A1, A10.

Ho, Kin Yip, and Albert K. C. Tsui. 2004. Analysis of Real GDP Growth Rates of Greater China: An Asymmetric Condition Volatility Approach. *China Economic Review* (15): 424–42.

Hong Kong Trade Development Council (HKTDC). 2004. *Guide to Doing Business in China.* Hong Kong: H.K. Trade Development Council.

Hong Kong Port Development Council (HKPDC) Website. 2006. http://www.pdc.gov.hk/eng/home/index.htm

Hu, Jingyan. 2005. The General Situation of China's FDI Absorption in 2004. http://www.yearbook.org.cn

Japan External Trade Organization (JETRO). 2004. Japan Identifies New Policy Challenges to Stustain Its Economic Progress. JETRO website. http://www.jetro.go.jp/usa/newyork/focusnewsletter/focus30.html

———. 2005a. *The 2005 White Paper on International Trade and Foreign Direct Investment.* Tokyo: JETRO.

———. 2005b. Japan's M&A Activity Continues to Grow. JETRO WEBSITE. http://www.jetro.org/index2.php?option=com_contents&task=view&id=264&Ite

Jönsson, Anette. 2005. Asia-Pacific Share of M&A Soars. *South China Morning Post* (June 20): B4.

Kageyama, Yuri. 2006. Japan's Growth Signals Recovery. *The Ann Arbor News* (February 18): A9.

Kennett, David. 2004. *A New View of Comparative Economics.* Mason, OH: Thomson and South-Western.

Kinsey, Sandra. 2002. The Balancing Act in Cross-border Dealmaking. *Mergers & Acquisitions* (October): 35–9.

Lampton, David M. 2005. Paradigm Lost, The Demise of "Weak China." *The National Interest* (Fall): 73–80.

Lee, Jane Lanhee. 2005. GM's China Sales Increase by 19%. *Wall Street Journal* (July 7): A2.

Linebaugh, Kate. 2006a. How Foreign Banks Scaled the Chinese Wall. *Wall Street Journal* (February 23): C1, C5.

———. 2006b. China Eases Rules on Stock Buying By Foreign Holders. *Wall Street Journal* (January 5): A6.

———. 2006c. Banks Line Up To Run Big Chinese IPO. *Wall Street Journal* (February 27): C4

McGregor, James. 2005. *One Billion Customers.* New York: Free Press.

Metwalli, Ali M. and Roger Y. W. Tang. 2002. Southeast Asia: The Next M&A Hotspot? *Journal of Corporate Accounting and Finance* (January/February): 39–47.

———. 2003. Euro M&A: Dealmakers Rethink Their Strategies. *Journal of Corporate Accounting and Finance* (September/October): 61–72.

Milman, Claudio D., James P. DeMello, and David J. Flanagan. 1996. A Review of Merger and Acquisition Activity in Asia: 1985–95. *Journal of Transnational Management Development* (2): 87–103.

The Ministry of Commerce of China. 2006. Chinese Economy Grows 9.9% in 2005. http://english.mofcom.gov.cn/aarticle/newsrelease/commonnews/200603/200603

The Ministry of Finance (MOF) of Japan. 2005. Financial System Reform. MOF website. http://www.mof.go.jp/english/big-bang/ebb32.htm.

Mody, Ashoka and Shoko Negishi. 2001. Cross-Border Mergers and Acquisitions in East Asia: Trends and Implications. *Finance & Development.* (March): 6–9.

Morrison, Wayne M. 2005. *China-U.S. Trade Issues.* Congressional Research Service of the Library of Congress. Updated July 1, 2005.

Nakamura, H. Richard. 2002. Preliminary Report on the Current State of Mergers and Acquisitions in Japan. Working Paper, The European Institute of Japanese Studies, Stockholm School of Economics.

Norton, Patrick M. and Howard Chao. 2001. Mergers and Acquisitions in China. *China Business Review.* http://www.chinabusinessreview.com/public/0109/mergers.html

Oster, Shai. 2006. China Hints At Shift in Its U.S. Treasury Assets. *Wall Street Journal* (January 6): A2.

Platt, Gordon. 2002. Japan's Economic Woes Spur Cross-border Deals. *Global Finance* (March): 22.

Pricewaterhouse Coopers. 2002a. *Doing Business and Investing in the People's Republic of China*. New York: Pricewaterhouse Coopers.

——. 2002b. *Doing Business and Investing in the Philippines*. New York: Pricewaterhouse Coopers.

——. 2003a. *Doing Business and Investing in Indonesia*. New York: Pricewaterhouse Coopers.

——. 2003b. *Doing Business and Investing in Japan*. New York: Pricewaterhouse Coopers.

——. 2005. *China M&A: Regulatory Uncertainty, Underlying Growth*. PWC Hong Kong Website. http://www.pwchk.com/home/printeng/pr 060905.html

Ross, Stephen A., Randolph W. Westerfield, and Jeffrey Jaffe. 2005. *Corporate Finance*. New York: McGraw Hill.

Salter, M. S. and W. A. Weinhold. 1979. *Diversification Through Acquisition*. New York: Free Press.

Sender, Henny. 2005. Meet China Inc.: Topping Japan Inc. of 1980's *Wall Street Journal* (June 24): C1.

Shenkar, Oded. 2005. *The Chinese Century*. Upper Saddle River, NJ: Wharton School Publishing and Pearson Education.

Smith, Elliot Blair. 2006. China Task Force to Wield Trade Rules. *USA Today* (February 15): 3B.

Sudarsanam, Sudi. 2003. *Creating Value from Mergers and Acquisitions*. New York: FT Prentice Hall.

Sull, Donald N. and Yong Wang. 2005. *Made in China, What Western Managers Can Learn from Trailblazing Chinese Entrepeneurs*. Boston, MA: Harvard Business School Press.

Sung, Yung Wing. 2005. *The Emergence of Greater China*. New York: Palgrave Macmillan.

Tang, Roger Y. W. and Ali M. Metwalli. 2003. M&A in Greater China. *Journal of Corporate Accounting and Finance* (January/February): 45–54.

United Nations Conference on Trade and Development (UNCTAD). 2004. *World Investment Report 2004, The Shift Towards Services*. New York: The United Nations.

——. 2005. *World Investment Report 2005, Transnational Corporations and the Internationalization of R&D*. New York: The United Nations.

Wall Street Journal (WSJ). 2005. Overseas Outlook: Mergers in Europe, New Tensions in China. *Wall Street Journal* (December 31): A10.

——. 2006. China Raises 2005 Growth Figure to 9.8%. *Wall Street Journal* (January 4): A9.

Weston, J. Fred and Samuel C. Weaver. 2001. *Mergers & Acquisitions*. New York: McGraw-Hill.

Wonacott, Peter and Neil King, Jr. 2005. China Irks U.S. As It Uses Trade to Embellish Newfound Clout. *Wall Street Journal* (October 3): A1, A14.

Woodard, Kim and Anita, Qingli Wang. 2004. Acquisition in China: A View of the Field. *The Online China Business Review* (November–December). http://www.chinabusinessreview.com/public/0411/woodward.html

Zhan, James Xiaoning and Terutomo Ozawa. 2001. *Business Restructuring in Asia*. Copenhagen, Denmark: Copenhagen Business School Press.

Zheng, Bijan. 2005. "China's Peaceful Rise" to Great-Power Status. *Foreign Affairs* (September/October): 18–24.

Index

eBooks

eBooks – at www.eBookstore.tandf.co.uk

A library at your fingertips!

eBooks are electronic versions of printed books. You can store them on your PC/laptop or browse them online.

They have advantages for anyone needing rapid access to a wide variety of published, copyright information.

eBooks can help your research by enabling you to bookmark chapters, annotate text and use instant searches to find specific words or phrases. Several eBook files would fit on even a small laptop or PDA.

NEW: Save money by eSubscribing: cheap, online access to any eBook for as long as you need it.

Annual subscription packages

We now offer special low-cost bulk subscriptions to packages of eBooks in certain subject areas. These are available to libraries or to individuals.

For more information please contact webmaster.ebooks@tandf.co.uk

We're continually developing the eBook concept, so keep up to date by visiting the website.

www.eBookstore.tandf.co.uk